DYNAMICS 365 PROJECT ACCOUNTING & CONTROLLING (PART 2)

A Comprehensive Guide to Master the Microsoft Dynamics 365 Project Management and Accounting Module

Ludwig Reinhard, Ph.D.

Copyright

Library of Congress Control Number: 2017908911
CreateSpace Independent Publishing Platform, North Charleston, SC
Copyright © 2017 Dr. Ludwig Franz Martin Reinhard
All rights reserved.

ISBN: 1542793939
ISBN 13: 9781542793933

About the Author

Dr. Ludwig Reinhard is a senior Dynamics 365 consultant from Germany, specializing in the finance and project area. Dr. Reinhard holds a bachelor's degree in business administration, an MBA, and a PhD in finance, as well as a number of Microsoft Dynamics certificates. He is an active member in the Microsoft Dynamics community and has his own Dynamics blog (https://dynamicsax-fico.com). In June 2017, he was awarded the Microsoft MVP award for business applications. More information about Dr. Reinhard can be found on his blog and LinkedIn.

About the Reviewers

Jürgen Weber

Jürgen Weber is a senior Dynamics 365 consultant from Germany, working mainly in the supply-chain-management, production, and project-accounting sector. With more than twenty-five years of industrial background in logistics and controlling, he further implemented different ERP systems on customer sites while serving as project manager. More information about Jürgen Weber can be found on LinkedIn.

Jörg Newy

Jörg is a senior Dynamics 365 consultant, with a focus on finance processes and a specialization in controlling. In his more than twenty years' experience as a consultant, he worked with several financial solutions from different providers. For the last ten years, he implemented Dynamics 365 at many companies from many different branches.

Georg Bauerochse

Georg Bauerochse is a senior Dynamics 365 consultant, working mainly in the finance area. With almost twenty years of experience in the IT business and thirteen years of experience with Dynamics 365, he has worked on a wide range of AX implementations, serving as senior consultant as well as subproject manager. More information about Georg Bauerochse can be found on LinkedIn.

Acknowledgments

This book would not have been possible without the help of the following people: Jan Timphaus, Karlin Reinhard, and Sebastian Duckwitz, who helped me by reviewing and improving the different parts of this book.

At this point, I would also like to express special thanks to my employer, who provided me the time, support, and means to finish this book.

The Sycor Group is an international full-service partner and solution integrator (SI) for Microsoft Dynamics 365 (AX & CRM) and a Microsoft Cloud Solution Provider. The experts consult, implement, optimize, and operate cloud, on premises, and hybrid scenarios. For major implementation and rollout projects, the Sycor Group is a reliable partner, based on expertise in more than eighty countries and with large systems up to five thousand users. Six hundred fifty employees and nineteen locations worldwide (Europe, Asia, and America) assure international delivery capabilities.

As an ISV, Sycor is a Microsoft Strategic Development Partner for rental, trade, service, and maintenance of mobile goods and fleet management. Its industry solutions—Sycor.Rental and Sycor.Fleet—are genuine Microsoft Dynamics 365 solutions and available at the Microsoft AppSource. The comprehensive Microsoft Dynamics 365 portfolio is backed by extensive hosting services (full Microsoft stack) and complemented by solutions and services for Microsoft Azure, Microsoft Cortana Intelligence Suite, Power BI, Microsoft Office 365, Microsoft SharePoint, Skype for Business, and other online Microsoft products. In addition to that, Sycor offers software asset management and license consulting. In the fields of manufacturing, retail, and professional services, Sycor has consulting and development teams with many years of Microsoft Dynamics AX and industry expertise. Sycor is a member of the Microsoft Dynamics Industry Partner Program EMEA in the areas of professional services and manufacturing.

Table of Contents

Preface iii

Abbreviations v

1. Introduction 1

2. Project Accounting 2

    2.1. Ledger-Posting Setup 2

    2.2. Time Projects 13

        2.2.1. Record Hour Transactions 14

        2.2.2. Record Other Transactions 16

    2.3. Cost Projects 18

        2.3.1. Record Hour Transactions 19

        2.3.2. Record Expense Transactions 21

        2.3.3. Record Item Transactions 22

        2.3.4. Record Fee Transactions 23

        2.3.5. Summary 24

    2.4. Internal Projects 25

        2.4.1. Internal Projects with P&L Accounting 26

        2.4.2. Internal Projects with BS Accounting 32

        2.4.3. Special Issues 38

    2.5. Investment Projects 41

        2.5.1. Project-Estimate Functionality 42

        2.5.2. Investment Projects with P&L Accounting 44

        2.5.3. Investment Projects with BS Accounting 53

        2.5.4. Special Issues 61

    2.6. Time and Material (T&M) Projects 66

        2.6.1. Basic T&M Projects 66

        2.6.2. T&M Projects with Accruals 81

        2.6.3. T&M Projects with BS Accounting 91

    2.7. Fix-Price (FP) Projects 101

        2.7.1. Basic Fix-Price Projects 101

        2.7.2. Advanced Fix-Price Projects 110

    2.8.   Summary Project-Group Setup 212

3.   Project Reporting and Analysis 215

    3.1.   Standard Reporting Tools 215

        3.1.1.   Project Specific Inquiry Forms 215

        3.1.2.   General Inquiry Forms and Reports 220

        3.1.3.   Financial Accounts and Dimensions 223

        3.1.4.   BI Tools 227

    3.2.   Earned Value Analysis (EVA) 229

        3.2.1.   Sample Data 232

        3.2.2.   Setup 234

        3.2.3.   Process and Analysis 240

        3.2.4.   Special Issues 252

    3.3.   Parallel Accounting 272

        3.3.1.   Setup 272

        3.3.2.   Example 275

        3.3.3.   Summary 289

    3.4.   Activity-Based Costing (ABC) 290

        3.4.1.   Background 290

        3.4.2.   Application D365 294

        3.4.3.   Summary 338

    3.5.   Indirect Cost Allocations 339

        3.5.1.   Background 339

        3.5.2.   Application D365 339

        3.5.3.   Summary 356

4.   Conclusion 357

Index 358

Preface

What This Book Covers

As the title of the book indicates, the main focus of this book is on accounting- and controlling-related topics around the project-management and accounting module in Dynamics 365. The book is thereby not industry specific but rather applies to a number of different industries. Due to the fact that almost every project transaction is, to a greater or lesser extent, related to accounting and controlling, essentially all aspects of the project-management and accounting module are covered in this book.

This wide coverage resulted in an issue in regard to the number of pages of the different chapters and resulted in lengthy discussions with the reviewers about how best to arrange and separate the different chapters. Finally, it was decided not to compromise on the quality and content but rather to split the topics into two separate books.

The first book thereby covers the major accounting- and controlling-related topics around the project-module setup and project-related processes. The second book, on the other hand, focuses on special accounting- and controlling-related topics, such as earned value management analyses and project-related cost allocations.

After describing what this book covers and how it is arranged, let's briefly focus on what it does not cover. The first thing that is not covered explicitly are questions around different kinds of project methodologies and approaches, such as Waterfall and Agile project-management techniques. In addition, purchase, production, and item-specific setups are also not in the major focus of this book. It is rather assumed that the reader is familiar with the basic setup of items, purchase orders, and the like.

What You Need for This Book

All examples illustrated are processed on the Dynamics 365 for Operations (D365) Update 4 demo machines available for download, for example, through Lifecycle Services (LCS). No specific software add-ons or code modifications are required to replicate and follow the illustrations and explanations below.

Who This Book Is For

This book is intended for application consultants, financial controllers, project managers, and project accountants as well as other professionals who are involved in the Microsoft Dynamics 365 project implementation. A basic knowledge of financial terms and concepts and Microsoft Dynamics 365 terminology is required.

Conventions

In this book, you will find a number of text styles that distinguish between the different kinds of information:

- Warnings and important notes are indicated by the following symbol:

- Best-practice recommendations from the author are indicated by the following symbol:

Reader Feedback

Feedback from our readers is always welcome. Let us know what you think about this book—what you like or dislike. Reader feedback is important for us, as it helps us develop titles that you really get the most out of. To send us general feedback, simply e-mail to lreinhard7@live.de.

Errata

Although we have taken utmost care to ensure the accuracy of our content, mistakes do happen. If you find a mistake, we would be grateful if you would report this to us. By doing so, you can save other readers from frustration and help us improve subsequent versions of this book. If you find any errata, please report them by e-mailing lreinhard7@live.de.

Abbreviations

ABC	Activity-based costing
AP	Accounts payable
AR	Accounts receivable
BAC	Budget at completion
BI	Business intelligence
BS	Balance sheet
CA	Control account
CC	Completed contract
CV	Cost variance
D365	Dynamics 365
ELR	Effective-labor rate
EV	Earned value
EVM	Earned value management
FASB	Financial Accounting Standards Board
FP	Fixed price
FTI	Free text invoice
GL	General ledger
GPR	Gross profit rate
HR	Human resources
IASB	International Accounting Standards Board
IC	Intercompany
IS	Income statement
ISV	Independent software vendor
KPI	Key performance indicator
LCS	Lifecycle services
OTB	Over target baseline
MISC	Miscellaneous

P&L	Profit and loss
P&P	Production and profit
PCS	Pieces
PMB	Performance-measurement baseline
PMBOK	Project-Management Body of Knowledge
PO	Purchase order
POC	Percentage of completion
PRODO	Production order
PV	Planned value
PWP	Pay when paid
R&D	Research and development
SV	Schedule variance
T&M	Time and material
TV	Total variance
VAT	Value-added tax
WBS	Work breakdown structure
WIP	Work in progress

1. Introduction

The first part of this book primarily focused on the set up of the project-management and accounting module and processing expense, hour, item, and fee transactions that were subsequently invoiced.

In this second part, we will change the focus toward the accounting integration of the project-management and accounting module that establishes the basis for a more detailed analysis of the various projects.

The next chapter will consequently provide a deep dive into the project-accounting area that focuses on the ledger transactions created when posting expense, hour, item, and fee transactions. This investigation will establish the basis for the examination of the different project-related reporting and analysis instruments that will be introduced thereafter.

2. Project Accounting

2.1. Ledger-Posting Setup

Let's get started with investigating the project-accounting setup and the resulting vouchers. As mentioned in the first part of this book, the combination of

- the project type (T&M, fixed-price, investment, etc.),
- the project-group ledger-integration settings (balance sheet vs. income statement), and
- the project ledger-posting setup

determines the accounting vouchers that Dynamics 365 generates.

The next subchapters will follow this enumeration and detail the vouchers that are generated for the different project-type, project-group combinations available in the standard application.

Please note that all descriptions and explanations will be based on the following common ledger-posting setup that makes use of one single ledger account for each project posting type in order to keep things as easy as possible for the reader to follow.

Main Account Number	Main Account Name	Main Account Type
165100	WIP cost value	Balance sheet
165200	WIP cost value item	Balance sheet
165300	WIP-accrued loss	Balance sheet
165400	WIP sales value	Balance sheet
165500	WIP production	Balance sheet
165600	WIP profit	Balance sheet
165700	WIP invoiced—on-account	Balance sheet
165800	WIP subscription	Balance sheet
415100	Invoiced revenue	Profit and loss
415200	Invoiced revenue—on-account	Profit and loss
415300	Accrued revenue—sales value	Profit and loss
415400	Accrued revenue—production	Profit and loss
415500	Accrued revenue—profit	Profit and loss
415600	Accrued revenue—on-account	Profit and loss
415700	Accrued revenue—subscription	Profit and loss
415800	Intercompany revenue GBSI	Profit and loss
415900	Intercompany revenue FRSI	Profit and loss
545100	Cost	Profit and loss
545200	Cost item	Profit and loss
545300	Accrued loss	Profit and loss
545400	Intercompany cost GBSI	Profit and loss
545500	Intercompany cost FRSI	Profit and loss
605100	Payroll allocation	Profit and loss

Figure 2-1 Main accounts setup

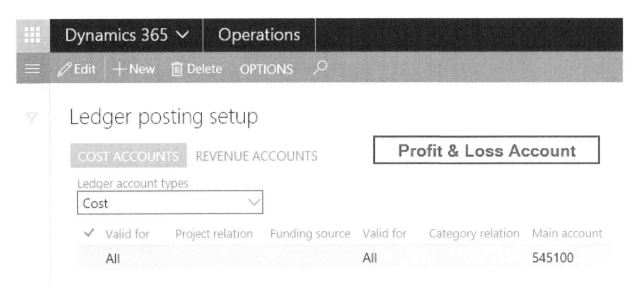

Figure 2-2 Project ledger-posting setup—Cost

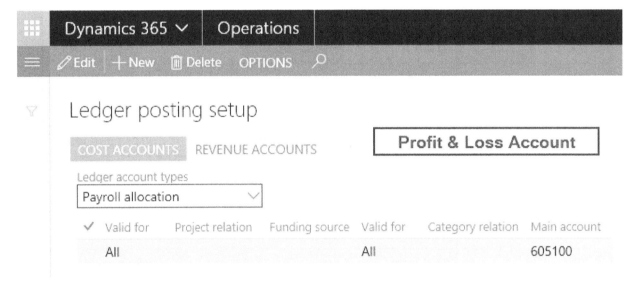

Figure 2-3 Project ledger-posting setup—Payroll allocation

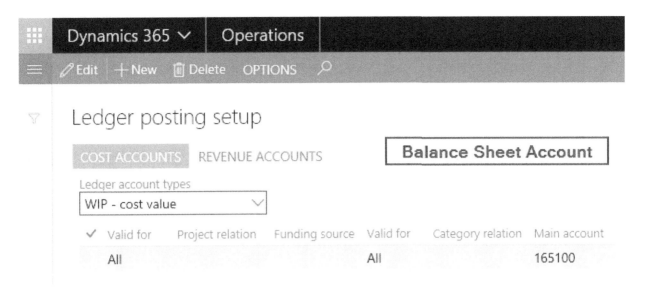

Figure 2-4 Project ledger-posting setup—WIP cost value

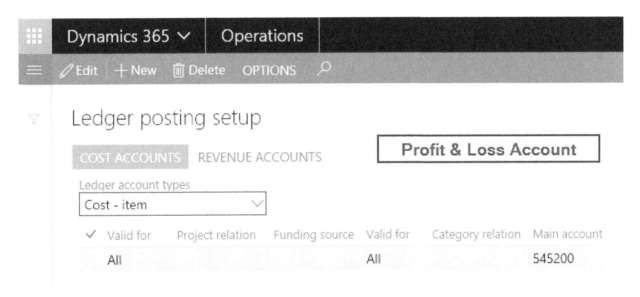

Figure 2-5 Project ledger-posting setup—Cost item

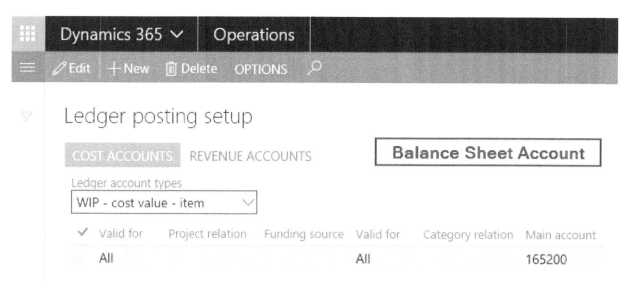

Figure 2-6 Project ledger-posting setup—WIP cost value item

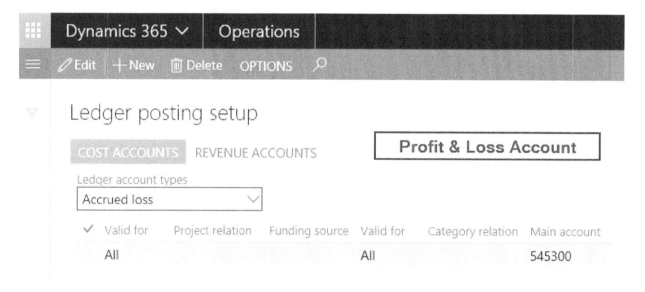

Figure 2-7 Project ledger-posting setup—Accrued loss

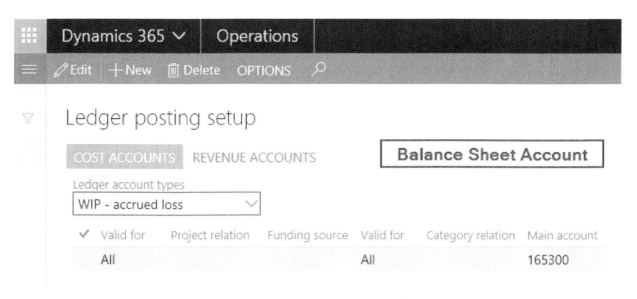

Figure 2-8 Project ledger-posting setup—WIP accrued loss

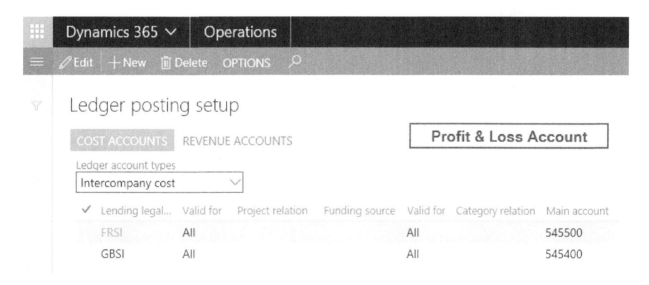

Figure 2-9 Project ledger-posting setup—Intercompany cost

Note Please note that the intercompany costing section has been enhanced by a legal entity column with the most recent Dynamics 365 for Operations update. This enhancement will alleviate the accounting set up in live environments because no reference to financial dimensions needs to be made to separate intercompany costs arising from different legal entities.

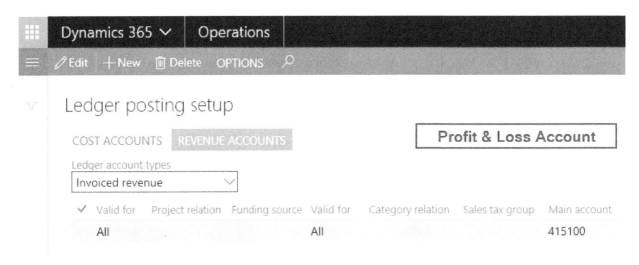

Figure 2-10 Project ledger-posting setup—Invoiced revenue

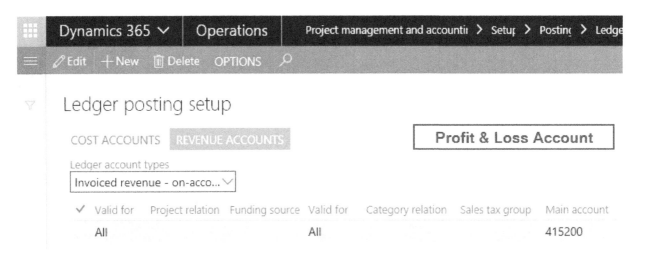

Figure 2-11 Project ledger-posting setup—Invoiced revenue on-account

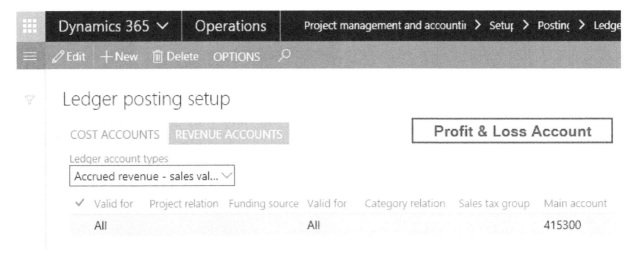

Figure 2-12 Project ledger-posting setup—Accrued revenue sales value

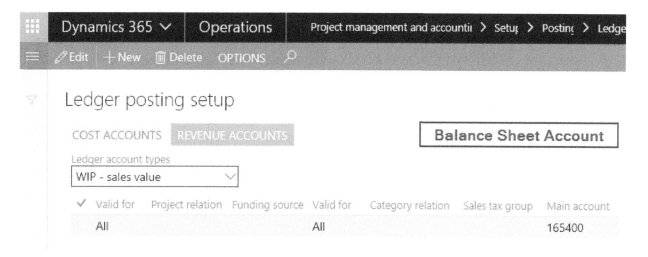

Figure 2-13 Project ledger-posting setup—WIP sales value

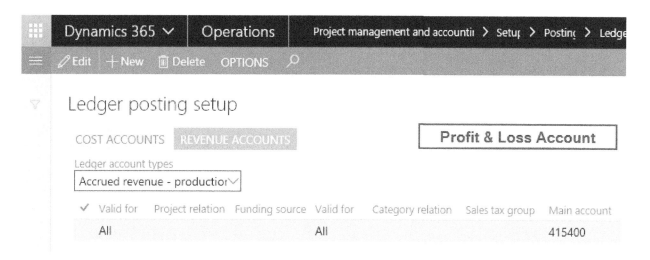

Figure 2-14 Project ledger-posting setup—Accrued revenue production

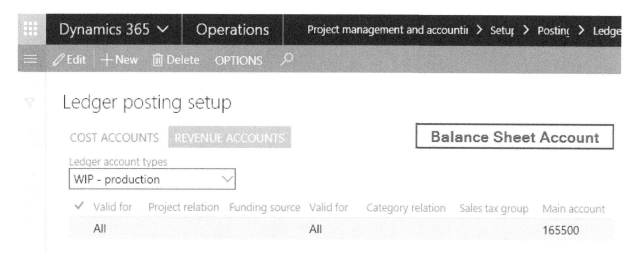

Figure 2-15 Project ledger-posting setup—WIP production

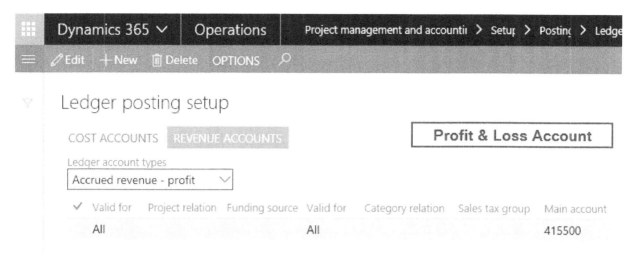

Figure 2-16 Project ledger-posting setup—Accrued revenue profit

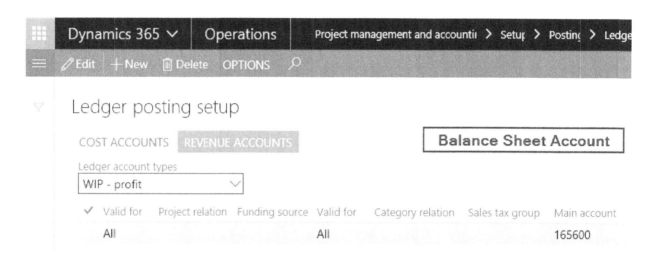

Figure 2-17 Project ledger-posting setup—WIP profit

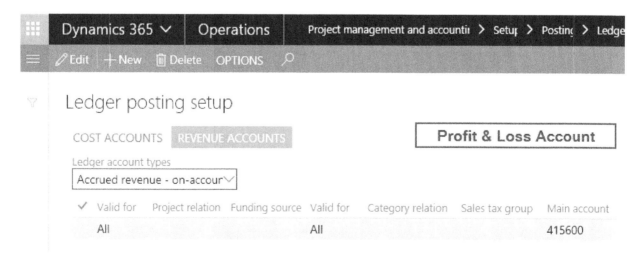

Figure 2-18 Project ledger-posting setup—Accrued revenue on-account

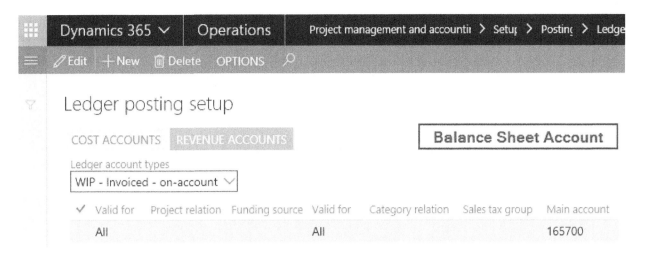

Figure 2-19 Project ledger-posting setup—WIP invoiced on-account

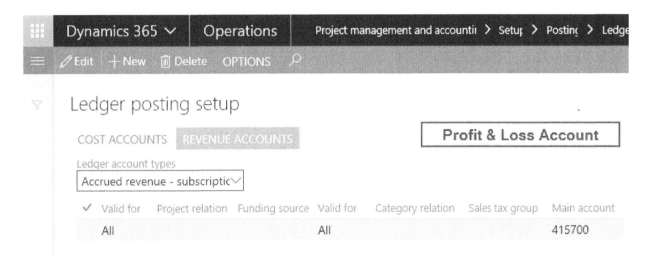

Figure 2-20 Project ledger-posting setup—Accrued revenue subscription

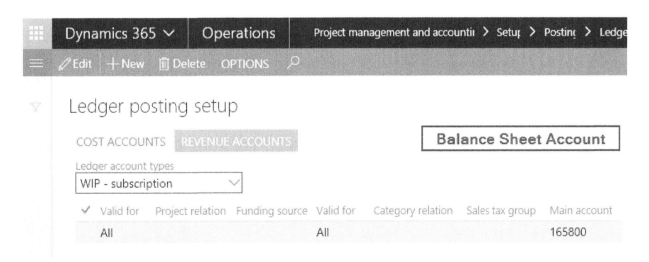

Figure 2-21 Project ledger-posting setup—WIP subscription

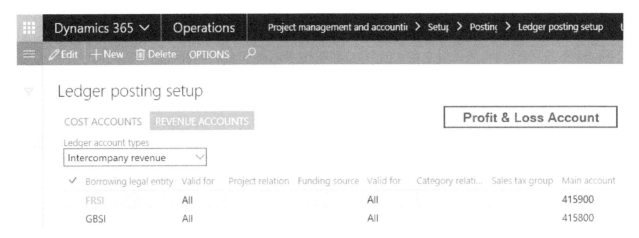

Figure 2-22 Project ledger-posting setup—Intercompany revenue

Note Please note that the intercompany revenue section has been enhanced by a legal entity column with the most recent Dynamics 365 for Operations update. This enhancement will alleviate the accounting set up in live environments because no reference to financial dimensions needs to be made to separate intercompany revenues arising from different legal entities.

2.2. Time Projects

The time project used next is set up with the following project-group settings.

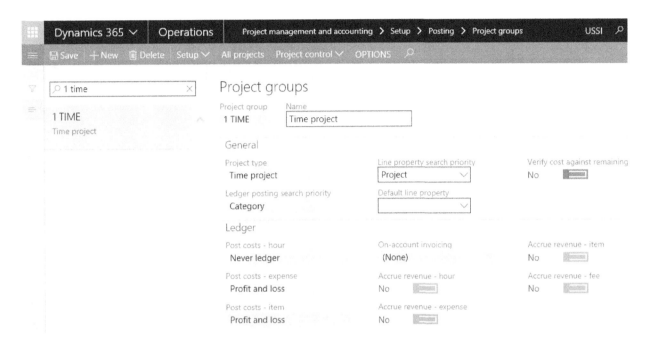

Figure 2-23 Time project-group setup

Note The ledger-integration parameters, *Never ledger* and *Profit and loss* that can be identified in the lower part of Figure 2-23, cannot be changed.

Note Within the following, the ledger-integration parameters, *Post costs—hour, Post costs—expense, and Post costs—item*, are analyzed and described in detail. The *On-account invoicing* ledger-integration parameter is described further below for project types that can be invoiced to customers.

2.2.1. Record Hour Transactions

In the hour journal illustrated next, ten hours of working time are recorded on the time project that has been set up. The resulting project transaction and ledger voucher are shown in Figures 2-24 and 2-25.

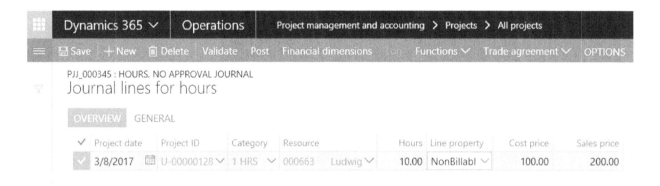

Figure 2-24 Recording hour transactions for a time project

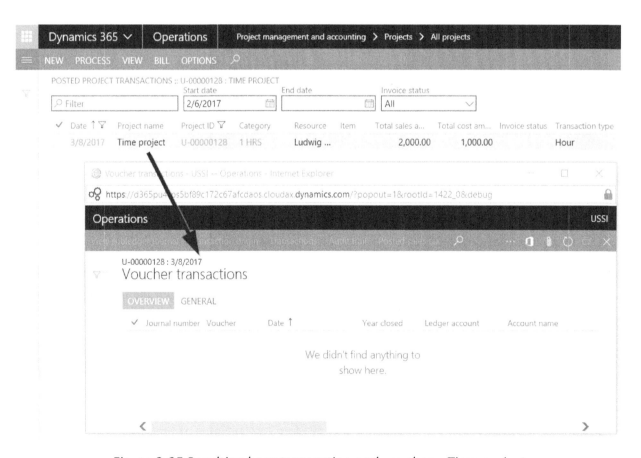

Figure 2-25 Resulting hour transaction and voucher—Time project

As one can identify from Figure 2-25, D365 creates a project transaction that does not result in the generation of a ledger voucher for a time project.

Note Even though no voucher is created, the costs associated with the hours posted on a time project can be identified and analyzed, for example, through the project cost control form. This can be identified in Figure 2-26.

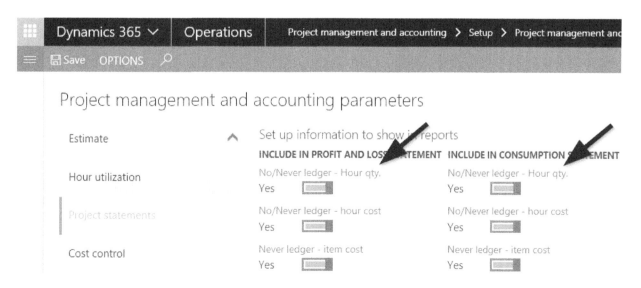

Cost line	Total budget...	Actual cost	Committed c...	Variance
Hour - quantity	0.00	10.00	0.00	-10.00
Hour - price average	0.00	100.00	0.00	-100.00
Expense	0.00	0.00	0.00	0.00
Hour	0.00	1,000.00	0.00	-1,000.00
Item	0.00	0.00	0.00	0.00
Total	0.00	1,000.00	0.00	-1,000.00

Figure 2-26 Costs associated with hours recorded for a time project

A prerequisite for analyzing those costs is the activation of the following project-module parameters.

Figure 2-27 Project statement parameter setup

2.2.2. Record Other Transactions

Project transactions other than hour transactions cannot be recorded on time projects. Figures 2-28, 2-29 and 2-30 demonstrate this by showing that D365 generates error messages if one tries to record expense, item, or fee transactions on time projects.

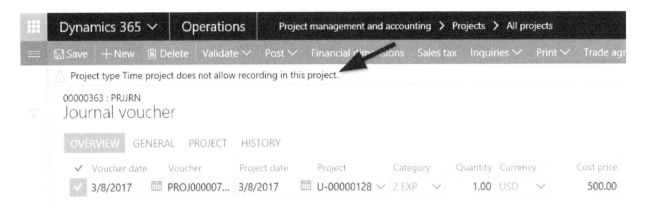

Figure 2-28 Recording expense transaction for a time project

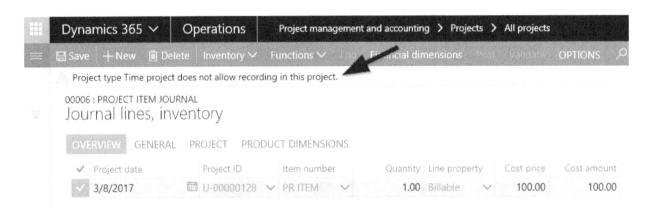

Figure 2-29 Recording item transaction for a time project

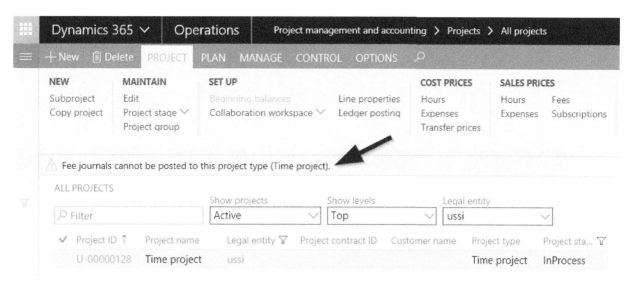

Figure 2-30 Recording fee transaction for a time project

2.3. Cost Projects

The cost project used in this subchapter is set up with the following project-group parameters.

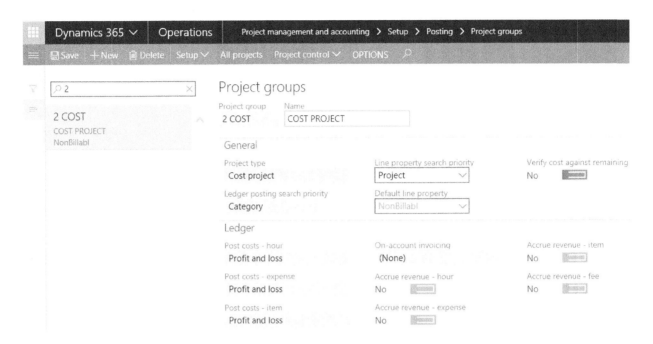

Figure 2-31 Cost project-group setup

Note The ledger-integration parameters *Profit and loss* that can be identified in Figure 2-31 cannot be changed. In other words, cost projects only allow recording transactions on P&L accounts.

2.3.1. Record Hour Transactions

Recording hour transactions on a cost project results in a voucher that debits the project cost account and that credits the payroll allocation account. Figures 2-32 and 2-33 summarize the sample project hours posted on a cost project.

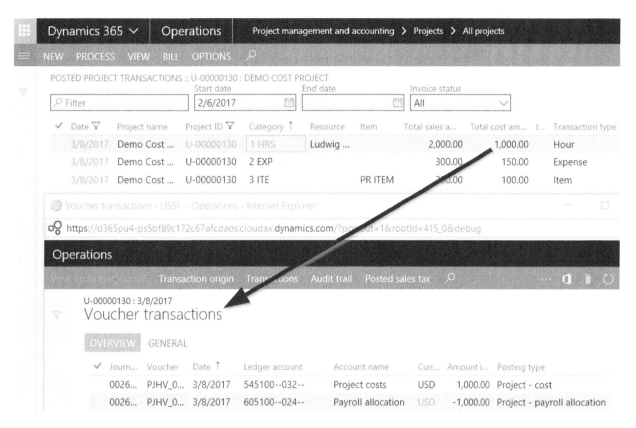

Figure 2-32 Resulting hour transaction and voucher—Cost project

DEBIT	CREDIT	AMOUNT
545100 Project costs [Profit&Loss—Project cost]	605100 Payroll allocation [Profit&Loss—Project payroll allocation]	$1,000

Figure 2-33 Accounting voucher hour transactions—Cost project

Note The expression that can be identified in square brackets below the account name identifies the main account type and—separated by a dash—the posting type.

Note Please note that the project cost is recorded together with department *032 Project Operations*, which is set up as financial dimension with the cost project. Department *024 Finance* that is used for the credit transaction is set up at the employee level. As both, the debit and the credit transactions are recorded on P&L accounts; there is no overall effect on the profit of the company. However, because the voucher debits and credits different financial dimensions (departments), a cost allocation from department *024* to department *032* materializes.

2.3.2. Record Expense Transactions

Different from time projects, cost projects allow posting expenses. Figures 2-34 and 2-35 show a sample expense transaction and the resulting accounting voucher.

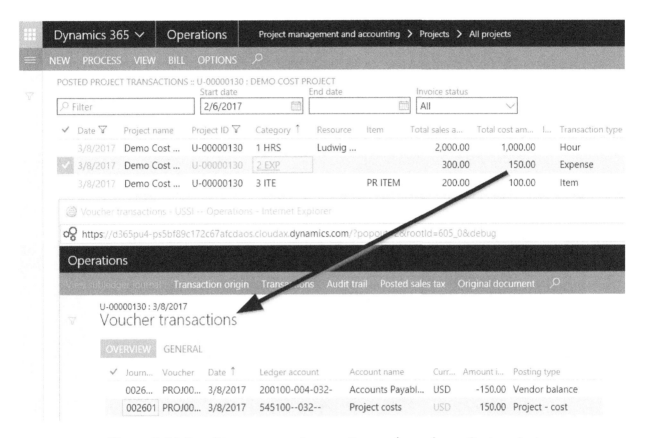

Figure 2-34 Resulting expense transaction and voucher—Cost project

DEBIT	CREDIT	AMOUNT
545100 Project costs [Profit&Loss—Project cost]	200100 Accounts Payable [BalanceSheet—Vendor balance]	$150

Figure 2-35 Accounting voucher expense transactions—Cost project

2.3.3. Record Item Transactions

Figures 2-36 and 2-37 show the vouchers resulting from items consumed on a cost project through the posting of a project item journal.

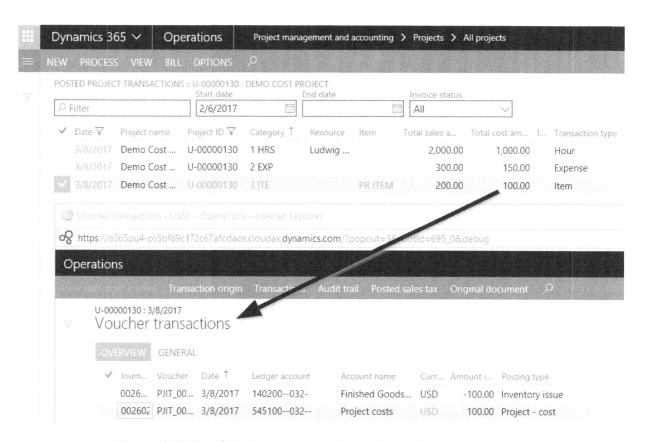

Figure 2-36 Resulting item transaction and voucher—Cost project

DEBIT	CREDIT	AMOUNT
545100 Project costs [Profit&Loss—Project cost]	140200 Finished Goods [BalanceSheet—Inventory issue]	$100

Figure 2-37 Accounting voucher item transactions—Cost project

2.3.4. Record Fee Transactions

As cost projects do not allow invoicing customers, fee transactions cannot be recorded for cost projects. Trying to post a fee transaction on a cost project is consequently interrupted with an error message identical to the one that is shown in Figure 2-38.

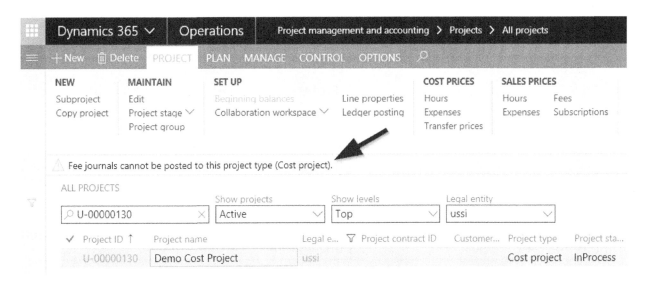

Figure 2-38 Recording fee transactions for a cost project

2.3.5. Summary

Figure 2-39 summarizes the vouchers that are generated for the sample transactions recorded on a cost project.

DEBIT	CREDIT	AMOUNT
Hour transactions		
545100 Project costs [Profit&Loss—Project cost]	605100 Payroll allocation [Profit&Loss—Project payroll allocation]	$1,000
Expense transactions		
545100 Project costs [Profit&Loss—Project cost]	200100 Accounts Payable [BalanceSheet—Vendor balance]	$150
Item transactions		
545100 Project costs [Profit&Loss—Project cost]	140200 Finished Goods [BalanceSheet—Inventory issue]	$100
Fee transactions		
Not possible		

Figure 2-39 Summary vouchers—Cost project

2.4. Internal Projects

The major difference between internal projects and cost projects is that internal projects allow recording transactions on BS or P&L accounts. This chapter is consequently subdivided into two parts where the P&L accounting setup and the resulting vouchers are presented first, before the BS accounting setup and the created vouchers are investigated in more detail.

Note Internal projects can be set up with a mixed BS and P&L accounting integration for the different transaction types. For reasons of brevity, such combined accounting setups are not presented in the following, as they merely represent a combination of the accounting principles and transactions illustrated next.

2.4.1.   Internal Projects with P&L Accounting

The internal project used in this subsection is set up with the following project-group parameters, which ensure that all transactions are recorded on P&L accounts.

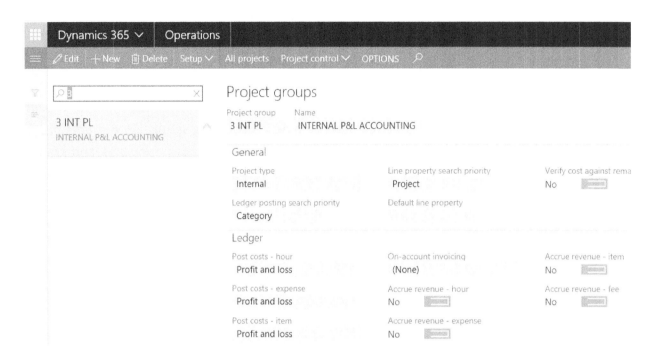

Figure 2-40 Internal project group with P&L accounting setup

2.4.1.1.   Record Hour Transactions

Because of the P&L accounting setup, recording hour transactions on internal projects with a P&L ledger accounting integration results in a voucher that is identical to the one created for cost projects. For details, please compare the results in Figure 2-41 and 2-42 with the ones shown in Figures 2-32 and 2-33.

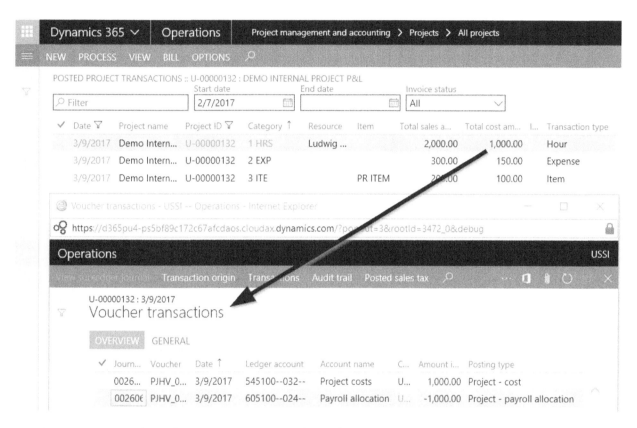

Figure 2-41 Resulting hour transaction and voucher—internal project with P&L accounting

DEBIT	CREDIT	AMOUNT
545100 Project costs [Profit&Loss—Project cost]	605100 Payroll allocation [Profit&Loss—Project payroll allocation]	$1,000

Figure 2-42 Accounting voucher hour transaction—internal project with P&L accounting

2.4.1.2.   Record Expense Transactions

What has been said for hour transactions recorded on the internal project with a P&L accounting integration also applies for recording expense and item transactions. That is, the resulting vouchers are identical to the ones presented for cost projects. For that reason, reference is made to the prior explanations.

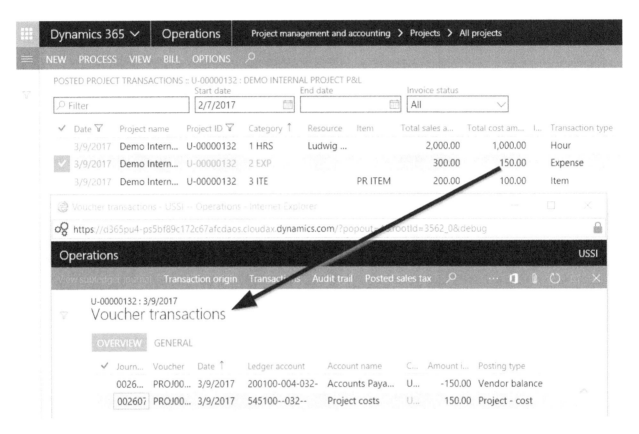

Figure 2-43 Resulting expense transaction and voucher—internal project with P&L accounting

DEBIT	CREDIT	AMOUNT
545100 Project costs [Profit&Loss—Project cost]	200100 Accounts Payable [BalanceSheet—Vendor balance]	$150

Figure 2-44 Accounting voucher expense transaction—internal project with P&L accounting

2.4.1.3.   Record Item Transactions

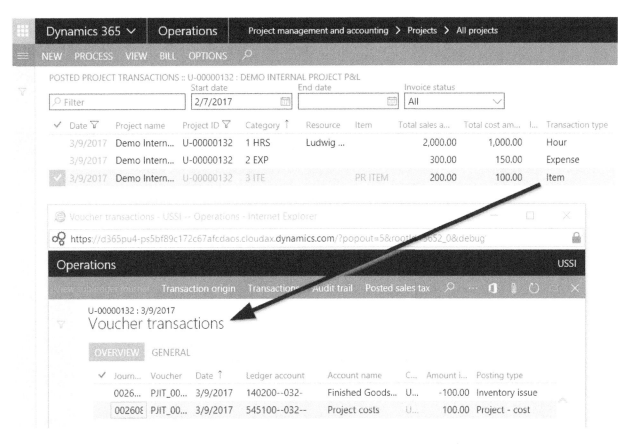

Figure 2-45 Resulting item transaction and voucher—internal project with P&L accounting

DEBIT	CREDIT	AMOUNT
545100 Project costs [Profit&Loss—Project cost]	140200 Finished Goods [BalanceSheet—Inventory issue]	$100

Figure 2-46 Accounting voucher item transactions—internal project with P&L accounting

2.4.1.4.   Record Fee Transactions

Internal projects cannot be used for invoicing customers. As a result, fee transactions cannot be recorded for internal projects and trying to post fees on internal projects is consequently interrupted with the following error message.

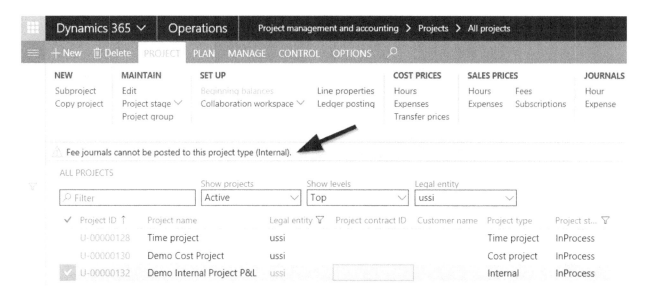

Figure 2-47 Recording fee transactions for an internal project with P&L accounting

2.4.1.5.   Summary

Figure 2-48 summarizes all vouchers that are generated when posting-hour, expense, and item transactions for internal projects with a P&L ledger accounting integration. A comparison of the vouchers with those that are generated for cost projects—please see Figure 2-39—shows that the vouchers are identical for both project types.

DEBIT	CREDIT	AMOUNT
Hour transactions		
545100 Project costs [Profit&Loss—Project cost]	605100 Payroll allocation [Profit&Loss—Project payroll allocation]	$1,000
Expense transactions		
545100 Project costs [Profit&Loss—Project cost]	200100 Accounts Payable [BalanceSheet—Vendor balance]	$150
Item transactions		
545100 Project costs [Profit&Loss—Project cost]	140200 Finished Goods [BalanceSheet—Inventory issue]	$100
Fee transactions		
Not possible		

Figure 2-48 Summary vouchers—internal project with P&L accounting

Note Given that the cost project and the internal project with P&L accounting integration generate identical vouchers, the question arises why one would use internal projects with P&L accounting integration at all. This question will be answered further below after internal projects with a BS ledger accounting integration are described.

2.4.2.   Internal Projects with BS Accounting

The project-group settings for the internal project with BS accounting integration are presented in Figure 2-49, which differs from the previous one by the account type used.

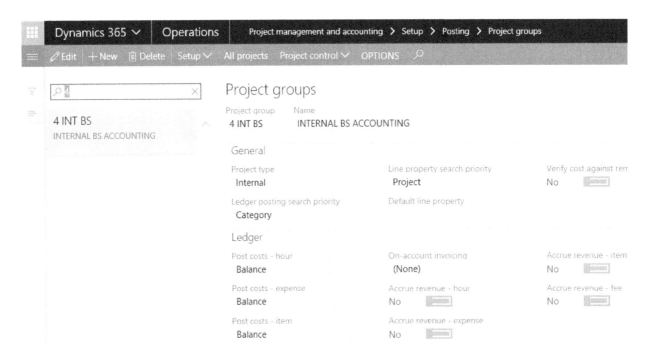

Figure 2-49 Internal project group with BS accounting setup

2.4.2.1. Record Hour Transactions

Due to the BS accounting integration, hour transactions recorded on an internal project with BS accounting integration are posted on a WIP (Work in Progress) account and are thus stored in the company's balance sheet. Figures 2-50 and 2-51 show this for the sample hour transactions recorded on the demo project.

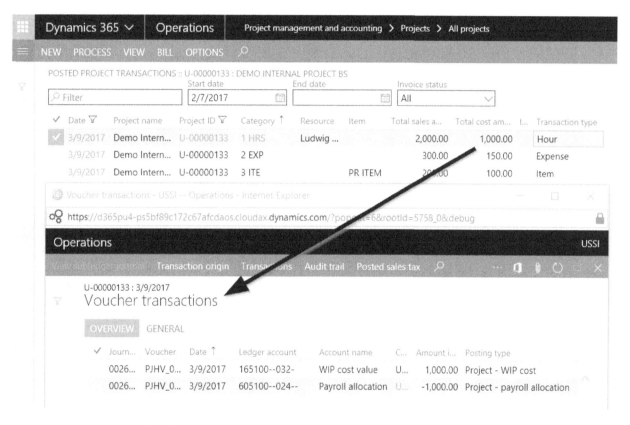

Figure 2-50 Resulting hour transaction and voucher—internal project with BS accounting

DEBIT	CREDIT	AMOUNT
165100 WIP cost value [BalanceSheet—Project WIP cost]	605100 Payroll allocation [Profit&Loss—Project payroll allocation]	$1,000

Figure 2-51 Accounting voucher hour transaction—internal project with BS accounting

Note Different from what has been explained before for the other project types, posting hours on an internal project with a BS accounting integration results in an immediate increase of a company's profit because costs are shifted from the company's income statement to its balance sheet.

2.4.2.2. Record Expense Transactions

Recording expense transactions on the internal project with BS accounting integration results in a voucher that makes use of the same WIP account that has already been used for recording the hour transaction. For details, please see the sample transaction in Figure 2-51.

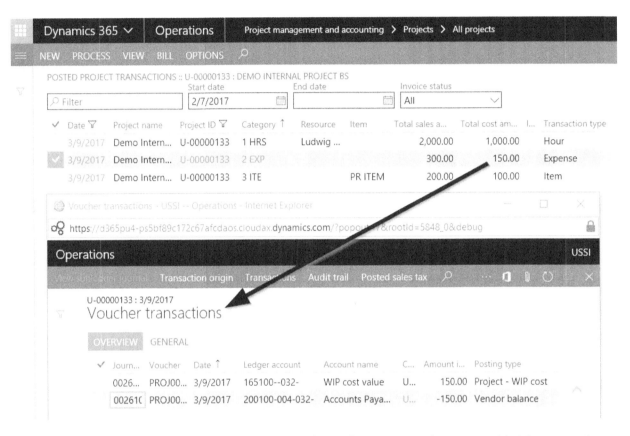

Figure 2-52 Resulting expense transaction and voucher—internal project with BS accounting

DEBIT	CREDIT	AMOUNT
165100 WIP cost value [BalanceSheet—Project WIP cost]	200100 Accounts Payable [BalanceSheet—Vendor balance]	$150

Figure 2-53 Accounting voucher expense transaction—internal project with BS accounting

2.4.2.3.   Record Item Transactions

The consumption of items on internal projects with a BS ledger integration creates a voucher, which posts the item costs first on the project cost account that has been used for the internal project with the P&L accounting integration. For details, please see Figures 2-45 and 2-46. This initial item consumption posting is then—in a second accounting step—nullified through a credit posting on the cost item ledger account no. 545200. Finally, all costs moved to the company's balance sheet through the debit posting on the WIP cost value item account no. 165200. This two-step accounting procedure is illustrated in Figures 2-54 and 2-55.

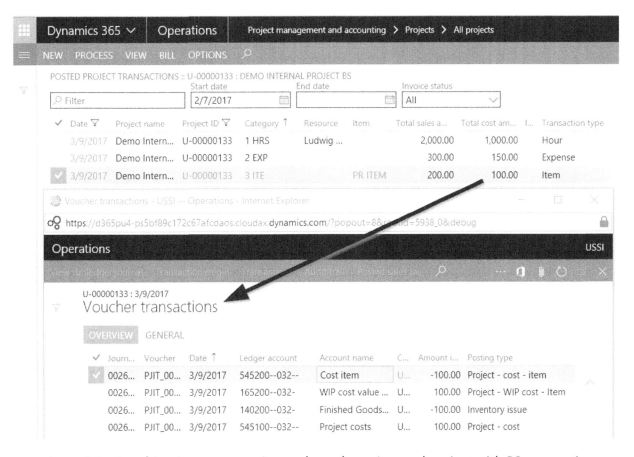

Figure 2-54 Resulting item transaction and voucher—internal project with BS accounting

DEBIT	CREDIT	AMOUNT
545100 Project costs [Profit&Loss—Project cost]	140200 Finished goods [BalanceSheet—Inventory issue]	$100
165200 WIP cost value item [BalanceSheet—Project WIP cost item]	545200 Cost item [Profit&Loss—Project cost item]	$100

Figure 2-55 Accounting voucher item transaction—internal project with BS accounting

2.4.2.4.   Record Fee Transactions

What has been said for the internal project with P&L accounting integration also applies for the internal project with BS accounting integration. That is, fee transactions cannot be recorded on internal projects because they cannot be used for invoicing customers.

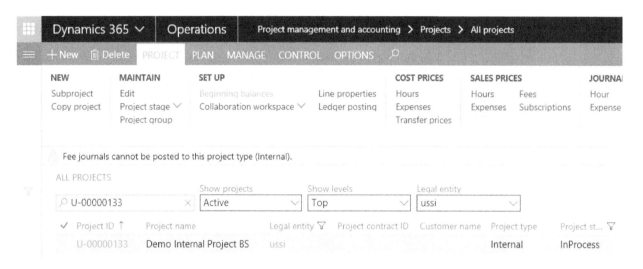

Figure 2-56 Recording fee transaction on an internal project with BS accounting

2.4.2.5.   Summary

Figure 2-57 summarizes all vouchers recorded on the internal project with BS accounting integration and shows that the costs are stored in the company's balance sheet through the debit postings on the respective WIP accounts.

DEBIT	CREDIT	AMOUNT
Hour transactions		
165100 WIP cost value [BalanceSheet—Project WIP cost]	605100 Payroll allocation [Profit&Loss—Project payroll allocation]	$1,000
Expense transactions		
165100 WIP cost value [BalanceSheet—Project WIP cost]	200100 Accounts Payable [BalanceSheet—Vendor balance]	$150
Item transactions		
545100 Project costs [Profit&Loss—Project cost]	140200 Finished goods [BalanceSheet—Inventory issue]	$100
165200 WIP cost value item [BalanceSheet—Project WIP cost item]	545200 Cost item [Profit&Loss—Project cost item]	$100
Fee transactions		
Not possible		

Figure 2-57 Summary vouchers—internal project with BS accounting

Note: As mentioned before, the hour transaction posting influences (increases) a company's profit through the credit posting on the payroll allocation account. If companies want to avoid such an influence, the ledger integration for hour transactions needs to be set, for example, to *No ledger, Never ledger*, or *Profit and loss*. Details of those alternative setups are further explained in chapter 2.7.2.10.

2.4.3.   Special Issues

Further above, the question was raised why one would use internal projects with P&L ledger integration if those projects result in the same vouchers that are generated for cost projects. The answer to this question is that only internal projects allow shifting costs from P&L accounts to BS accounts and vice versa through the *Post costs* functionality shown in Figure 2-58.

Figure 2-58 Post cost functionality—Internal projects (1)

Applied to the internal project with BS accounting integration, the *Post costs* function allows shifting costs that have initially been recorded on WIP accounts in the balance sheet to P&L accounts in the income statement. Figures 2-59 and 2-60 exemplify how this can be realized.

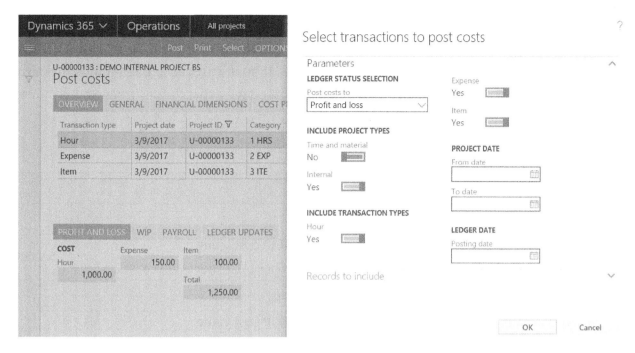

Figure 2-59 Post cost functionality—Internal projects (2)

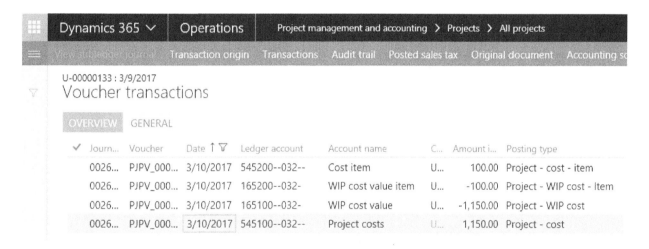

Figure 2-60 Post cost functionality—Internal projects (3)

Figure 2-61 summarizes the accounting voucher that results from using the *Post costs* functionality for the internal project with a BS accounting integration. A comparison of this summary with the original vouchers that are shown in Figure 2-57 demonstrates that all costs have been moved from the WIP accounts to the project cost accounts. This is equivalent to saying that the costs have been moved from the company's balance sheet to its income statement.

DEBIT	CREDIT	AMOUNT
Hour transactions		
545100 Project costs [Profit&Loss—Project cost]	165100 WIP cost value [BalanceSheet—Project WIP cost]	$1,000
Expense transactions		
545100 Project costs [Profit&Loss—Project cost]	165100 WIP cost value [BalanceSheet—Project WIP cost]	$150
Item transactions		
545200 Cost item [Profit&Loss—Project cost item]	165200 WIP cost value item [BalanceSheet—Project WIP cost item]	$100

Figure 2-61 Post cost functionality—internal projects (4)

Note In regard to the *Post costs* functionality—that has already been introduced in the first part of this book—the reader is reminded that the access to this functionality should tightly be controlled, as it allows users influencing financial statements and project results.

2.5. Investment Projects

Investment projects represent another type of internal projects that cannot directly be invoiced to customers. For that reason, only costs for hour, expense, and item transactions can be recorded for investment projects.

Investment projects are typically used for long-term investments, such as the construction of buildings or the development of new products, where the costs incurred today are later on transferred to either a fixed asset or a ledger account or another project.

In order to capitalize the costs that have been accumulated, investment projects make use of the estimate functionality. For investment projects with P&L accounting setup, posting the estimates transfers all costs accumulated on the P&L accounts to the WIP accounts in the balance sheet. This transfer does not occur for investment projects with BS posting setup, as all costs are immediately recorded on WIP accounts in the company's balance sheet.

Once the project is completed, all costs are eliminated, which means that the accumulated costs are transferred to a fixed asset, a ledger account, or another project.

The next subsections show the additional setups required for using the aforementioned estimate project functionality and illustrate the differences in the accounting of investment projects with a P&L and BS accounting setup.

2.5.1. Project-Estimate Functionality

To make use of the project-estimate functionality, two additional setups are required.

2.5.1.1. Setup Cost Template

The first additional setup relates to the creation of a cost template, which does not serve a specific purpose other than calculating the costs that have been accumulated for the investment project over a given period. Figure 2-62 shows the cost template used for the sample transactions.

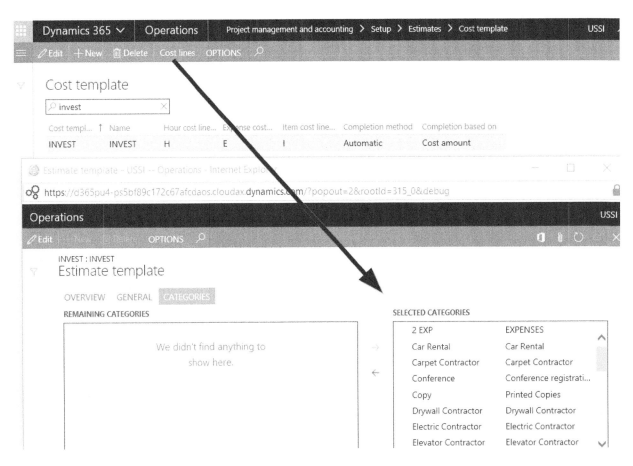

Figure 2-62 Sample cost template

Note Only the costs for the categories selected will be considered in the estimate process. This is why one typically selects all available project categories unless special accounting or valuation requirements necessitate the deselection of the one or the other category.

2.5.1.2. Setup Period Code

The second setup requires the establishment of a period code, which is needed for the periodic estimate calculation process.

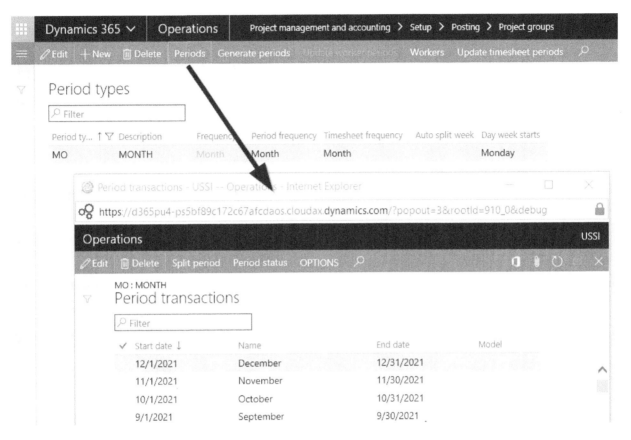

Figure 2-63 Period code used for the project-estimate calculation

2.5.2. Investment Projects with P&L Accounting

With those additional setups in place, a project group for an investment project can be created. Please note that one has to establish a link to the previously setup cost template and project group when setting up the project group. Figure 2-64 illustrates this for the set up of the investment project group with a P&L accounting integration.

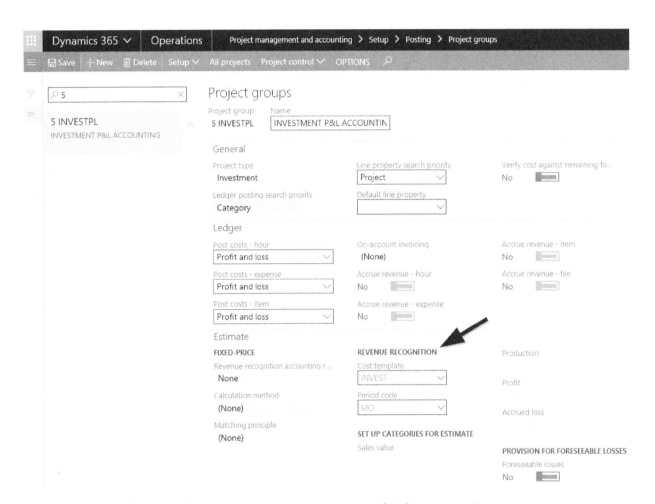

Figure 2-64 Investment project group with P&L accounting setup

To keep things as easy as possible, all project transactions exemplified below are posted within a single period (month), which requires the estimate process to be run and posted only once.

For longer running projects, the estimate process needs to be executed for each period that the project is running until the end of the project when the estimate is eliminated. This repetitive process is illustrated in Figure 2-65 and summarizes the process flow of an investment project with a P&L accounting setup.

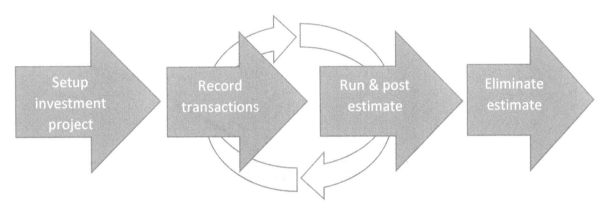

Figure 2-65 Process flow investment projects with P&L accounting setup

2.5.2.1. Record Hour Transactions

Recording hour transactions on an investment project with P&L accounting integration results in a voucher identical to the one that has been created for the cost project and the internal project with P&L accounting integration. For details, please see Figures 2-66 and 2-67.

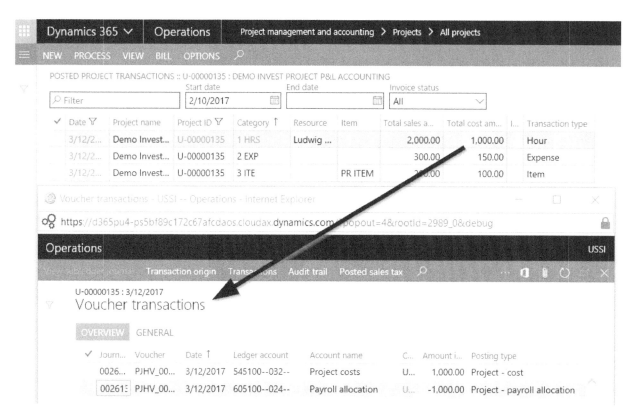

Figure 2-66 Resulting hour transaction and voucher—Investment project with P&L accounting

DEBIT	CREDIT	AMOUNT
545100 Project costs [Profit&Loss—Project cost]	605100 Payroll allocation [Profit&Loss—Project payroll allocation]	$1,000

Figure 2-67 Accounting voucher hour transaction—Investment project with P&L accounting

2.5.2.2.   Record Expense Transactions

Expense transactions recorded on investment projects with P&L accounting integration similarly result in a voucher identical to the one that has been shown for cost and internal projects with a P&L accounting integration. The same holds for item transactions shown in the following subsection.

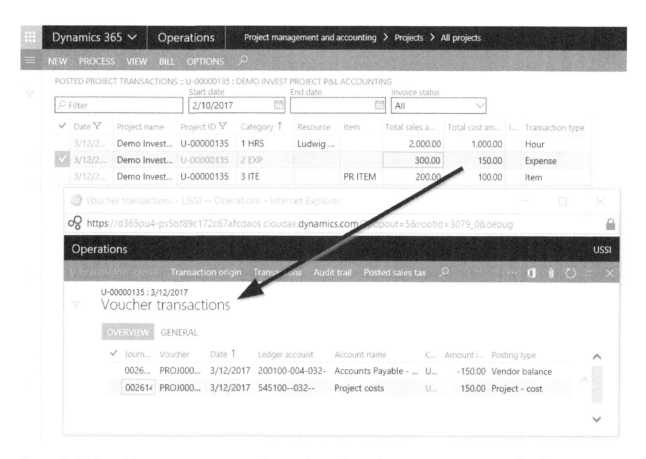

Figure 2-68 Resulting expense transaction and voucher—Investment project with P&L accounting

DEBIT	CREDIT	AMOUNT
545100 Project costs [Profit&Loss—Project cost]	200100 Accounts Payable [BalanceSheet—Vendor balance]	$150

Figure 2-69 Accounting voucher expense transaction—Investment project with P&L accounting

2.5.2.3.   Record Item Transactions

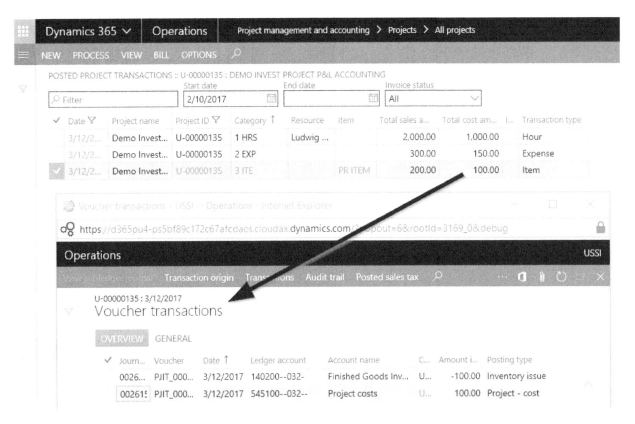

Figure 2-70 Resulting item transaction and voucher—Investment project with P&L accounting

DEBIT	CREDIT	AMOUNT
545100 Project costs [Profit&Loss—Project cost]	140200 Finished Goods [BalanceSheet—Inventory issue]	$100

Figure 2-71 Accounting voucher item transaction—Investment project with P&L accounting

2.5.2.4.   Record Fee Transactions

As mentioned in the introductory part, fees cannot be recorded for investment projects because they cannot be invoiced to customers.

2.5.2.5. Run, Post, and Eliminate Estimate

Once all transactions for a given period are recorded, the project estimate needs to be created posted and—at the end of the project—eliminated. The creation of the project estimate for the last period after all costs have been posted is shown in Figure 2-72.

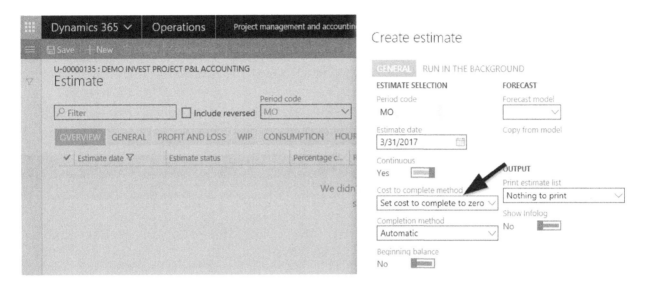

Figure 2-72 Create project estimate

Note The previously set up period code and cost template come into play with the creation of the project estimates. That is, each estimate needs to be created with reference to a specific period code and cost template. While the period code can easily be identified from Figure 2-72, the cost template cannot directly be identified because it is referenced from the project-group setup.

Note The estimate process shown above needs to be run for each period (as illustrated in Figure 2-65 above) with a cost to complete method that shifts the project costs of a specific period to the WIP accounts in the company's balance sheet. For this purpose, a cost to complete method such as *Total cost—actual* can be used. The completion method *set cost to complete zero* is only used for the last estimate before the costs are transferred to a fixed asset, another project, or a ledger account.

Posting the estimate results in the following ledger voucher that shifts all costs from the project cost accounts to the project WIP accounts.

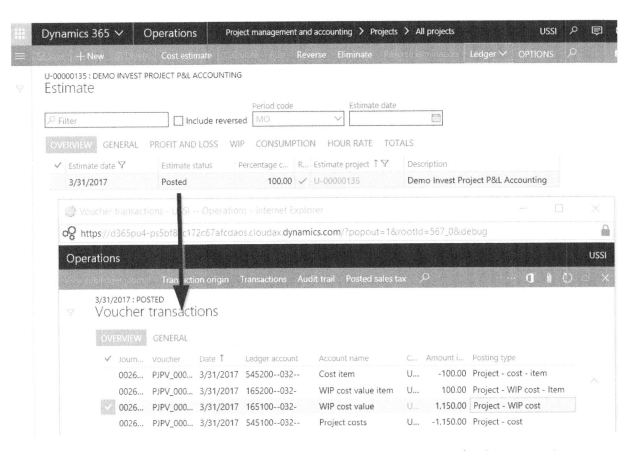

Figure 2-73 Resulting estimate voucher—Investment project with P&L accounting

DEBIT	CREDIT	AMOUNT
165100 WIP cost value [BalanceSheet—Project WIP cost]	545100 Project costs [Profit&Loss—Project cost]	$1,150
165200 WIP cost value item [BalanceSheet—Project WIP cost item]	545200 Cost item [Profit&Loss—Project-cost item]	$100

Figure 2-74 Estimate posting voucher—Investment project with P&L accounting

Eliminating the estimate(s)—for example to a fixed asset—results in the following transaction and voucher.

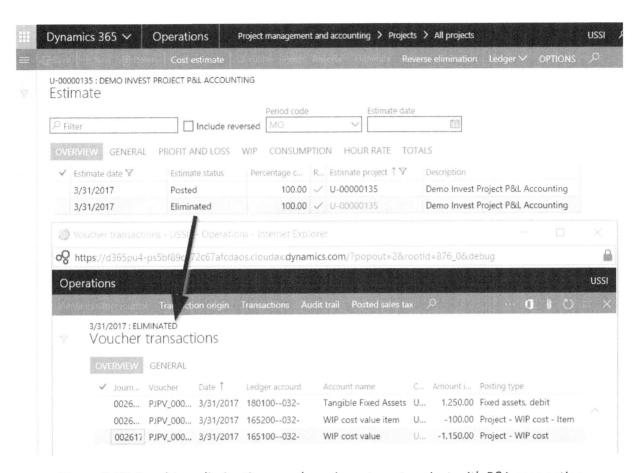

Figure 2-75 Resulting elimination voucher—investment project with P&L accounting

DEBIT	CREDIT	AMOUNT
180100 Tangible Fixed Assets [BalanceSheet—Fixed assets, debit]	165100 WIP cost value [BalanceSheet—Project WIP cost]	$1,150
	165200 WIP cost value item [BalanceSheet—Project WIP cost item]	$100

Figure 2-76 Elimination posting voucher—investment project with P&L accounting

2.5.2.6.   Summary

Figure 2-77 summarizes all vouchers for the different transactions recorded on the sample investment project with a P&L accounting integration.

DEBIT	CREDIT	AMOUNT
Hour transactions		
545100 Project costs [Profit&Loss—Project cost]	605100 Payroll allocation [Profit&Loss—Project payroll allocation]	$1,000
Expense transactions		
545100 Project costs [Profit&Loss—Project cost]	200100 Accounts Payable [BalanceSheet—Vendor balance]	$150
Item transactions		
545100 Project costs [Profit&Loss—Project cost]	140200 Finished goods [BalanceSheet—Inventory issue]	$100
Fee transactions		
Not possible		
Post estimates		
165100 WIP cost value [BalanceSheet—Project WIP cost]	545100 Project costs [Profit&Loss—Project cost]	$1,150
165200 WIP cost value item [BalanceSheet—Project WIP cost item]	545200 Cost item [Profit&Loss—Project-cost item]	$100
Eliminate estimates		
180100 Tangible Fixed Assets [BalanceSheet—Fixed assets, debit]	165100 WIP cost value [BalanceSheet—Project WIP cost]	$1,150
	165200 WIP cost value item [BalanceSheet—Project WIP cost item]	$100

Figure 2-77 Summary vouchers—investment project with P&L accounting

2.5.3. Investment Projects with BS Accounting

The set up of the investment project group used in the following is identical to the one shown in the previous chapter except for the ledger integration that records all transactions on BS accounts.

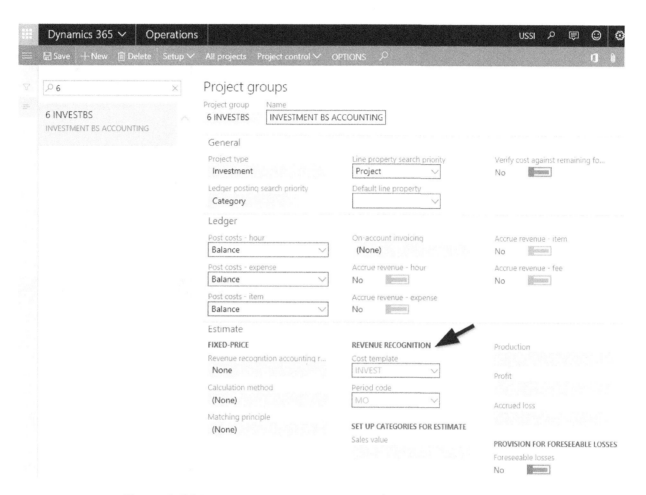

Figure 2-78 Investment project group with BS accounting setup

2.5.3.1. Record Hour Transactions

The vouchers that are created when posting-hour, expense, and item transactions on an investment project with a BS accounting setup are identical to the ones that are created for internal projects with a BS accounting setup. For that reason, only screen-prints and the resulting ledger vouchers are presented below without any additional comments or remarks.

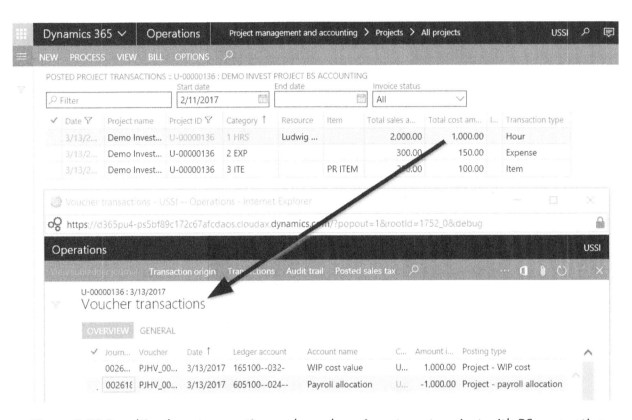

Figure 2-79 Resulting hour transaction and voucher—investment project with BS accounting

DEBIT	CREDIT	AMOUNT
165100 WIP cost value [BalanceSheet—Project WIP cost]	605100 Payroll allocation [Profit&Loss—Project payroll allocation]	$1,000

Figure 2-80 Accounting voucher hour transaction—investment project with BS accounting

2.5.3.2.   Record Expense Transactions

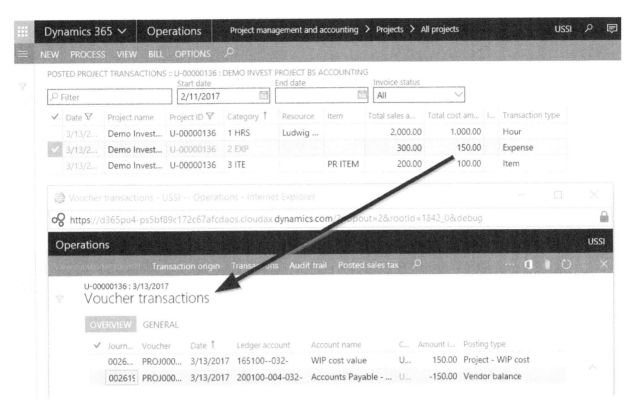

Figure 2-81 Resulting expense transaction and voucher—investment project with BS accounting

DEBIT	CREDIT	AMOUNT
165100 WIP cost value [BalanceSheet—Project WIP cost]	200100 Accounts Payable [BalanceSheet—Vendor balance]	$150

Figure 2-82 Accounting voucher expense transaction—investment project with BS accounting

2.5.3.3.   Record Item Transactions

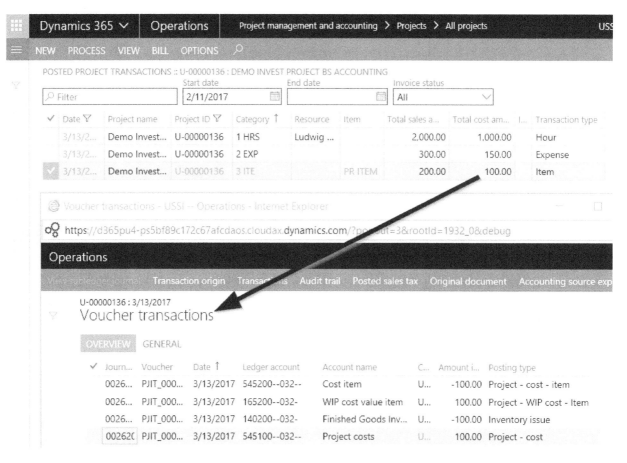

Figure 2-83 Resulting item transaction and voucher—investment project with BS accounting

DEBIT	CREDIT	AMOUNT
545100 Project costs [Profit&Loss—Project cost]	140200 Finished goods [BalanceSheet—Inventory issue]	$100
165200 WIP cost value item [BalanceSheet—Project WIP cost item]	545200 Cost item [Profit&Loss—Project cost item]	$100

Figure 2-84 Accounting voucher item transaction—investment project with BS accounting

2.5.3.4.   Record Fee Transactions

As mentioned before, fee transactions cannot be recorded on investment projects, as those projects cannot be invoiced to customers.

2.5.3.5.   Run, Post, and Eliminate Estimate

The major difference between the internal projects with a BS accounting setup and the ones with a P&L accounting setup materializes in the creation and posting of project estimates, which is exemplified in Figure 2-85.

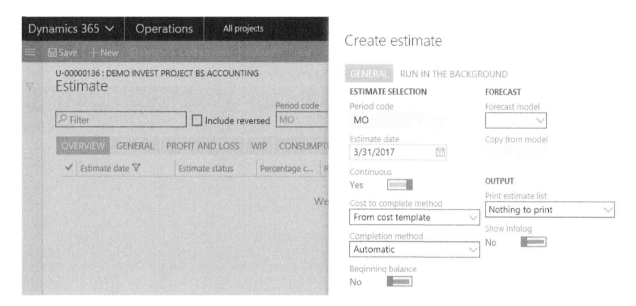

Figure 2-85 Create project estimate

The first major difference between the investment projects with a BS and a P&L accounting integration can be identified when comparing the vouchers posted for the project estimates. Whereas a voucher is generated when posting estimates for an investment project with a P&L accounting integration, no voucher is generated for investment projects with a BS accounting integration. That is because investment projects with a BS accounting setup immediately post all costs to project WIP accounts. For that reason, no additional voucher needs to be created for investment projects with a BS accounting integration when posting estimates. Figure 2-86 illustrates this.

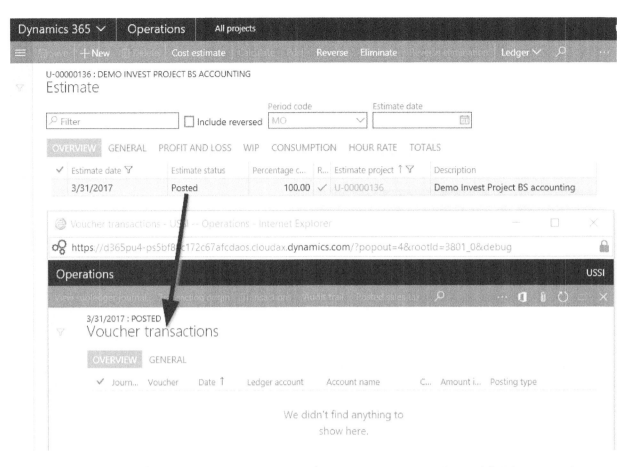

Figure 2-86 Resulting estimate posting voucher—investment project with BS accounting

Against the background of what has been said in regard to the creation of estimate vouchers, setting up investment projects with a BS accounting integration appears to be superior to setting up investment projects with a P&L accounting setup. That is because investment projects with a P&L accounting setup regularly require the creation and posting of estimates in order to move the accumulated costs from the project cost to the WIP accounts, which is not required for investment projects with a BS accounting setup.

Eliminating the estimate(s) to a fixed asset results in the very same transaction, respectively, voucher that has been created for the investment project with the P&L accounting setup. For details, please see Figures 2-87 and 2-88.

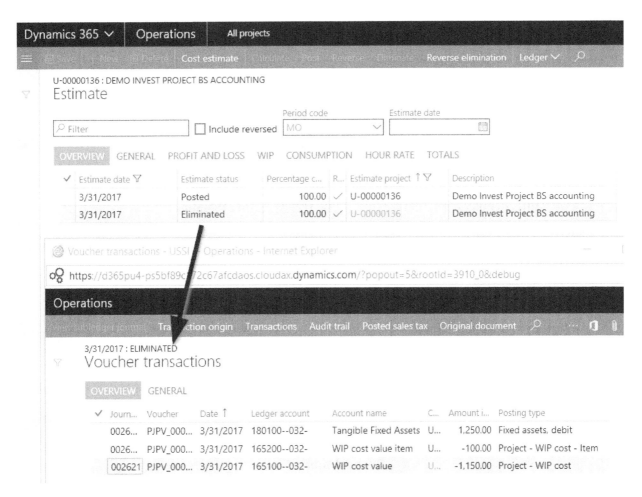

Figure 2-87 Resulting elimination voucher—investment project with BS accounting

DEBIT	CREDIT	AMOUNT
180100 Tangible Fixed Assets [BalanceSheet—Fixed assets, debit]	165100 WIP cost value [BalanceSheet—Project WIP cost]	$1,150
	165200 WIP cost value item [BalanceSheet—Project WIP cost item]	$100

Figure 2-88 Elimination posting voucher—investment project with P&L accounting

2.5.3.6.   Summary

As before, Figure 2-89 summarizes all vouchers for the different transactions recorded on the sample investment project with BS accounting integration.

DEBIT	CREDIT	AMOUNT
Hour transactions		
165100 WIP cost value [BalanceSheet—WIP cost value]	605100 Payroll allocation [Profit&Loss—Project payroll allocation]	$1,000
Expense transactions		
165100 WIP cost value [BalanceSheet—Project cost]	200100 Accounts Payable [BalanceSheet–Vendor balance]	$150
Item transactions		
545100 Project costs [Profit&Loss—Project cost]	140200 Finished goods [BalanceSheet—Inventory issue]	$100
165200 WIP cost value item [BalanceSheet—Project WIP cost item]	545200 Cost item [Profit&Loss—Project cost item]	$100
Fee transactions		
Not possible		
Post estimates		
No voucher generated		
Eliminate estimates		
180100 Tangible Fixed Assets [BalanceSheet—Fixed assets, debit]	165100 WIP cost value [BalanceSheet—Project WIP cost]	$1,150
	165200 WIP cost value item [BalanceSheet—Project WIP cost item]	$100

Figure 2-89 Summary vouchers—investment project with BS accounting

2.5.4. Special Issues

Sometimes companies do not want or are not allowed to capitalize all costs that are accumulated on an investment project. Within this section, we will have a look at an example where only a part of the total accumulated costs will be transferred to a fixed asset and the remainder will be expensed.

To realize this, the project-group parameter for foreseeable losses is activated and an accrued loss category is selected in the previously used category form. Details of this setup can be found in Figure 2-90.

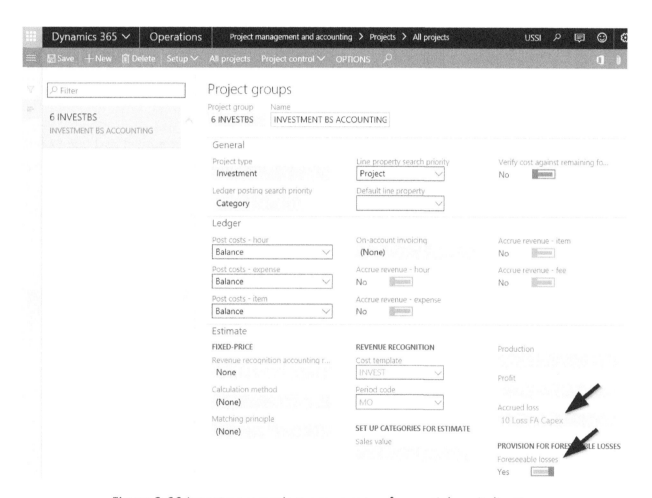

Figure 2-90 Investment project-group setup for partial capitalization

Note Please note that the project category that is used for recording the so-called accrued loss must be linked to an expense-related project category and must have the estimate parameter turned on.

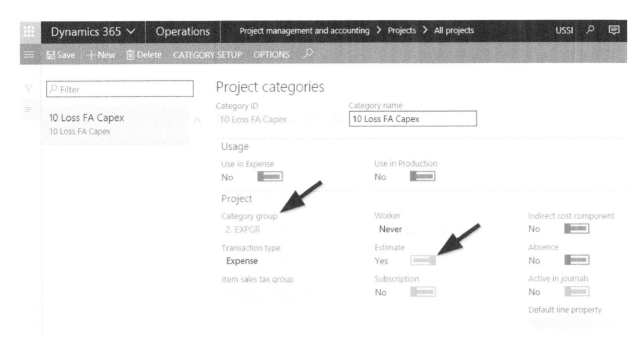

Figure 2-91 Accrued loss project category setup

To illustrate how one can capitalize only a part of the total accumulated project costs, the same hour, expense, and item transactions that have been posted in the previous section are recorded on a newly set up investment project. In addition, a project estimate has been created in the same way as exemplified in the previous section. However, before posting the estimate, a capitalization threshold of $1,000 is specified in the *totals* tab of the project-estimate form.

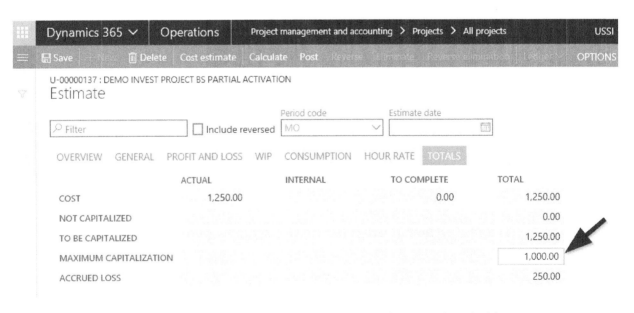

Figure 2-92 Project estimate with capitalization threshold

If the estimate is posted, a voucher that accounts for the costs that are not going to be capitalized is created. This voucher is shown next.

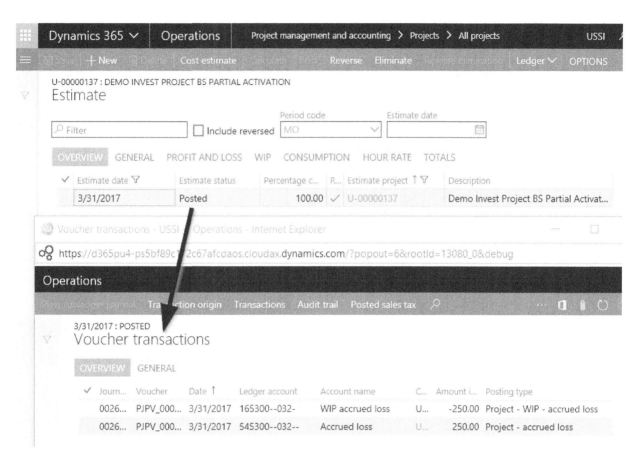

Figure 2-93 Resulting estimate voucher—investment project with BS accounting and specified capitalization threshold

DEBIT	CREDIT	AMOUNT
545300 Accrued loss [Profit&Loss—Project accrued loss]	165300 WIP accrued loss [BalanceSheet—Project WIP accrued loss]	$250

Figure 2-94 Estimate posting voucher—investment project with BS accounting and specified capitalization threshold

As one can identify from Figures 2-93 and 2-94, the costs that are not capitalized ($250) are expensed on the accrued loss account. The elimination of the estimate finally results in a voucher that shifts the specified maximum capitalization amount to the fixed asset ($1,000) and clears all WIP account balances. Figures 2-95 and 2-96 illustrate this in detail.

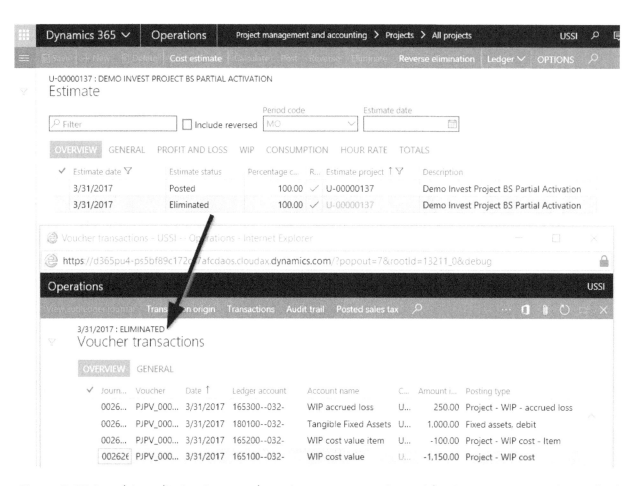

Figure 2-95 Resulting elimination voucher—investment project with BS accounting and specified capitalization threshold

DEBIT	CREDIT	AMOUNT
165300 WIP accrued loss [BalanceSheet—Project WIP accrued loss]		$250
180100 Tangible Fixed Assets [BalanceSheet—Fixed assets, debit]		$1,000
	165200 WIP cost value item [BalanceSheet—Project WIP cost item]	$100
	165100 WIP cost value [BalanceSheet—Project WIP cost]	$1,150

Figure 2-96 Elimination posting voucher—investment project with BS accounting and specified capitalization threshold

2.6. Time and Material (T&M) Projects

All project types introduced before were characterized by the fact that they could not be invoiced to customers. This is different for the T&M projects described in this chapter, as well as the fix-price projects described further below.

2.6.1. Basic T&M Projects

A basic T&M project can be characterized as follows:

- There is a direct (periodic) match between project cost and revenues,
- invoices are created for the actual expenses incurred, and
- all costs and revenues are posted to P&L accounts.

Figure 2-97 shows the project-group settings that will be used for the subsequent illustration of the different transactions.

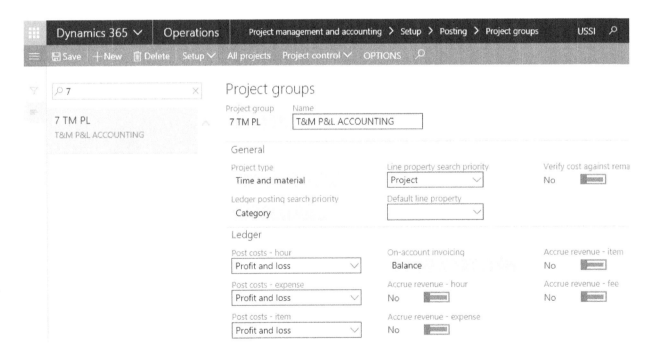

Figure 2-97 Basic T&M project group with P&L accounting setup

Note Creating new T&M projects requires referencing a project contract, which is needed for invoicing the customer.

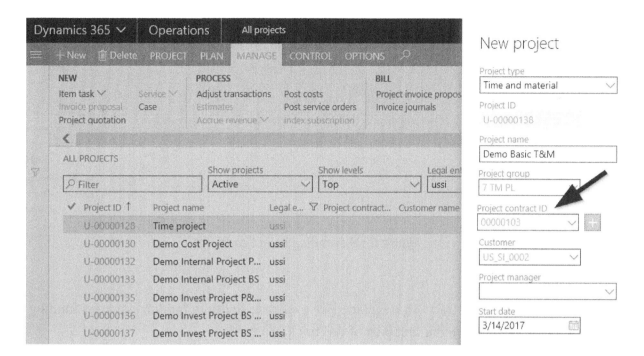

Figure 2-98 Basic T&M project creation

Project contracts hold all the information—such as currency, customer address, and terms of payment—that is necessary for creating project invoices. Once a project is linked to a project contract, customer invoices can be created either from the individual project or from the project contract. Using the project contract for invoicing customers has the advantage that several projects can be invoiced at the same time. Figure 2-99 illustrates a sample project contract that is linked to a number of different projects.

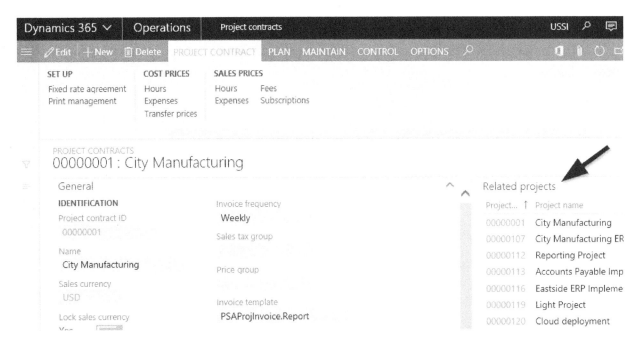

Figure 2-99 Sample project contract

More complex project contracts that include, for example, multiple funding sources, funding limits, and so forth can be found in the first part of this book.

2.6.1.1.   Record Hour Transactions

The ledger vouchers created for hour, expense, and item transactions are identical to those shown for cost projects. For that reason, only screen-prints and the resulting vouchers are presented in the following.

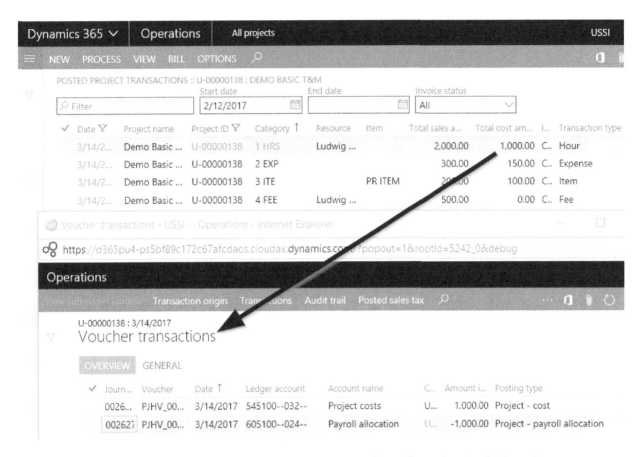

Figure 2-100 Resulting hour transactions and voucher—basic T&M project

DEBIT	CREDIT	AMOUNT
545100 Project costs [Profit&Loss—Project cost]	605100 Payroll allocation [Profit&Loss—Project payroll allocation]	$1,000

Figure 2-101 Accounting voucher hour transactions—basic T&M project

2.6.1.2. Record Expense Transactions

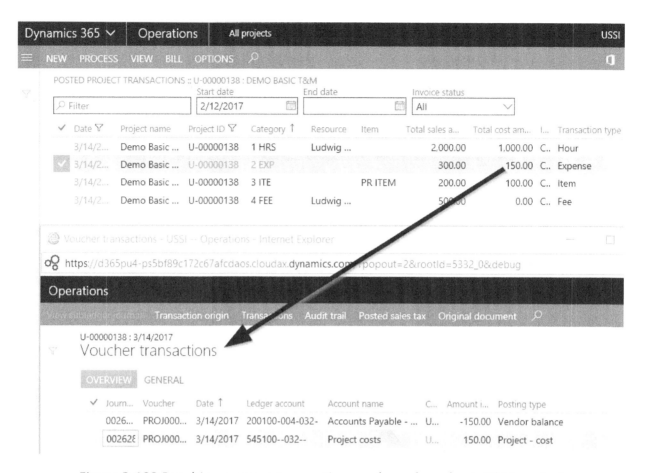

Figure 2-102 Resulting expense transactions and voucher—basic T&M project

DEBIT	CREDIT	AMOUNT
545100 Project costs [Profit&Loss—Project cost]	200100 Accounts Payable [BalanceSheet—Vendor balance]	$150

Figure 2-103 Accounting voucher expense transactions—basic T&M project

2.6.1.3. Record Item Transactions

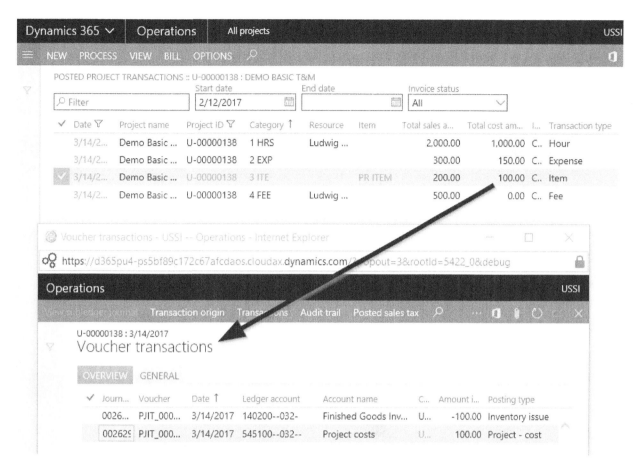

Figure 2-104 Resulting item transaction and voucher—basic T&M project

DEBIT	CREDIT	AMOUNT
545100 Project costs [Profit&Loss—Project cost]	140200 Finished Goods [BalanceSheet—Inventory issue]	$100

Figure 2-105 Accounting voucher item transactions—basic T&M project

2.6.1.4.   Record Fee Transactions

Previously, it was explained that project fees do not have costs associated and can only be used for posting project revenues. For that reason, recording a fee transaction on a T&M project does not result in the creation of a voucher, as Figure 2-106 illustrates.

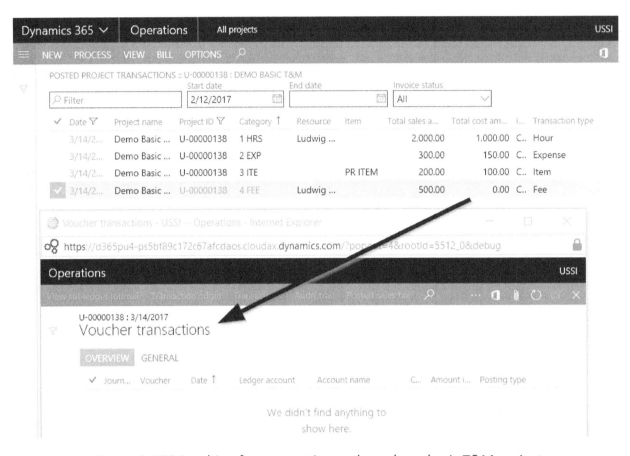

Figure 2-106 Resulting fee transaction and voucher—basic T&M project

DEBIT	CREDIT	AMOUNT
No voucher generated		

Figure 2-107 Accounting voucher fee transactions—basic T&M project

2.6.1.5. Generate Customer Invoices

Once billable project transactions have been recorded, project invoices can be created by initiating the project invoice proposal process. Figure 2-108 shows the respective form in D365 that allows including and excluding specific transactions from the invoice.

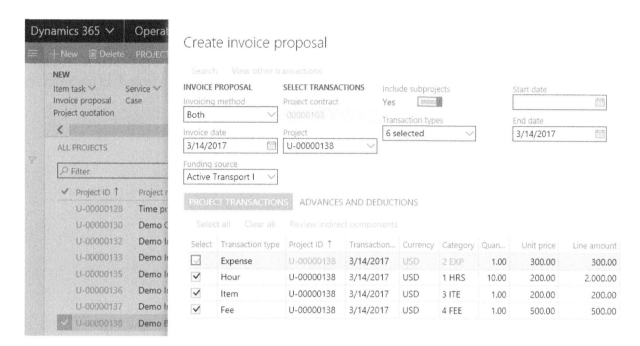

Figure 2-108 Project invoice proposal form

Posting the project invoice for the four transaction types used, results in the following voucher that is summarized in the accounting overview in Figure 2-110.

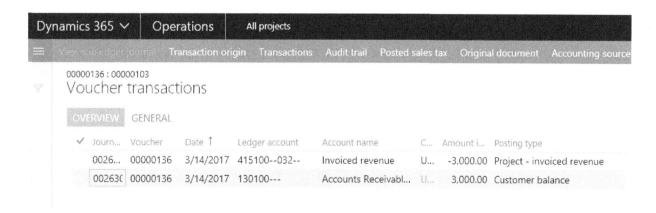

Figure 2-109 Resulting invoice transaction and voucher—basic T&M project

DEBIT	CREDIT	AMOUNT
130100 Accounts Receivable [BalanceSheet—Customer Balance]	415100 Invoiced revenue [Profit&Loss—Project invoiced revenue]	$3,000

Figure 2-110 Accounting voucher invoice transaction—basic T&M project

Note
Whether the project invoice voucher includes separate voucher lines for each of the transaction types recorded or whether it summarizes the different revenue voucher lines into a single voucher depends on the ledger-posting detail level parameter specified in the project-module parameters form.

2.6.1.6.   Summary

Figure 2-111 summarizes all vouchers for the different transactions recorded on the sample T&M project with a P&L accounting setup.

DEBIT	CREDIT	AMOUNT
Hour transactions		
545100 Project costs [Profit&Loss—Project cost]	605100 Payroll allocation [Profit&Loss—Project payroll allocation]	$1,000
Expense transactions		
545100 Project costs [Profit&Loss—Project cost]	200100 Accounts Payable [BalanceSheet—Vendor balance]	$150
Item transactions		
545100 Project costs [Profit&Loss—Project cost]	140200 Finished Goods [BalanceSheet—Inventory issue]	$100
Fee transactions		
No voucher generated		
Project invoice		
130100 Accounts Receivable [BalanceSheet—Customer Balance]	415100 Invoiced revenue [Profit&Loss—Project invoiced revenue]	$3,000

Figure 2-111 Summary vouchers—basic T&M project

2.6.1.7. Special Issues

Within the prior sections, the on-account invoicing parameters have not been examined. This loophole will be closed now by comparing the project-group setup shown in Figure 2-97—that makes use of a *Balance* setup for the on-account invoicing parameter—with the setup shown in Figure 2-112, which make use of a *Profit and loss* setup.

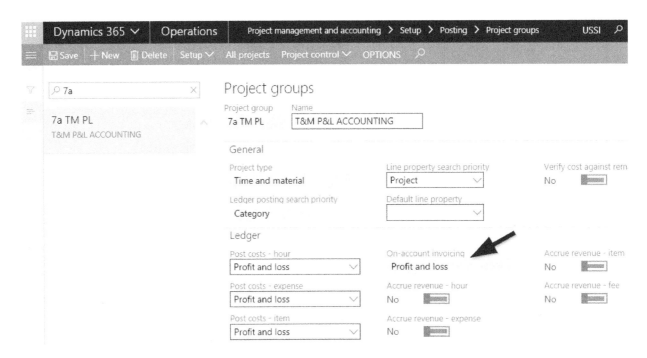

Figure 2-112 Basic T&M project group with BS accounting setup for on-account invoicing

In order to identify what difference the setup of the on-account invoicing parameter makes, two projects linked to the different project groups are created. For each of those projects, prepayment and deduction on-account transactions are set up, as exemplified in Figure 2-113.

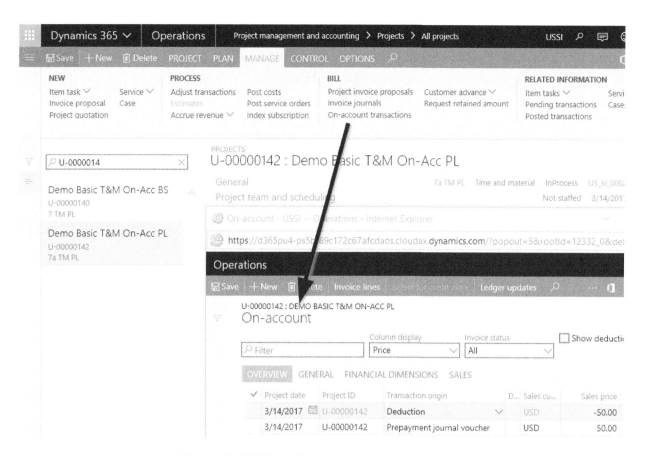

Figure 2-113 Sample on-account transactions

Posting the prepayment on-account transactions for the project with the *Balance* on-account setup results in a voucher that is exemplified in the upper part of Figure 2-114. The lower part shows the transaction created when the prepayment is deducted.

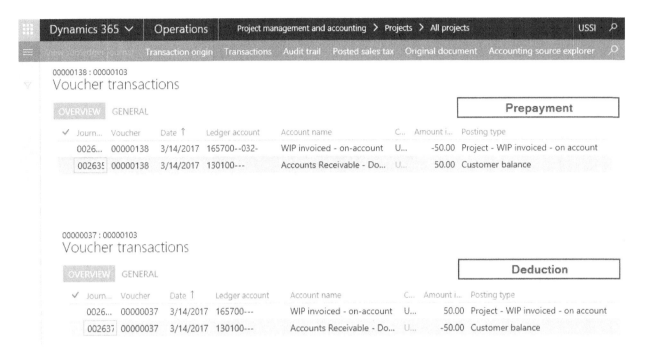

Figure 2-114 On-account vouchers with BS on-accounting setup

DEBIT	CREDIT	AMOUNT
Prepayment		
130100 Accounts Receivable [BalanceSheet—Customer Balance]	165700 WIP invoiced on-account [BalanceSheet—Project WIP invoiced on-account]	$50
Deduction		
165700 WIP invoiced on-account [BalanceSheet—Project WIP invoiced on-account]	130100 Accounts Receivable [BalanceSheet—Customer Balance]	$50

Figure 2-115 On-account vouchers with BS on-accounting setup

Figures 2-116 and 2-117 summarize the same on-account transactions for the project with a *Profit and loss* on-account parameter setup.

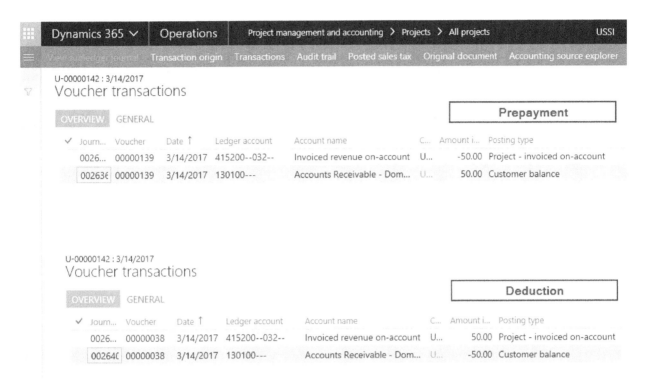

Figure 2-116 On-account vouchers with P&L on-accounting setup

DEBIT	CREDIT	AMOUNT
Prepayment		
130100 Accounts Receivable [BalanceSheet—Customer Balance]	415200 Invoiced revenue on account [Profit&Loss—Project—invoiced on account]	$50
Deduction		
415200 Invoiced revenue on account [Profit&Loss—Project-invoiced on account]	130100 Accounts Receivable [BalanceSheet—Customer Balance]	$50

Figure 2-117 On-account vouchers with P&L on-accounting setup

Comparing the results for the on-account transactions posted with the *Balance* and the *Profit and loss* setup demonstrates that the *Balance* setup makes use of the ledger account that is set up in the WIP invoiced on-account section, whereas the *Profit and loss* setup makes use of the ledger account that is set up in the *invoiced revenue—on-account* section.

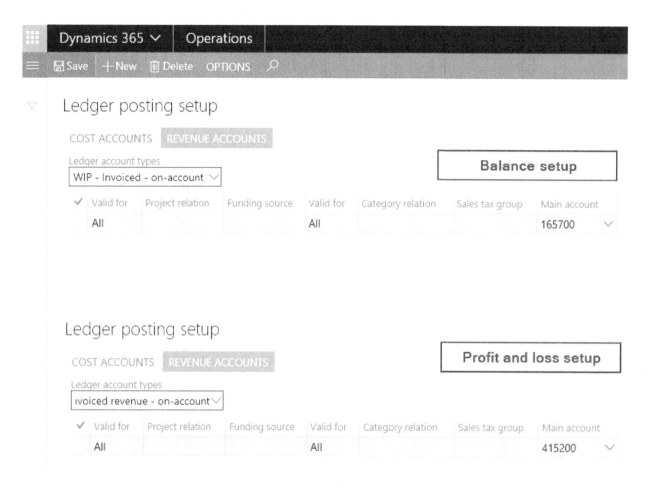

Figure 2-118 On-account ledger accounts used

After illustrating the difference that the set up of the on-account invoicing parameter makes, the question about the preferable setup has not been answered. From the author's perspective, the parameter setup that makes use of the *Balance* on-account parameter is preferable over a setup that tracks on-account transactions on a P&L account because of the cash-related nature of on-account transactions that do by themselves not influence a company's profit.

2.6.2.   T&M Projects with Accruals

T&M projects with accruals are typically used when there is no direct (periodic) match between project costs and project revenues. This is usually the case for longer running projects where costs and revenues arise in different periods.

Figure 2-119 illustrates the project-group setup that will be used for recording the sample transactions shown in the next subchapters.

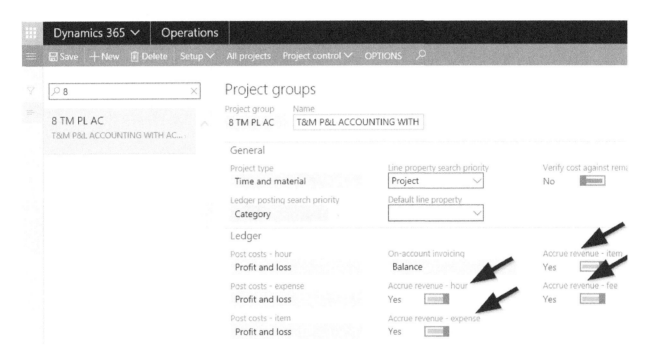

Figure 2-119 T&M project group with P&L accounting setup and accruals

2.6.2.1.   Record Hour Transactions

Recording project hours on a T&M project with accruals results in a voucher that debits the project cost account and credits the payroll allocation account in a first step. Whereas vouchers are identical to the ones shown before, the accrual posting that debits the *WIP sales-value* account no. 165400 and credits an *accrued revenue* account no. 415300 with the prospective sales amount, differs from everything that has been shown previously.

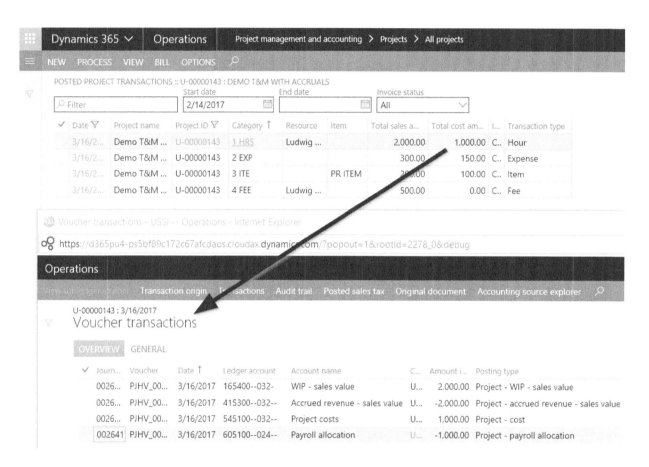

Figure 2-120 Resulting hour transaction and voucher—T&M project with P&L accounting and accruals

The next accounting overview summarizes the voucher in an accounting-like way and shows that the accrual parameters ensure a periodic match of project costs and expected project revenues, which is important for a contemporary and permanent project controlling.

DEBIT	CREDIT	AMOUNT
545100 Project costs [Profit&Loss—Project cost]	605100 Payroll allocation [Profit&Loss—Project payroll allocation]	$1,000
165400 WIP sales value [BalanceSheet—Project WIP sales value]	415300 Accrued revenue sales value [Profit&Loss—Project accrued revenue-sales value]	$2,000

Figure 2-121 Accounting voucher hour transaction—T&M project with P&L accounting and accruals

2.6.2.2.   Record Expense Transactions

The additional accrual posting line that has been identified for the hour transactions can also be identified for the expense and item-related project transactions. Details thereof can be found in Figures 2-122 and 2-123.

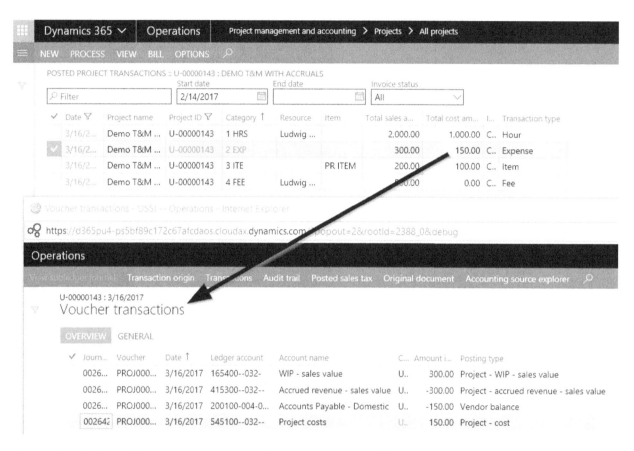

Figure 2-122 Resulting expense transaction and voucher—T&M project with P&L accounting and accruals

DEBIT	CREDIT	AMOUNT
545100 Project costs [Profit&Loss—Project cost]	200100 Accounts Payable [BalanceSheet—Vendor balance]	$150
165400 WIP sales value [BalanceSheet—Project WIP sales value]	415300 Accrued revenue sales value [Profit&Loss—Project accrued revenue-sales value]	$300

Figure 2-123 Accounting voucher expense transaction—T&M project with P&L accounting and accruals

2.6.2.3. Record Item Transactions

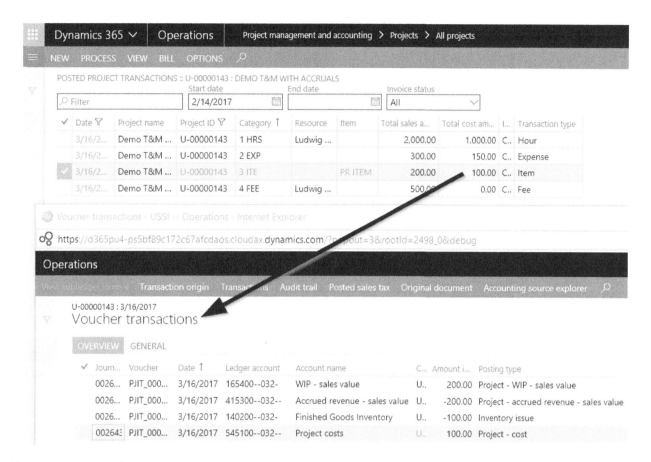

Figure 2-124 Resulting item transaction and voucher—T&M project with P&L accounting and accruals

DEBIT	CREDIT	AMOUNT
545100 Project costs [Profit&Loss—Project cost]	140200 Finished goods [BalanceSheet—Inventory issue]	$100
165400 WIP sales value [BalanceSheet—Project WIP sales value]	415300 Accrued revenue sales value [Profit&Loss—Project accrued revenue-sales value]	$200

Figure 2-125 Accounting voucher item transaction—T&M project with P&L accounting and accruals

2.6.2.4.　Record Fee Transactions

Given the project-group setup, an accrual posting for the expected sales amount is recorded even for the fee transaction that does not have a cost amount attached.

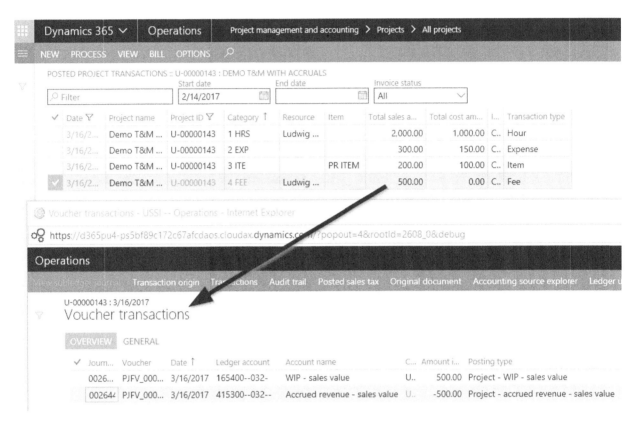

Figure 2-126 Resulting fee transaction and voucher—T&M project with P&L accounting and accruals

DEBIT	CREDIT	AMOUNT
165400 WIP sales value [BalanceSheet—Project WIP sales value]	415300 Accrued revenue sales value [Profit&Loss—Project accrued revenue-sales value]	$500

Figure 2-127 Accounting voucher fee transaction—T&M project with P&L accounting and accruals

Against the background of what has been said before in regard to matching costs and revenues on a periodic basis, the activation of the *accrued revenue-fee* parameter should be avoided from the author's perspective. The underlying reason for this best-practice recommendation is the fact that fee transactions do not have a cost associated. Activating the fee-related accrual parameter consequently results in a comparatively too large revenue accrual, which might overshadow problems that arise during project execution.

2.6.2.5.   Generate Customer Invoices

Invoicing the customer for the hours, expense, and so forth transactions results in a voucher that reverses the previously posted revenue accruals and replaces them with the realized project revenue. Figures 2-128 and 2-129 illustrate this replacement of the accrued revenue by the realized project revenue.

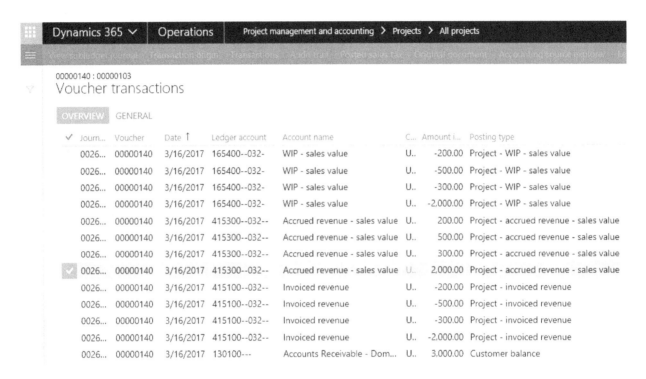

Figure 2-128 Resulting invoice transaction and voucher—T&M project with P&L accounting and accruals

DEBIT	CREDIT	AMOUNT
415300 Accrued revenue sales value [Profit&Loss—Project accrued revenue-sales value]	165400 WIP sales value [BalanceSheet—Project WIP sales value]	$3,000
130100 Accounts Receivable [BalanceSheet—Customer balance]	415100 Invoiced Revenue [Profit&Loss—Project invoice revenue]	$3,000

Figure 2-129 Accounting voucher invoice transaction—T&M project with P&L accounting and accruals

2.6.2.6.   Summary

As before, Figure 2-130 summarizes the transactions posted for the T&M project with accruals.

DEBIT	CREDIT	AMOUNT
Hour transactions		
545100 Project costs [Profit&Loss—Project cost]	605100 Payroll allocation [Profit&Loss—Project payroll allocation]	$1,000
165400 WIP sales value [BalanceSheet—Project WIP sales value]	415300 Accrued revenue sales value [Profit&Loss—Project accrued revenue-sales value]	$2,000
Expense transactions		
545100 Project costs [Profit&Loss—Project cost]	200100 Accounts Payable [BalanceSheet—Vendor balance]	$150
165400 WIP sales value [BalanceSheet—Project WIP sales value]	415300 Accrued revenue sales value [Profit&Loss—Project accrued revenue-sales value]	$300
Item transactions		
545100 Project costs [Profit&Loss—Project cost]	140200 Finished goods [BalanceSheet—Inventory issue]	$100
165400 WIP sales value [BalanceSheet—Project WIP sales value]	415300 Accrued revenue sales value [Profit&Loss—Project accrued revenue-sales value]	$200
Fee transactions		
165400 WIP sales value [BalanceSheet—Project WIP sales value]	415300 Accrued revenue sales value [Profit&Loss—Project accrued revenue-sales value]	$500
Project invoice		
415300 Accrued revenue sales value [Profit&Loss—Project accrued revenue-sales value]	165400 WIP sales value [BalanceSheet—Project WIP sales value]	$3,000
130100 Accounts Receivable [BalanceSheet—Customer balance]	415100 Invoiced Revenue [Profit&Loss—Project invoice revenue]	$3,000

Figure 2-130 Summary vouchers—T&M project with P&L accounting and accruals

2.6.2.7.   Special Issues

When using T&M projects with accruals, one needs to ensure that those accruals are in line with the accounting regulations in one's company and country. Please note that not all accounting standard setters allow recording accruals in the way presented for reasons of prudence and the *recognition of loss principle*.

Note If a company or accounting standard setter does not allow recording accruals in the way presented, one can still make use of accruals by using statistical ledger accounts that are not included in external accounting statements or reports.

2.6.3. T&M Projects with BS Accounting

T&M projects with BS accounting setup store all costs on WIP accounts in the company's balance sheet until the project invoice is recorded. At the time the project invoice is posted, all costs are moved from the WIP accounts to the P&L accounts to establish a match between project costs and revenues. The project-group setup required to realize this project accounting method is shown in Figure 2-131.

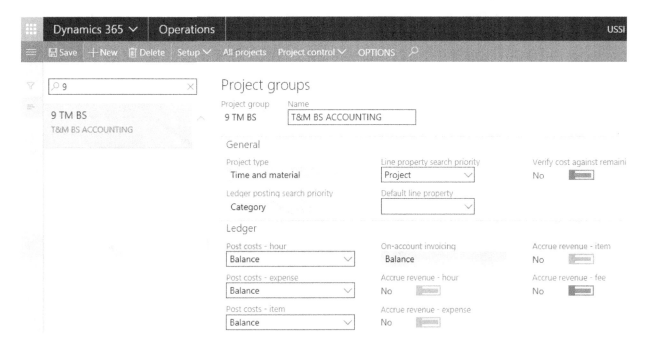

Figure 2-131 T&M project group with BS accounting setup

2.6.3.1.   Record Hour Transactions

The ledger vouchers created for hour, expense, and item transactions are identical to those shown further above for internal projects with BS accounting. For that reason, only screen-prints and the resulting ledger vouchers are shown next.

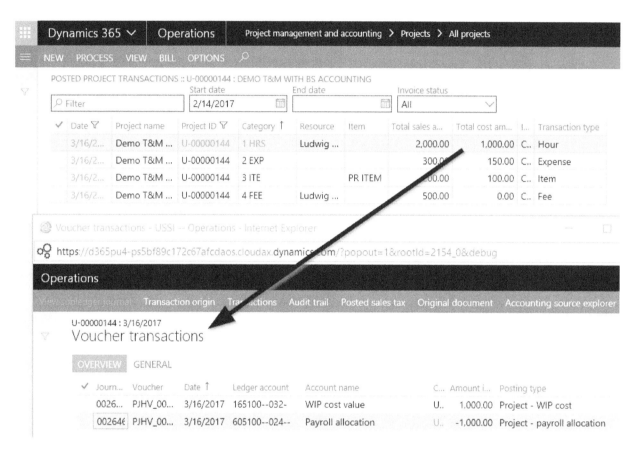

Figure 2-132 Resulting hour transaction and voucher—T&M project with BS accounting

DEBIT	CREDIT	AMOUNT
165100 WIP cost value [BalanceSheet—Project WIP cost]	605100 Payroll allocation [Profit&Loss—Project payroll allocation]	$1,000

Figure 2-133 Accounting voucher hour transaction—T&M project with BS accounting

2.6.3.2. Record Expense Transactions

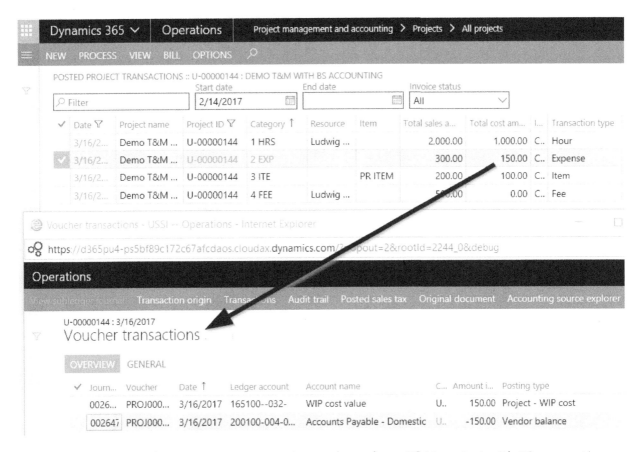

Figure 2-134 Resulting expense transaction and voucher—T&M project with BS accounting

DEBIT	CREDIT	AMOUNT
165100 WIP cost value [BalanceSheet—Project WIP cost]	200100 Accounts Payable [BalanceSheet—Vendor balance]	$150

Figure 2-135 Accounting voucher expense transaction—T&M project with BS accounting

2.6.3.3.   Record Item Transactions

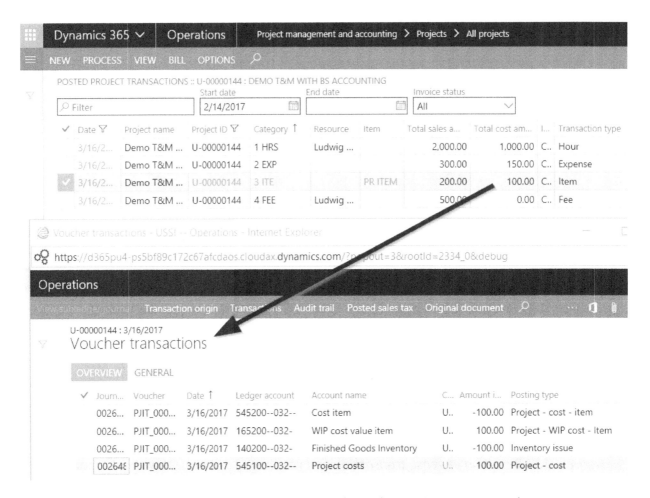

Figure 2-136 Resulting item transaction and voucher—T&M project with BS accounting

DEBIT	CREDIT	AMOUNT
545100 Project costs [Profit&Loss—Project cost]	140200 Finished goods [BalanceSheet—Inventory issue]	$100
165200 WIP cost value item [BalanceSheet—Project WIP cost item]	545200 Cost item [Profit&Loss—Project cost item]	$100

Figure 2-137 Accounting voucher item transaction—T&M project with BS accounting

2.6.3.4.   Record Fee Transactions

Fee transactions recorded on T&M projects with BS accounting integration do not result in any voucher because fees do not have costs associated. The next illustration proves this standard behavior.

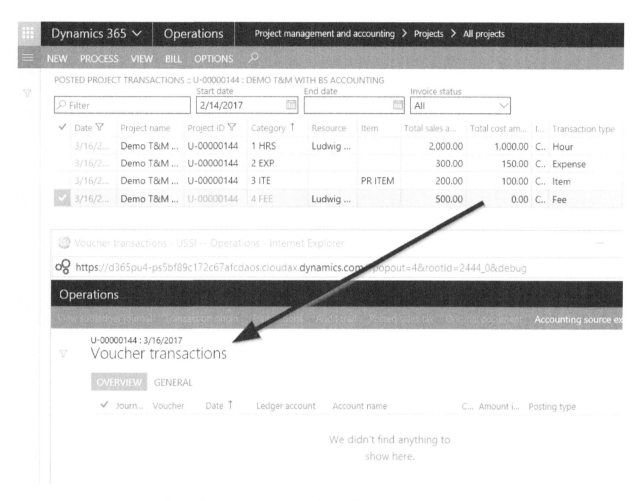

Figure 2-138 Resulting fee transaction and voucher—T&M project with BS accounting

DEBIT	CREDIT	AMOUNT
No voucher generated		

Figure 2-139 Accounting voucher fee transaction—T&M project with BS accounting

2.6.3.5.   Generate Customer Invoices

Posting the project invoice results in a voucher that clears all WIP transactions recorded before and shifts all costs to the project cost accounts in the company's income statement. In addition to this shift, the realized project revenue is recorded on the ordinary project revenue account. For details, please see the following illustrations.

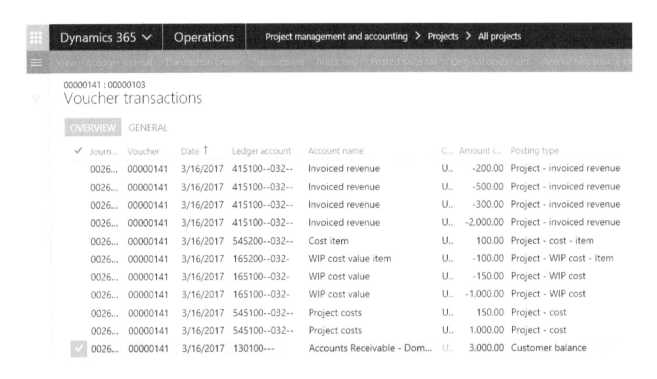

Figure 2-140 Resulting invoice transaction and voucher—T&M project with BS accounting

DEBIT	CREDIT	AMOUNT
545100 Project costs [Profit&Loss—Project cost]	165100 WIP cost value [BalanceSheet—Project WIP cost]	$1,150
545100 Project costs item [Profit&Loss—Project cost item]	165200 WIP cost value item [BalanceSheet—Project WIP cost item]	$100
130100 Accounts Receivable [BalanceSheet—Customer balance]	415100 Invoiced Revenue [Profit&Loss—Project invoice revenue]	$3,000

Figure 2-141 Accounting voucher invoice transaction—T&M project with BS accounting

2.6.3.6. Summary

As before, Figure 2-142 summarizes all transactions that are recorded for the sample T&M project with a BS accounting setup.

DEBIT	CREDIT	AMOUNT
Hour transactions		
165100 WIP cost value [BalanceSheet—Project WIP cost]	605100 Payroll allocation [Profit&Loss—Project payroll allocation]	$1,000
Expense transactions		
165100 WIP cost value [BalanceSheet—Project WIP cost]	200100 Accounts Payable [BalanceSheet—Vendor balance]	$150
Item transactions		
545100 Project costs [Profit&Loss—Project cost]	140200 Finished goods [BalanceSheet—Inventory issue]	$100
165200 WIP cost value item [BalanceSheet—Project WIP cost item]	545200 Cost item [Profit&Loss—Project cost item]	$100
Fee transactions		
No voucher generated		
Project invoice		
545100 Project costs [Profit&Loss—Project cost]	165100 WIP cost value [BalanceSheet—Project WIP cost]	$1,150
545100 Project costs item [Profit&Loss—Project cost item]	165200 WIP cost value item [BalanceSheet—Project WIP cost item]	$100
130100 Accounts Receivable [BalanceSheet—Customer Balance]	415100 Invoiced revenue [Profit&Loss—Project invoiced revenue]	$3,000

Figure 2-142 Summary vouchers—T&M project with BS accounting

2.6.3.7. Special Issues

Figures 2-143 to 2-145 summarize the T&M project transactions in a graphical way assuming that all project costs and revenues arise in different periods (Jan–May).

Figure 2-143 shows how project costs and revenues match for projects with a basic T&M project-group setup.

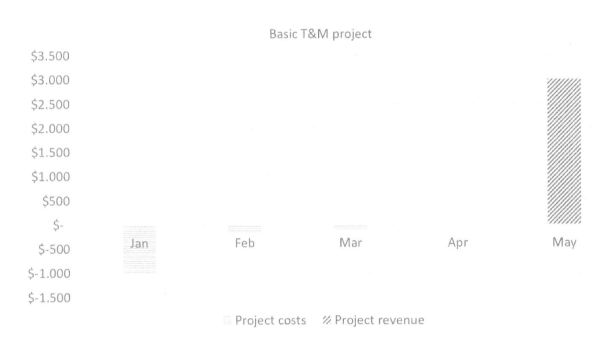

Figure 2-143 Basic T&M project with P&L accounting

As one can identify from Figure 2-143, costs and revenues do not match with a basic T&M project setup, which makes basic T&M projects unsuitable for controlling projects that run over an extended period.

On the other hand, T&M projects that use a P&L accounting setup are able to provide a continuous controlling of project cost and revenues over the lifetime of a project because (actual) costs and (expected) revenues are matched on a periodic basis.

Figure 2-144 T&M project with P&L accounting and accruals

For a T&M project with a BS accounting setup, costs and revenues are matched at the end of the project, respectively, when project invoices are created. This fact makes them—from a project-controlling perspective—somehow unsuitable for longer running projects where project invoices are not created on a regular basis.

Figure 2-145 T&M project with BS accounting

2.7. Fix-Price (FP) Projects

2.7.1. Basic Fix-Price Projects

The basic fix-price project type can be used for short-term projects where the costs and revenues arise in the same period. This type of FP project does not require a periodic match of costs and revenues because the project lifetime is short. For that reason *No WIP* is selected in the revenue recognition accounting rule field in the project-group form and the complete ledger integration is set to *Profit and loss*. Details of the basic FP project-group setup that is used for the following illustrations can be found in Figure 2-146.

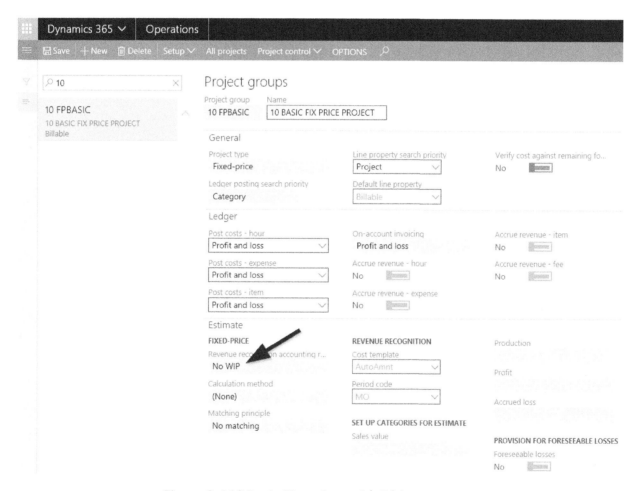

Figure 2-146 Basic FP project with P&L accounting

Please note that all ledger-integration principles are automatically set to *Profit and loss* and cannot be changed. Trying to change them results in an error message that is illustrated in Figure 2-147.

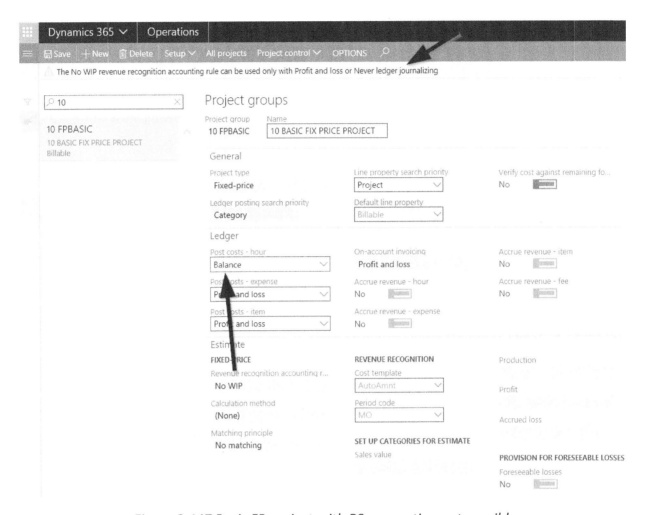

Figure 2-147 Basic FP project with BS accounting not possible

As users cannot change the ledger integration of a basic FP project, a basic FP project resembles a project with P&L accounting integration. For that reason, the next subchapters merely document the generated hours, expense, item, and fee transactions for reasons of completeness.

2.7.1.1. Record Hour Transactions

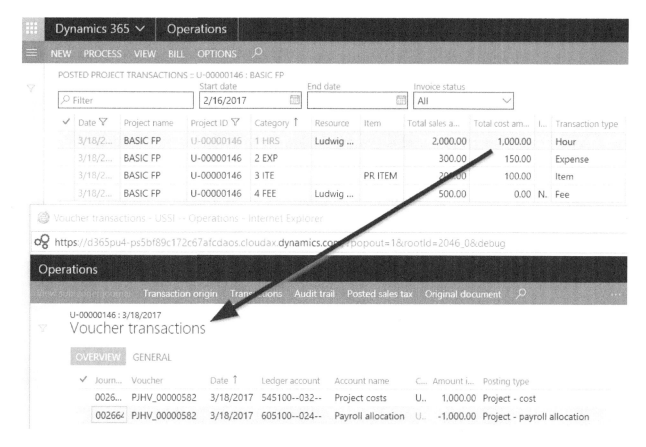

Figure 2-148 Resulting hour transaction and voucher—basic FP project

DEBIT	CREDIT	AMOUNT
545100 Project costs [Profit&Loss—Project cost]	605100 Payroll allocation [Profit&Loss—Project payroll allocation]	$1,000

Figure 2-149 Accounting voucher hour transaction—basic FP project

2.7.1.2.   Record Expense Transactions

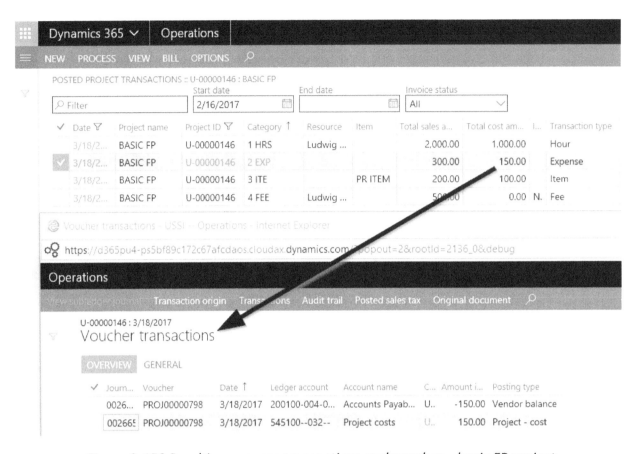

Figure 2-150 Resulting expense transactions and voucher—basic FP project

DEBIT	CREDIT	AMOUNT
545100 Project costs [Profit&Loss—Project cost]	200100 Accounts Payable [BalanceSheet—Vendor balance]	$150

Figure 2-151 Accounting voucher expense transactions—basic FP project

2.7.1.3.   Record Item Transactions

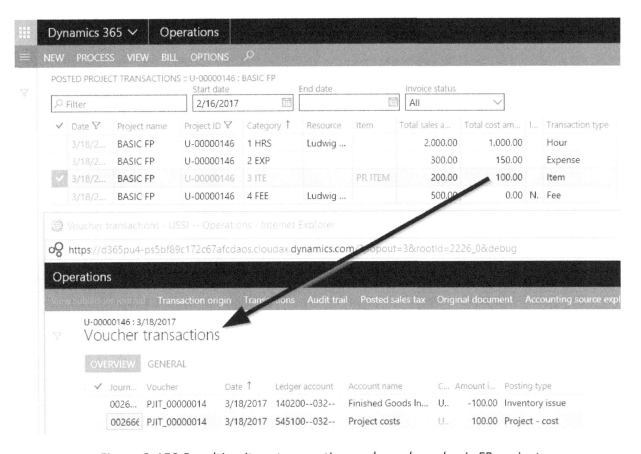

Figure 2-152 Resulting item transaction and voucher—basic FP project

DEBIT	CREDIT	AMOUNT
545100 Project costs [Profit&Loss—Project cost]	140200 Finished Goods [BalanceSheet—Inventory issue]	$100

Figure 2-153 Accounting voucher item transactions—basic FP project

2.7.1.4.   Record Fee Transactions

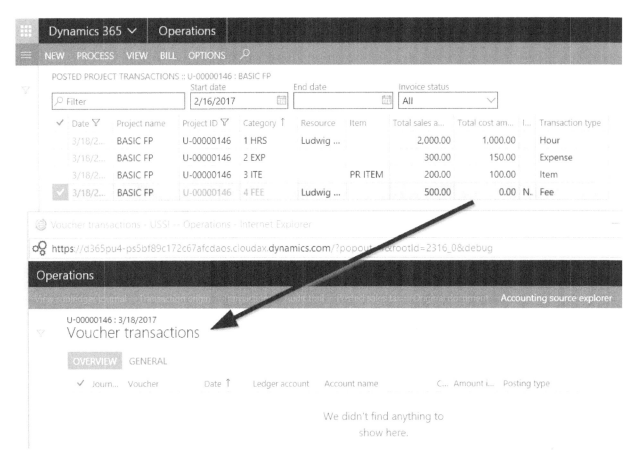

Figure 2-154 Resulting fee transaction and voucher—basic FP project

DEBIT	CREDIT	AMOUNT
No voucher generated		

Figure 2-155 Accounting voucher fee transactions—basic FP project

2.7.1.5.   Generate Customer Invoices

Even though all transactions recorded on the basic FP project have been recorded with a billable line-property, the project invoice proposal form does not suggest invoicing any of those transactions. Figure 2-156 illustrates this by showing that none of the previously recorded transactions can be selected in the invoice proposal form.

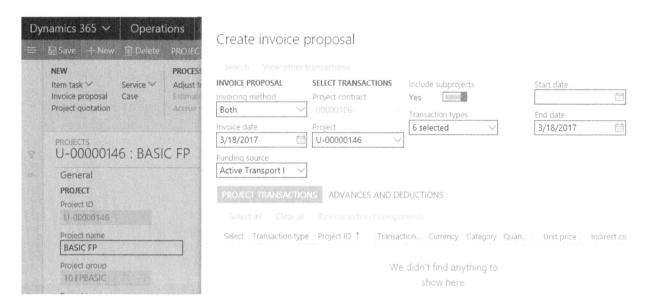

Figure 2-156 Invoice proposal basic FP project (1)

The underlying reason for this standard system behavior is caused by the fact that customers are not invoiced for actual consumption on basic FP projects but rather for fixed agreed upon milestones that need to be set up first in the on-account form, as exemplified in Figure 2-157.

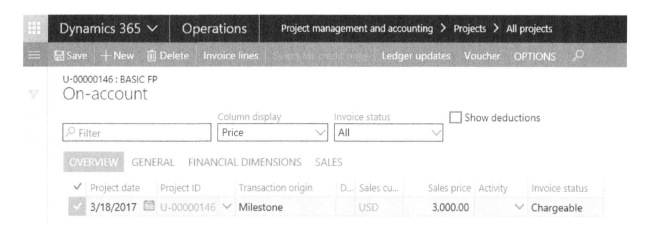

Figure 2-157 Milestone on-account position basic FP project

Once a chargeable milestone position is set up, it is picked up by the invoice proposal process and can be invoiced to the customer. Figures 2-158 to 2-160 illustrate the project invoice generation and the resulting ledger voucher.

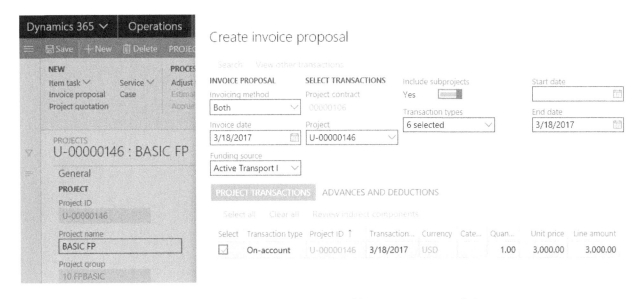

Figure 2-158 Invoice proposal basic FP project (2)

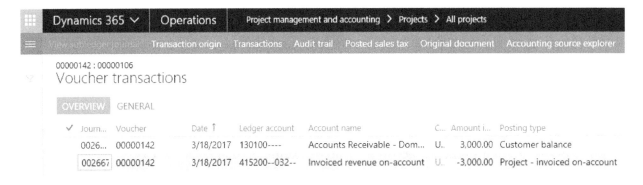

Figure 2-159 Resulting invoice transaction and voucher—basic FP project

DEBIT	CREDIT	AMOUNT
130100 Accounts Receivable [BalanceSheet—Customer Balance]	415100 Invoiced revenue [Profit&Loss—Project invoiced revenue]	$3,000

Figure 2-160 Accounting voucher invoice transaction—basic FP project

2.7.1.6.   Summary

As in the previous chapters, Figure 2-161 summarizes all transactions that have been recorded for the basic FP project.

DEBIT	CREDIT	AMOUNT
Hour transactions		
545100 Project costs [Profit&Loss—Project cost]	605100 Payroll allocation [Profit&Loss—Project payroll allocation]	$1,000
Expense transactions		
545100 Project costs [Profit&Loss—Project cost]	200100 Accounts Payable [BalanceSheet—Vendor balance]	$150
Item transactions		
545100 Project costs [Profit&Loss—Project cost]	140200 Finished Goods [BalanceSheet—Inventory issue]	$100
Fee transactions		
No voucher generated		
Project invoice		
130100 Accounts Receivable [BalanceSheet—Customer Balance]	415100 Invoiced revenue [Profit&Loss—Project invoiced revenue]	$3,000

Figure 2-161 Summary vouchers—basic FP project

2.7.2.   Advanced Fix-Price Projects

Advanced FP projects are characterized by their duration, which surpass a short and foreseeable time span, as it is the case for basic FP projects. Because of their longer duration and the agreed upon fixed contract price—where the customer is not invoiced for actual consumption—costs and revenues do not match.

To get costs and revenues matched, a number of assessment principles have been developed by accounting standard setters in the form of accounting methods, respectively, accounting principles, which can be classified into two groups.

The first group—often considered being the more conservative approach—is the so-called completed contract (CC) accounting method that tracks all costs and revenues on WIP accounts in the company's balance sheet until the end of the project when costs and revenues are realized and matched.

The second group—the so-called percentage of completion method (POC)—continuously matches costs and revenues over the lifetime of the project and thus allows a contemporary and early control of a project's prospective profit or loss.

Note From a finance and controlling perspective, the POC method seems to be superior to the CC method. However, not all accounting standard setters allow applying the POC method. For that reason, it is recommendable consulting a company's auditors before applying the POC method in a live environment.

2.7.2.1.   Prerequisites

To run advanced FP projects, a number of things need to be set up before those projects can be processed. Within the following subchapters, those setups will be explained in more detail together with the sample data that will be used for running and comparing different CC and POC projects.

2.7.2.1.1.   Period Code

The first thing required to run advanced FP projects is the setup of a period code that determines in which intervals (e.g. month, week, and quarter) projects will be assessed or controlled. As the setup of period codes is straightforward and has already been explained in chapter 2.5.1.2., reference is made to the explanations there.

2.7.2.1.2.   Cost Template

FP projects require—as investment projects—cost templates that determine what project categories will be taken into consideration when assessing the project through the estimate process. To keep things as simple and comparable as possible, the following cost template will be used for the sample transactions presented further below.

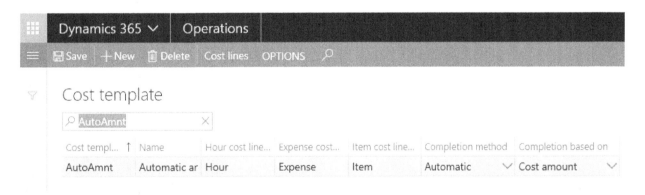

Figure 2-162 Sample cost template used for advanced FP projects

2.7.2.1.3.   Estimate Categories

Estimate categories are required to post temporary revenue accruals for FP projects in order to match cost and revenues over the lifetime of the project. Figure 2-163 illustrates the set up of a so-called sales value estimate category.

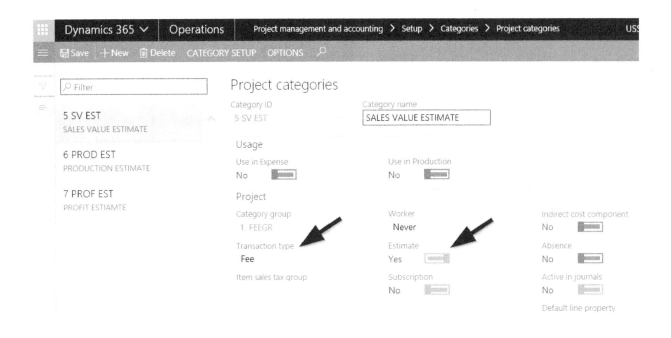

Figure 2-163 Project-estimate category setup

Note Project-estimate categories need to be linked to a fee category group and have the estimate parameter turned on.

2.7.2.1.4. Forecast Model

The last setup required relates to the set up of a forecast model, which is needed for determining how much revenue can be accrued based on the completion principle specified in the cost template.

In other words, the forecast model holds the planned cost values that are compared against the actual cost values in order to determine the percentage of completion (POC) that is used for calculating how much revenue can be accrued given the specific progress of a project.

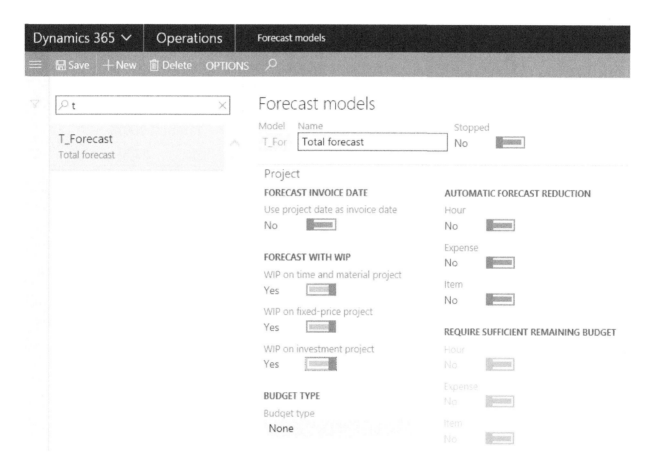

Figure 2-164 Sample forecast model

2.7.2.1.5.   Sample Transactions

All the sample transactions illustrated in the following chapters are based on the same planned and actual cost data that are illustrated in Figure 2-165.

	Period 1	Period 2	Period 3	Total
Planned cost				
Hour	5 hours ($500)		2 hours ($200)	$700
Expense		$100		$100
Item			2 items ($200)	$200
Total	**$500**	**$100**	**$400**	**$1,000**
Actual cost				
Hour	5 hours ($500)	4 hours ($400)	1 hour ($100)	$1,000
Expense		$150		$150
Item			1 item ($100)	$100
Total	**$500**	**$550**	**$200**	**$1,250**

Figure 2-165 Sample data FP projects

Note The actual cost data are identical to the data that have been used in the previous chapters except for the period in which they are recorded. In addition, to allow comparing the transactions and vouchers that are generated in the following chapters with those that have been recorded for the project types analyzed before, the customer will be invoiced $3,000 through an on-account milestone transaction in the first period.

2.7.2.2. CC-Method—P&L Accounting—SV Estimation

With all those setups in place, a first FP project is created with the following project-group settings.

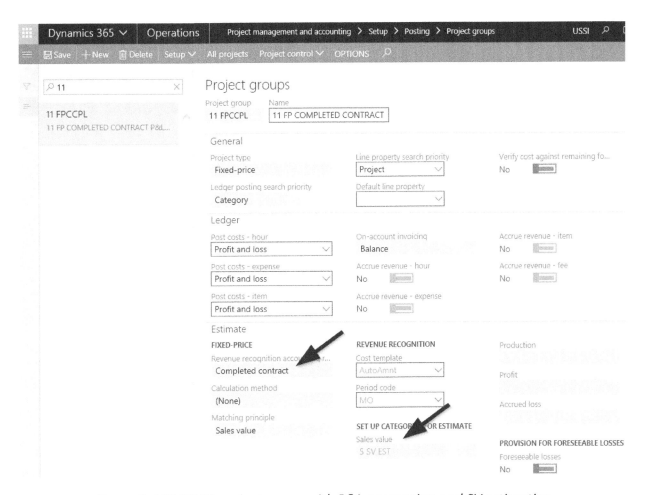

Figure 2-166 CC FP project group with P&L accounting and SV estimation

2.7.2.2.1.   Enter Forecast Values

Different from the projects run before, the first project step for the advanced FP project consists of recording the planned project costs for the different periods in the project forecast form. This is exemplified in Figure 2-167.

Figure 2-167 Project forecast recorded

In the first part of this book, it was mentioned that plan data are recorded in the Work Breakdown Structure (WBS) form first. Once they are entered there, they can be transferred to the forecast and budget forms. What has been mentioned in the first part is still valid. However, to conserve space and maintain simplicity, the plan data are in the following directly and only recorded in the forecast forms.

2.7.2.2.2.   Record and Invoice Milestones

Next, a milestone on-account transaction for the agreed upon sales price of $3,000 is recorded and immediately invoiced. The Figures 2-168 to 2-170 show the resulting ledger voucher generated.

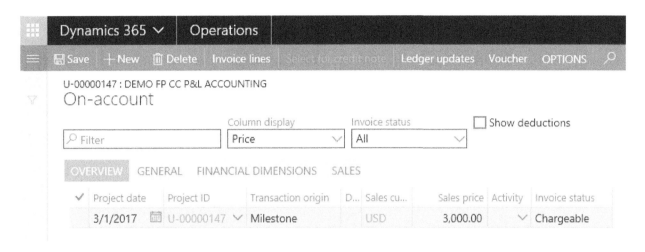

Figure 2-168 Milestone on-account record

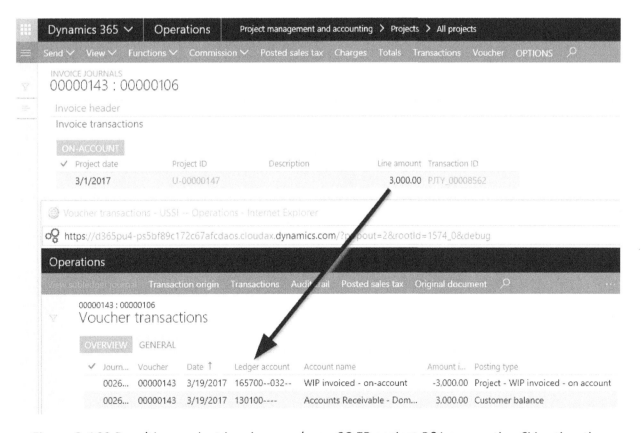

Figure 2-169 Resulting project invoice voucher—CC FP project P&L accounting SV estimation

DEBIT	CREDIT	AMOUNT
PERIOD 1		
130100 Accounts Receivable [BalanceSheet—Customer Balance]	165700 WIP Invoiced on-account [BalanceSheet—Project WIP invoiced on-account]	$3,000

Figure 2-170 Accounting invoice voucher—CC FP project P&L accounting SV estimation

Note Please note that the customer invoice transaction does not result in a revenue posting but is rather recorded on a WIP account in the company's balance sheet. In other words, invoicing the customer does—at this stage—not influence the company's profit.

The next subchapters show the vouchers that are resulting from recording hour, expense, and item transactions on the FP project. As the vouchers generated resemble those of an ordinary cost project, no additional comments or remarks are made in the following.

2.7.2.2.3.   Record Hour Transactions

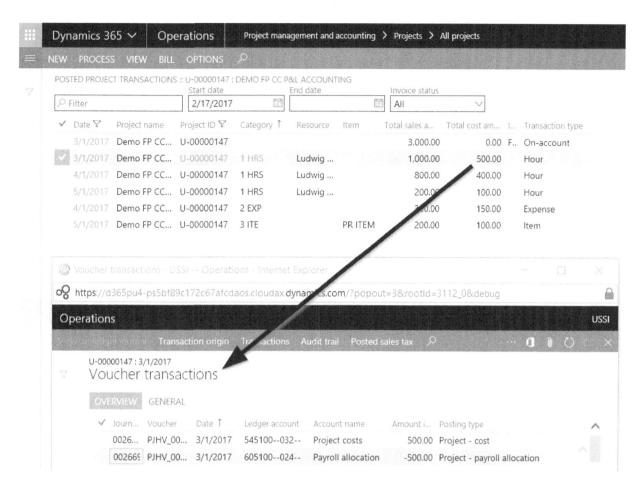

Figure 2-171 Resulting hour transaction and voucher—CC FP project P&L accounting SV estimation

DEBIT	CREDIT	AMOUNT
PERIOD 1		
545100 Project costs [Profit&Loss—Project cost]	605100 Payroll allocation [Profit&Loss—Project payroll allocation]	$500
PERIOD 2		
545100 Project costs [Profit&Loss—Project cost]	605100 Payroll allocation [Profit&Loss—Project payroll allocation]	$400
PERIOD 3		
545100 Project costs [Profit&Loss—Project cost]	605100 Payroll allocation [Profit&Loss—Project payroll allocation]	$100

Figure 2-172 Accounting voucher hour transaction—CC FP project P&L accounting SV estimation

2.7.2.2.4. Record Expense Transactions

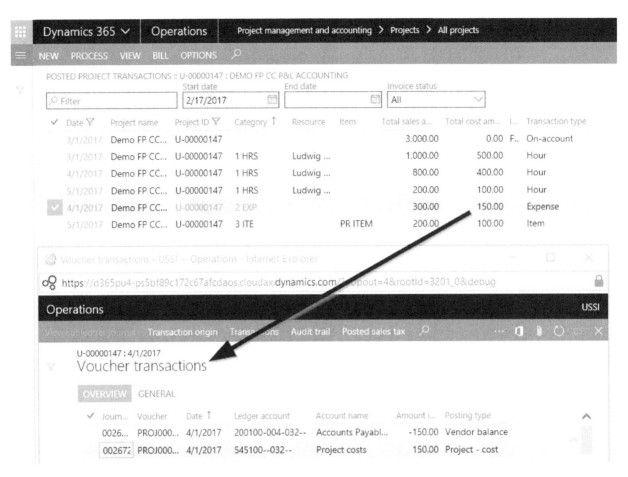

Figure 2-173 Resulting expense transaction and voucher—CC FP project P&L accounting SV estimation

DEBIT	CREDIT	AMOUNT
PERIOD 2		
545100 Project costs [Profit&Loss—Project cost]	200100 Accounts Payable [BalanceSheet—Vendor balance]	$150

Figure 2-174 Accounting voucher expense transaction—CC FP project P&L accounting SV estimation

2.7.2.2.5. Record Item Transactions

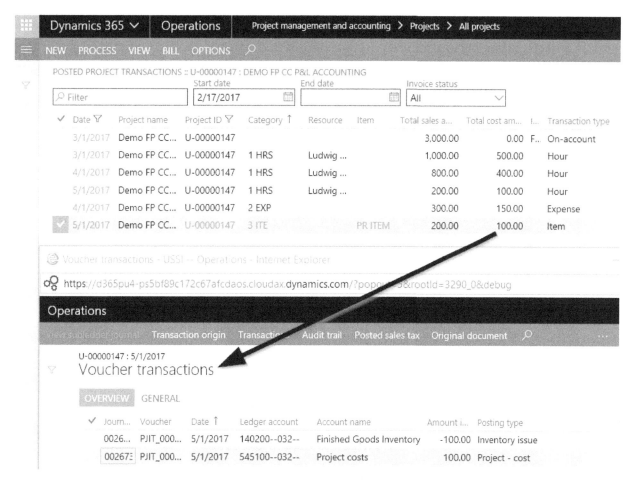

Figure 2-175 Resulting item transaction and voucher—CC FP project P&L accounting SV estimation

DEBIT	CREDIT	AMOUNT
PERIOD 3		
545100 Project costs [Profit&Loss—Project cost]	140200 Finished Goods [BalanceSheet—Inventory issue]	$100

Figure 2-176 Accounting voucher item transaction—CC FP project P&L accounting SV estimation

2.7.2.2.6.   Project Estimates

For FP projects, project estimates need to be created and posted on a periodic basis, typically at the end of an accounting period. Figures 2-177 and 2-178 illustrate the creation of those estimates that require the specification of an estimate date, a forecast model to compare the actual costs against and a completion method, such as *From cost template*.

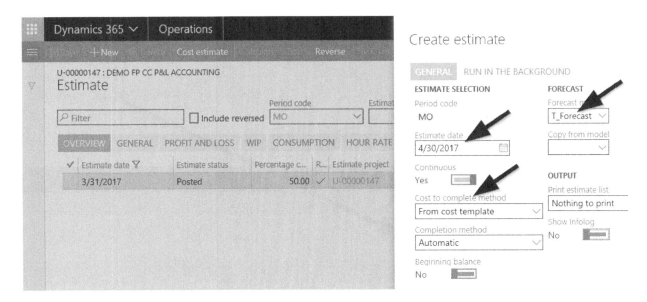

Figure 2-177 Estimate creation

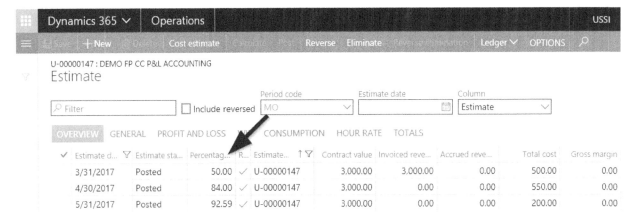

Figure 2-178 Calculated project estimates

The next formulas illustrate how the POC values that are shown in Figure 2-178 above are calculated.

POC in % = Actual costs / (Actual costs + Cost to complete) * 100%   (1)

POC (Period 1) = $500 /($500 + $200 planned hour costs + $100 planned expense costs + $200 planned item costs) * 100% = 50%   (2)

POC (Period 2) = $1,050 /($1,050 + $200 planned item costs) * 100% = 84%   (3)

POC (Period 3) = $1,250 /($1,250 + $200 planned item costs) * 100% = 92,59%   (4)

Posting the project estimates for the different months generates voucher transactions that are summarized in Figures 2-179 and 2-180.

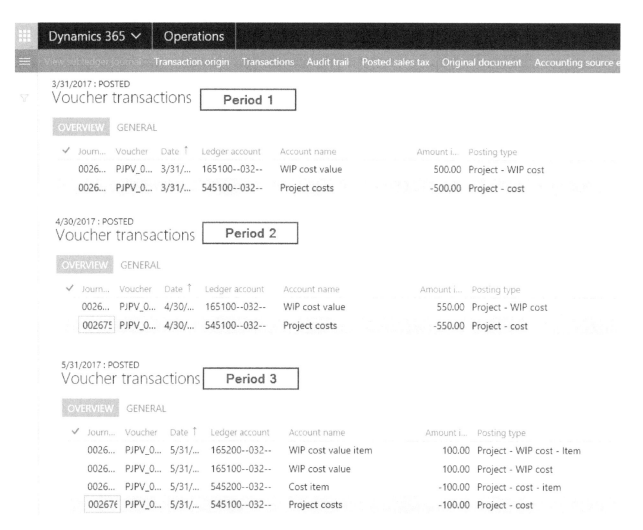

Figure 2-179 Resulting estimate transaction vouchers—CC FP project P&L accounting SV estimation

DEBIT	CREDIT	AMOUNT
PERIOD 1		
165100 WIP cost value [BalanceSheet—Project WIP cost]	545100 Project costs [Profit&Loss—Project cost]	$500
PERIOD 2		
165100 WIP cost value [BalanceSheet—Project WIP cost]	545100 Project costs [Profit&Loss—Project cost]	$550
PERIOD 3		
165100 WIP cost value [BalanceSheet—Project WIP cost]	545100 Project costs [Profit&Loss—Project cost]	$100
165200 WIP cost value item [BalanceSheet—Project WIP cost item]	545200 Cost item [Profit&Loss—Project-cost item]	$100

Figure 2-180 Accounting voucher estimate transactions—CC FP project P&L accounting SV estimation

An investigation of the project-estimate voucher postings shows that the estimate process neutralizes the costs posted through a transfer of those costs to WIP accounts in the company's balance sheet. In other words, the estimate process ensures that no costs arise at the project level.

2.7.2.2.7.   Elimination of Estimates

Once all transactions have been recorded and the project reached its end, the generated project estimates need to be eliminated in order to post the realized costs and revenues. Before the estimates can be eliminated, the POC must be set to 100%, which can be achieved by running another estimation with the cost to complete method *Set cost to complete to zero*. For details, please see Figure 2-181.

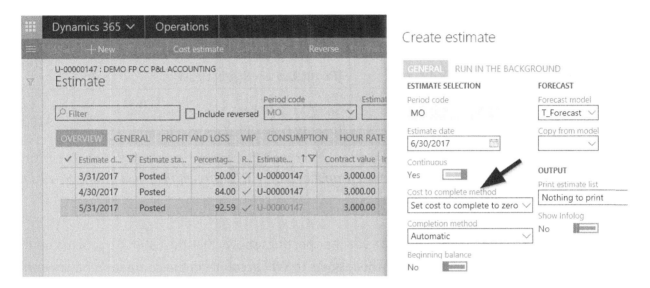

Figure 2-181 Estimate creation to set POC to 100%

Note As no other costs have been recorded, posting this last estimate does not generate a ledger voucher.

Once the POC reached 100%, the estimate button becomes available.

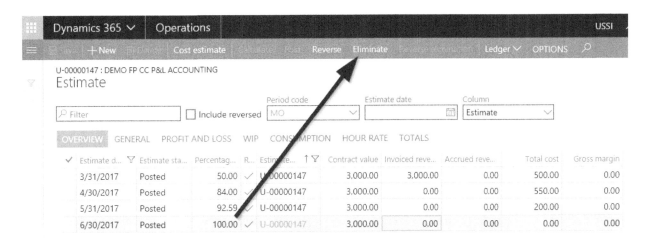

Figure 2-182 Estimate elimination

Posting the created elimination transaction results in a voucher that clears the WIP accounts and shifts all costs to P&L accounts in the company's income statement.

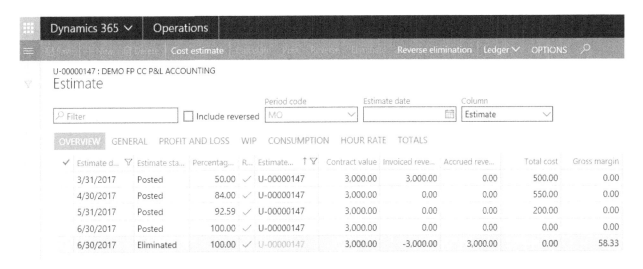

Figure 2-183 Created elimination transaction

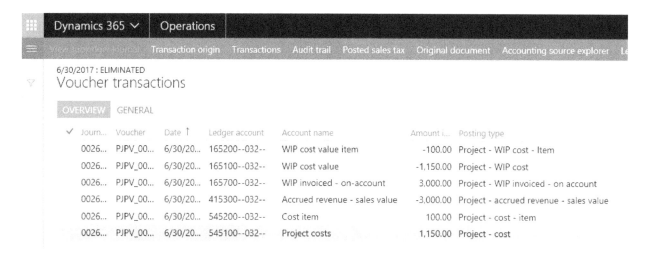

Figure 2-184 Resulting elimination transaction voucher—CC FP project P&L accounting SV estimation

DEBIT	CREDIT	AMOUNT
END OF PROJECT		
545200 Cost item [Profit&Loss—Project-cost item]	165200 WIP cost value item [BalanceSheet—Project WIP cost item]	$100
545100 Project costs [Profit&Loss—Project cost]	165100 WIP cost value [BalanceSheet—Project WIP cost]	$1,150
165700 WIP Invoiced on-account [BalanceSheet—Project WIP invoiced on-account]	415300 Accrued revenue sales value [Profit&Loss—Project accrued revenue sales value]	$3,000

Figure 2-185 Accounting voucher elimination transaction—CC FP project P&L accounting SV estimation

2.7.2.2.8. Summary

The following accounting summary shows how the recorded project costs are first neutralized through a transfer of all costs to the company's WIP accounts when posting the project estimates. Once the project ends and all estimates are eliminated, costs and revenues are realized and can be identified on the P&L accounts in the company's income statement.

DEBIT	CREDIT	AMOUNT
PERIOD 1		
Customer invoice		
130100 Accounts Receivable [BalanceSheet—Customer Balance]	165700 WIP Invoiced on-account [BalanceSheet—Project WIP invoiced on-account]	$3,000
Hours		
545100 Project costs [Profit&Loss—Project cost]	605100 Payroll allocation [Profit&Loss—Project payroll allocation]	$500
Estimate		
165100 WIP cost value [BalanceSheet—Project WIP cost]	545100 Project costs [Profit&Loss—Project cost]	$500
PERIOD 2		
Hours		
545100 Project costs [Profit&Loss—Project cost]	605100 Payroll allocation [Profit&Loss—Project payroll allocation]	$400
Expenses		
545100 Project costs [Profit&Loss—Project cost]	200100 Accounts Payable [BalanceSheet—Vendor balance]	$150
Estimate		
165100 WIP cost value [BalanceSheet—Project WIP cost]	545100 Project costs [Profit&Loss—Project cost]	$550

DEBIT	CREDIT	AMOUNT
PERIOD 3		
Hours		
545100 Project costs [Profit&Loss—Project cost]	605100 Payroll allocation [Profit&Loss—Project payroll allocation]	$100
Items		
545100 Project costs [Profit&Loss—Project cost]	140200 Finished Goods [BalanceSheet—Inventory issue]	$100
Estimate		
165100 WIP cost value [BalanceSheet—Project WIP cost]	545100 Project costs [Profit&Loss—Project cost]	$100
165200 WIP cost value item [BalanceSheet—Project WIP cost item]	545200 Cost item [Profit&Loss—Project-cost item]	$100
END OF PROJECT		
Elimination		
545200 Cost item [Profit&Loss—Project-cost item]	165200 WIP cost value item [BalanceSheet—Project WIP cost item]	$100
545100 Project costs [Profit&Loss—Project cost]	165100 WIP cost value [BalanceSheet—Project WIP cost]	$1,150
165700 WIP Invoiced on-account [BalanceSheet—Project WIP invoiced on-account]	415300 Accrued revenue sales value [Profit&Loss—Project accrued revenue sales value]	$3,000

Figure 2-186 Summary vouchers—CC FP project P&L accounting SV estimation

Note Despite the fact that the project costs are neutralized at the project level through the WIP postings created with the estimates, the overall profit of the company increases temporarily by the hour-related costs until the estimates are eliminated. That is because the hour-related costs are shifted (debited) to a WIP account whereas the credit posting is executed on a P&L account.

The following diagram illustrates the accounting process used by a CC FP project with P&L accounting and sales-value estimation graphically.

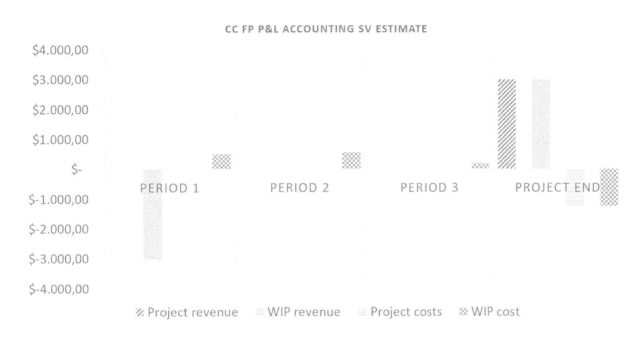

Figure 2-187 Graphical accounting summary—CC FP project P&L accounting SV estimation

An analysis of the graphical illustration provided in Figure 2-187 shows that all project costs and revenues are initially stored on WIP accounts in the company's balance sheet until the end of the project. Once the project reaches its end, all transactions recorded on those WIP accounts are reversed and transferred to the company's P&L accounts.

The graphical illustration shown in Figure 2-187 above demonstrates that a contemporary and early control of a project's progress cannot be achieved for CC FP projects with a P&L accounting setup except through a comparison of the planned costs with those temporarily stored on the WIP cost accounts. This comparison is shown in Figure 2-188, which illustrates the planned project costs—recorded in the project forecast form—side by side with the actual costs that are recorded on WIP accounts in the company's balance sheet.

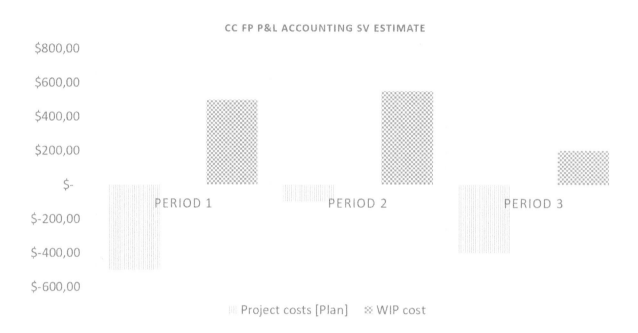

Figure 2-188 Project control—CC FP project P&L accounting SV estimation

Please note that the illustrated project control requires a very detailed and exact project planning. Changes in the scope require an immediate adjustment of the project forecast recorded in order to avoid comparing "apples and oranges".

2.7.2.3.   CC-Method—P&L Accounting—P&P Estimation

After analyzing the CC FP project with the sales-value estimation in the previous chapter, let's now have a look at what difference a production & profit (P&P) estimation makes. For that reason, the following project group has been set up and will be used for the illustrations and explanations in this subchapter.

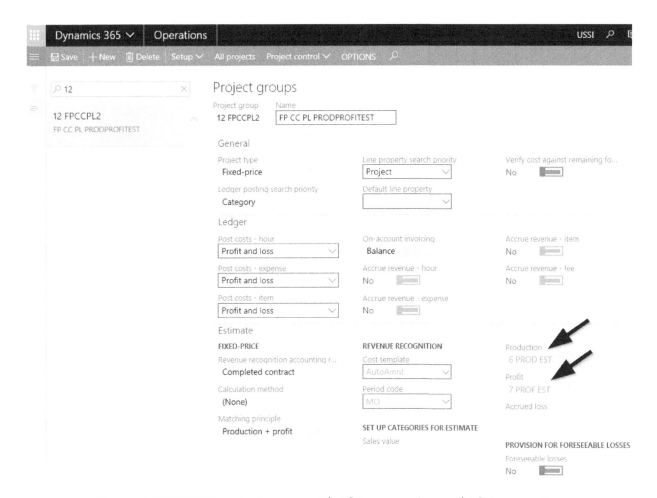

Figure 2-189 CC FP project group with P&L accounting and P&P estimation

Note To avoid unnecessary repetition of things that have already been described in the previous chapter, the following explanations and illustrations will focus only on differences that are caused by the varying project-group parameter settings.

2.7.2.3.1. Enter Forecast Values

Identical to the previous chapter.

2.7.2.3.2. Record and Invoice Milestones

Identical to the previous chapter.

2.7.2.3.3. Record Hour Transactions

Identical to the previous chapter.

2.7.2.3.4. Record Expense Transactions

Identical to the previous chapter.

2.7.2.3.5. Record Item Transactions

Identical to the previous chapter.

2.7.2.3.6. Project Estimates

Identical to the previous chapter.

2.7.2.3.7. Elimination of Estimates

The first and only difference caused by the P&P estimate relates to the elimination voucher that is illustrated in Figure 2-190.

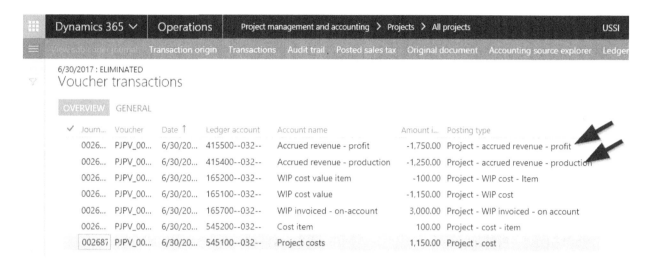

Figure 2-190 Resulting elimination transaction voucher—CC FP project P&L accounting P&P estimation

A comparison of this voucher with the one that has been shown in the previous chapter (please see Figure 2-184) shows that the previously used accrued revenue account is now split up into two parts: The first part (*production*) records the revenue amount that is identical to the realized actual cost amount, and the second part (*profit*) records the remaining profit.

2.7.2.3.8.   Summary

The next accounting summary shows the same vouchers that have already been reported in the previous chapter except for the revenue posting at the end of the project.

DEBIT	CREDIT	AMOUNT
PERIOD 1		
Customer invoice		
130100 Accounts Receivable [BalanceSheet—Customer Balance]	165700 WIP Invoiced on-account [BalanceSheet—Project WIP invoiced on-account]	$3,000
Hours		
545100 Project costs [Profit&Loss—Project cost]	605100 Payroll allocation [Profit&Loss—Project payroll allocation]	$500
Estimate		
165100 WIP cost value [BalanceSheet—Project WIP cost]	545100 Project costs [Profit&Loss—Project cost]	$500
PERIOD 2		
Hours		
545100 Project costs [Profit&Loss—Project cost]	605100 Payroll allocation [Profit&Loss—Project payroll allocation]	$400
Expenses		
545100 Project costs [Profit&Loss—Project cost]	200100 Accounts Payable [BalanceSheet—Vendor balance]	$150
Estimate		
165100 WIP cost value [BalanceSheet—Project WIP cost]	545100 Project costs [Profit&Loss—Project cost]	$550

DEBIT	CREDIT	AMOUNT
PERIOD 3		
Hours		
545100 Project costs [Profit&Loss—Project cost]	605100 Payroll allocation [Profit&Loss—Project payroll allocation]	$100
Items		
545100 Project costs [Profit&Loss—Project cost]	140200 Finished Goods [BalanceSheet—Inventory issue]	$100
Estimate		
165100 WIP cost value [BalanceSheet—Project WIP cost]	545100 Project costs [Profit&Loss—Project cost]	$100
165200 WIP cost value item [BalanceSheet—Project WIP cost item]	545200 Cost item [Profit&Loss—Project-cost item]	$100
END OF PROJECT		
Elimination		
545200 Cost item [Profit&Loss—Project-cost item]	165200 WIP cost value item [BalanceSheet—Project WIP cost item]	$100
545100 Project costs [Profit&Loss—Project cost]	165100 WIP cost value [BalanceSheet—Project WIP cost]	$1,150
165700 WIP Invoiced on-account [BalanceSheet—Project WIP invoiced on-account]	415400 Accrued revenue production [Profit&Loss—Project accrued revenue production]	$1,250
	415500 Accrued revenue profit [Profit&Loss—Project accrued revenue profit]	$1,750

Figure 2-191 Summary vouchers—CC FP project P&L accounting P&P estimation

Note Please note that what has been said in the previous chapter in regard to a temporary increase in the company's profitability because of the hour transactions also applies here.

2.7.2.4.   CC-Method—BS Accounting—SV Estimation

The transactions recorded in this chapter are based on the following project-group setup.

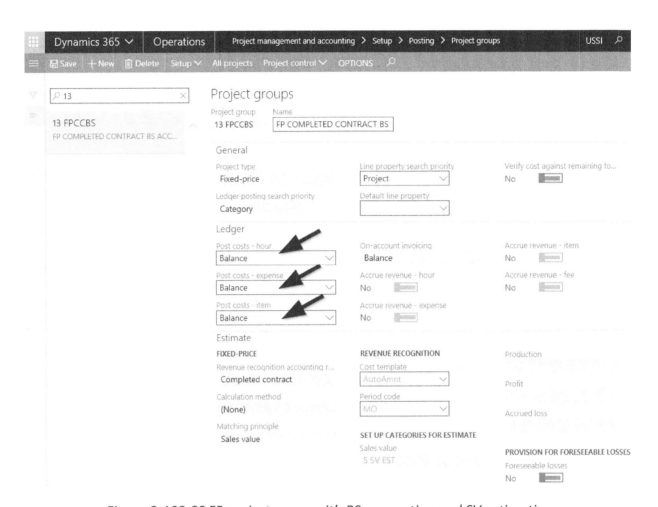

Figure 2-192 CC FP project group with BS accounting and SV estimation

Note Please note that the major difference to the previously illustrated project with an SV estimation (see chapter 2.7.2.2.) consists in the modified ledger integration that uses balance sheet rather than income statement accounts.

2.7.2.4.1. Enter Forecast Values

Identical to the previous chapter.

2.7.2.4.2. Record and Invoice Milestones

Identical to the previous chapter.

2.7.2.4.3. Record Hour Transactions

A first major difference to what has been shown in the previous chapters can be identified in the voucher transactions that are generated when project hours are recorded. That is, the vouchers generated for the hour transactions resemble those of a T&M project with BS accounting setup. For details, please see Figures 2-193 and 2-194.

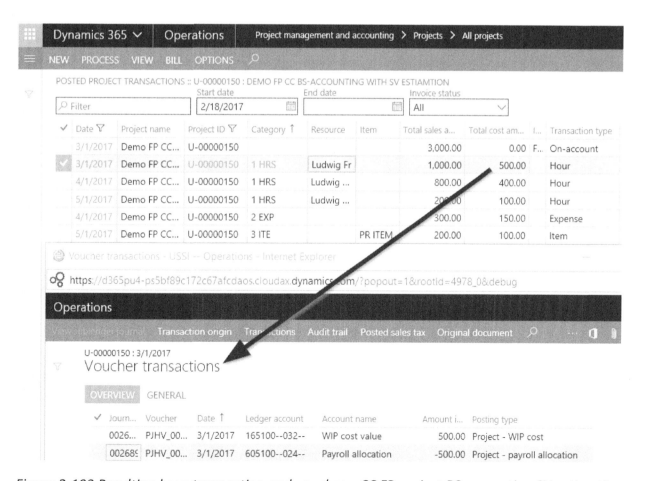

Figure 2-193 Resulting hour transaction and voucher—CC FP project BS accounting SV estimation

DEBIT	CREDIT	AMOUNT
PERIOD 1		
165100 WIP cost value [BalanceSheet—Project WIP cost]	605100 Payroll allocation [Profit&Loss—Project payroll allocation]	$500
PERIOD 2		
165100 WIP cost value [BalanceSheet—Project WIP cost]	605100 Payroll allocation [Profit&Loss—Project payroll allocation]	$400
PERIOD 3		
165100 WIP cost value [BalanceSheet—Project WIP cost]	605100 Payroll allocation [Profit&Loss—Project payroll allocation]	$100

Figure 2-194 Accounting voucher hour transaction—CC FP project BS accounting SV estimation

Note Please note that those hour transactions (temporarily) increase the company's profit because a balance sheet account is used for the debit and an income statement account for the credit transaction.

2.7.2.4.4. Record Expense Transactions

As also the expense and item transactions resemble those that have been recorded for T&M projects with a BS accounting setup, reference is made to the previous explanations in chapter 2.6.3. and only illustrative screen-prints are provided for reasons of completeness.

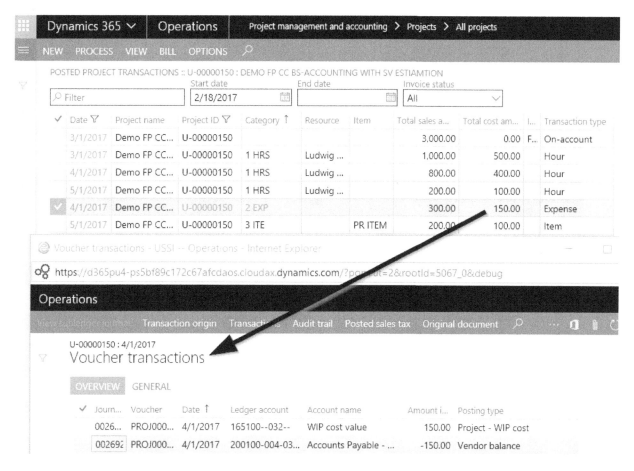

Figure 2-195 Resulting expense transaction and voucher—CC FP project BS accounting SV estimation

DEBIT	CREDIT	AMOUNT
PERIOD 2		
165100 WIP cost value [BalanceSheet—Project WIP cost]	200100 Accounts Payable [BalanceSheet—Vendor balance]	$150

Figure 2-196 Accounting voucher expense transaction—CC FP project BS accounting SV estimation

2.7.2.4.5.   Record Item Transactions

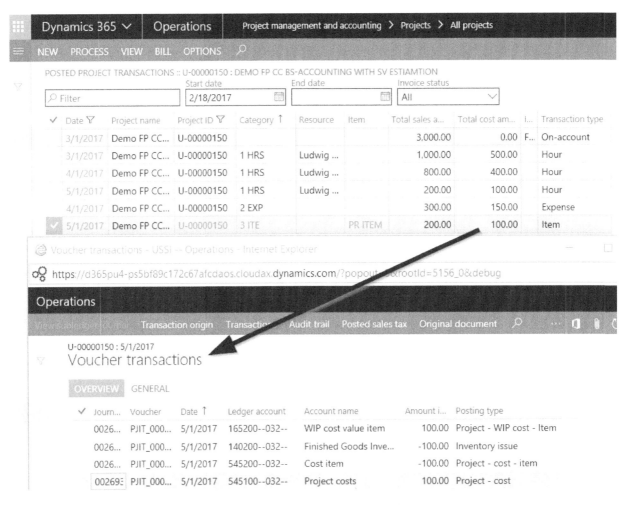

Figure 2-197 Resulting item transaction and voucher—CC FP project BS accounting SV estimation

DEBIT	CREDIT	AMOUNT
545100 Project costs [Profit&Loss—Project cost]	140200 Finished goods [BalanceSheet—Inventory issue]	$100
165200 WIP cost value item [BalanceSheet—Project WIP cost item]	545200 Cost item [Profit&Loss—Project-cost item]	$100

Figure 2-198 Accounting voucher item transaction—CC FP project BS accounting SV estimation

2.7.2.4.6.   Project Estimates

A major difference between the previously illustrated CC FP projects with the P&L accounting setup can be identified from analyzing the vouchers that are generated when project estimates are posted.

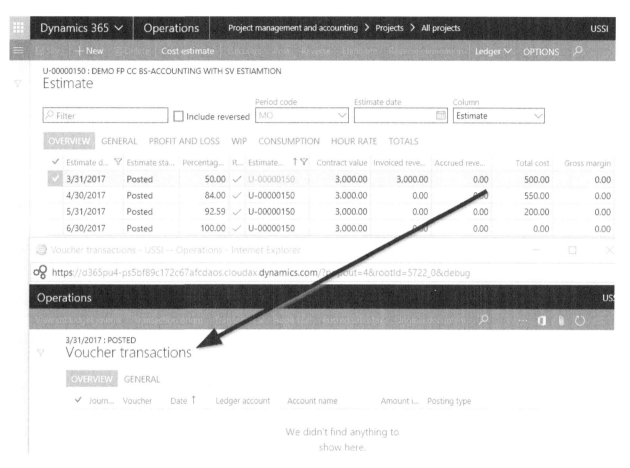

Figure 2-199 Resulting estimate transaction vouchers—CC FP project BS accounting SV estimation

As one can identify from Figure 2-199, no ledger vouchers are generated when posting project estimates for CC FP projects with a BS accounting integration. The underlying reason for this outcome is the fact that all costs are already recorded on WIP accounts in the company's balance sheet and that no further transaction is consequently required for shifting costs from P&L accounts in the company's income statement to WIP accounts in the company's balance sheet.

2.7.2.4.7.   Elimination of Estimates

Eliminating the project estimates at the end of the project results in the following voucher, which is identical to the one presented for the CC FP project with the P&L accounting setup and the SV estimation. Please see Figure 2-184.

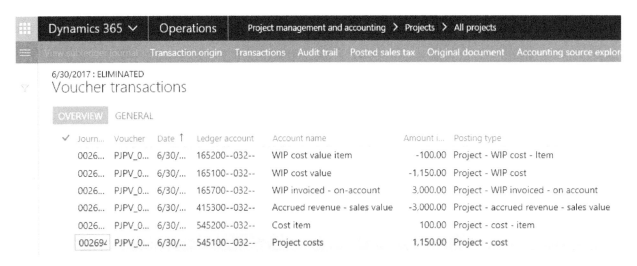

Figure 2-200 Resulting elimination voucher—CC FP project BS accounting SV estimation

DEBIT	CREDIT	AMOUNT
END OF PROJECT		
545200 Cost item [Profit&Loss—Project-cost item]	165200 WIP cost value item [BalanceSheet—Project WIP cost item]	$100
545100 Project costs [Profit&Loss—Project cost]	165100 WIP cost value [BalanceSheet—Project WIP cost]	$1,150
165700 WIP Invoiced on-account [BalanceSheet—Project WIP invoiced on-account]	415300 Accrued revenue sales value [Profit&Loss—Project accrued revenue sales value]	$3,000

Figure 2-201 Accounting voucher elimination transaction—CC FP project BS accounting SV estimation

2.7.2.4.8. Summary

As for the previously analyzed project types, Figure 2-202 summarizes all vouchers created for the CC FP project with BS accounting integration and SV estimation.

DEBIT	CREDIT	AMOUNT
PERIOD 1		
Customer invoice		
130100 Accounts Receivable [BalanceSheet—Customer Balance]	165700 WIP Invoiced on-account [BalanceSheet—Project WIP invoiced on-account]	$3,000
Hours		
165100 WIP cost value [BalanceSheet—Project WIP cost]	605100 Payroll allocation [Profit&Loss—Project payroll allocation]	$500
Estimate		
No voucher generated		
PERIOD 2		
Hours		
165100 WIP cost value [BalanceSheet—Project WIP cost]	605100 Payroll allocation [Profit&Loss—Project payroll allocation]	$400
Expenses		
165100 WIP cost value [BalanceSheet—Project WIP cost]	200100 Accounts Payable [BalanceSheet—Vendor balance]	$150
Estimate		
No voucher generated		

DEBIT	CREDIT	AMOUNT
PERIOD 3		
Hours		
165100 WIP cost value [BalanceSheet—Project WIP cost]	605100 Payroll allocation [Profit&Loss—Project payroll allocation]	$100
Items		
545100 Project costs [Profit&Loss—Project cost]	140200 Finished goods [BalanceSheet—Inventory issue]	$100
165200 WIP cost value item [BalanceSheet—Project WIP cost item]	545200 Cost item [Profit&Loss—Project-cost item]	$100
Estimate		
No voucher generated		
END OF PROJECT		
Elimination		
545200 Cost item [Profit&Loss—Project-cost item]	165200 WIP cost value item [BalanceSheet—Project WIP cost item]	$100
545100 Project costs [Profit&Loss—Project cost]	165100 WIP cost value [BalanceSheet—Project WIP cost]	$1,150
165700 WIP Invoiced on-account [BalanceSheet—Project WIP invoiced on-account]	415300 Accrued revenue sales value [Profit&Loss—Project accrued revenue sales value]	$3,000

Figure 2-202 Summary vouchers—CC FP project BS accounting SV estimation

Comparing the number of vouchers created and given the de facto identical outcome, a BS accounting setup for CC FP projects seems to be superior to a P&L accounting setup for FP CC projects.

2.7.2.5.   CC-Method—BS Accounting—P&P Estimation

The next project group analyzed does also make use of the CC accounting method and the BS accounting setup. Yet different from what has been shown in the previous chapter, the P&P rather than the SV estimate method is used. Figure 2-203 highlights the differences in the project-group setup compared to what has been used in the previous chapter.

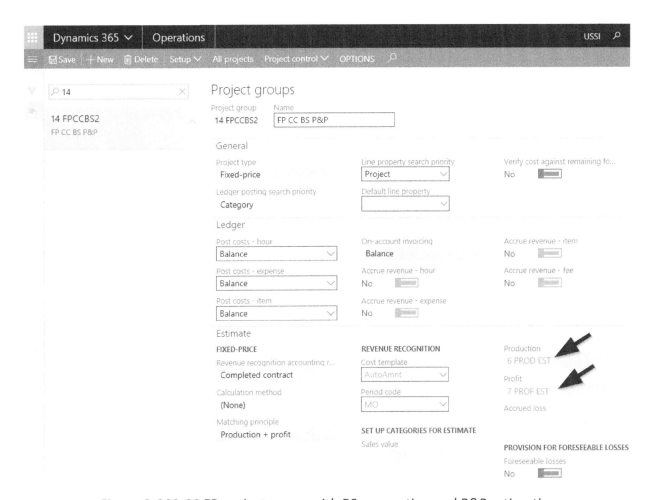

Figure 2-203 CC FP project group with BS accounting and P&P estimation

Note As before, the following explanations and illustrations will focus only on differences that are caused by the project-group parameter settings in this chapter compared to the ones in the previous chapter.

2.7.2.5.1.   Enter Forecast Values

Identical to the previous chapter.

2.7.2.5.2.   Record and Invoice Milestones

Identical to the previous chapter.

2.7.2.5.3.   Record Hour Transactions

Identical to the previous chapter.

2.7.2.5.4.   Record Expense Transactions

Identical to the previous chapter.

2.7.2.5.5.   Record Item Transactions

Identical to the previous chapter.

2.7.2.5.6.   Project Estimates

Identical to the previous chapter.

2.7.2.5.7.   Elimination of Estimates

As one would expect, the only difference that can be identified in the accounting entries generated compared to the ones shown in the previous chapter relates to the revenue posting of the elimination voucher. That is, whereas the SV estimation records the complete revenue on a single ledger account in one amount, the P&P splits the revenue into one part that is identical to the total project costs posted (*production*) and into a second (*profit*) part that records the remaining profit. The voucher transactions, shown in Figure 2-204, highlight this difference in the revenue recognition between the SV and the P&P estimation procedure.

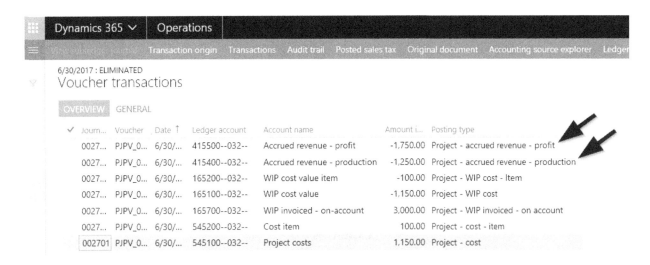

Figure 2-204 Resulting elimination transaction voucher—CC FP project BS accounting P&P estimation

2.7.2.5.8. Summary

DEBIT	CREDIT	AMOUNT
PERIOD 1		
Customer invoice		
130100 Accounts Receivable [BalanceSheet—Customer Balance]	165700 WIP Invoiced on-account [BalanceSheet—Project WIP invoiced on-account]	$3,000
Hours		
165100 WIP cost value [BalanceSheet—Project WIP cost]	605100 Payroll allocation [Profit&Loss—Project payroll allocation]	$500
Estimate		
No voucher generated		
PERIOD 2		
Hours		
165100 WIP cost value [BalanceSheet—Project WIP cost]	605100 Payroll allocation [Profit&Loss—Project payroll allocation]	$400
Expenses		
165100 WIP cost value [BalanceSheet—Project WIP cost]	200100 Accounts Payable [BalanceSheet—Vendor balance]	$150
Estimate		
. No voucher generated		

DEBIT	CREDIT	AMOUNT
PERIOD 3		
Hours		
165100 WIP cost value [BalanceSheet—Project WIP cost]	605100 Payroll allocation [Profit&Loss—Project payroll allocation]	$100
Items		
545100 Project costs [Profit&Loss—Project cost]	140200 Finished goods [BalanceSheet—Inventory issue]	$100
165200 WIP cost value item [BalanceSheet—Project WIP cost item]	545200 Cost item [Profit&Loss—Project-cost item]	$100
Estimate		
No voucher generated		
END OF PROJECT		
Elimination		
545200 Cost item [Profit&Loss—Project-cost item]	165200 WIP cost value item [BalanceSheet—Project WIP cost item]	$100
545100 Project costs [Profit&Loss—Project cost]	165100 WIP cost value [BalanceSheet—Project WIP cost]	$1,150
165700 WIP Invoiced on-account [BalanceSheet—Project WIP invoiced on-account]	415400 Accrued revenue production [Profit&Loss—Project accrued revenue production]	$1,250
	415500 Accrued revenue profit [Profit&Loss—Project accrued revenue profit]	$1,750

Figure 2-205 Summary vouchers—CC FP project BS accounting P&P estimation

2.7.2.6. POC-Method—P&L Accounting—SV Estimation

The next project type investigated in more detail are FP projects that make use of the percentage of completion (POC) revenue recognition method. As before, Figure 2-206 illustrates the project-group settings that are used for the subsequent posting and analysis of the project transactions shown below.

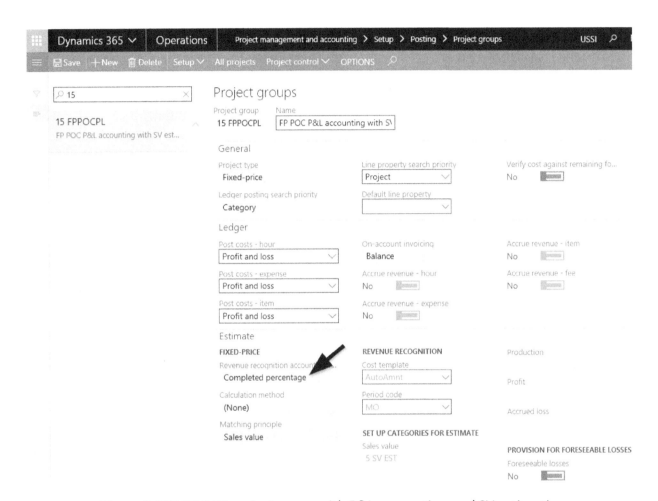

Figure 2-206 POC FP project group with P&L accounting and SV estimation

Note The POC FP project with P&L accounting integration resembles the CC FP project with P&L accounting integration shown further above. For that reason and in order to conserve space, only differences between those project types are illustrated in the following.

2.7.2.6.1. Enter Forecast Values

Same as CC FP project with P&L accounting and SV estimation.

2.7.2.6.2. Record and Invoice Milestones

Same as CC FP project with P&L accounting and SV estimation.

2.7.2.6.3. Record Hour Transactions

Same as CC FP project with P&L accounting and SV estimation.

2.7.2.6.4. Record Expense Transactions

Same as CC FP project with P&L accounting and SV estimation.

2.7.2.6.5. Record Item Transactions

Same as CC FP project with P&L accounting and SV estimation.

2.7.2.6.6. Project Estimates

The first noticeable difference between the POC and CC project can be identified in the project-estimate voucher exemplified in Figure 2-207.

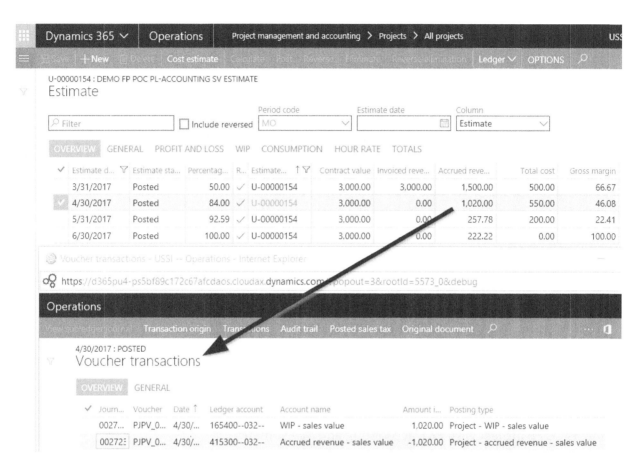

Figure 2-207 Resulting estimate transaction vouchers—POC FP project with P&L accounting SV estimation

The previously used CC accounting method shifted all project costs to a WIP account in the company's balance sheet and thereby neutralized the effects that the recorded transactions had on the company's income statement.

The POC accounting method does, on the other hand side, not move the project cost to a WIP account in the company's balance sheet but rather creates vouchers that accrue the corresponding project revenue. This is illustrated in Figure 2-208.

DEBIT	CREDIT	AMOUNT
PERIOD 1		
165400 WIP sales value [BalanceSheet—Project WIP sales value]	415300 Accrued revenue sales value [Profit&Loss—Project accrued revenue sales value]	$1,500
PERIOD 2		
165400 WIP sales value [BalanceSheet—Project WIP sales value]	415300 Accrued revenue sales value [Profit&Loss—Project accrued revenue sales value]	$1,020
PERIOD 3		
165400 WIP sales value [BalanceSheet—Project WIP sales value]	415300 Accrued revenue sales value [Profit&Loss—Project accrued revenue sales value]	$257.78
FINAL PERIOD		
165400 WIP sales value [BalanceSheet—Project WIP sales value]	415300 Accrued revenue sales value [Profit&Loss—Project accrued revenue sales value]	$222.22

Figure 2-208 Accounting voucher estimate transaction—POC FP project with P&L accounting SV estimation

An important question regarding the project revenue is how D365 calculates the accrued revenue for the different periods. The next formulas answer this question by providing details of the accrued revenue calculations.

Accrued revenue period = POC change * contract value (5)

Accrued revenue period 1 = (50%-0%) * $3,000 = $1,500 (6)

Accrued revenue period 2 = (84%-50%) * $3,000 = $1,020 (7)

Accrued revenue period 3 = (92,59%-84%) * $3,000 = $257.78 (8)

Accrued revenue final period = (100%-92,59%) * $3,000 = $222.22 (9)

2.7.2.6.7.   Elimination of Estimates

A second major difference between the CC and the POC FP project with P&L accounting integration can be identified in the ledger voucher that is generated with the elimination of the estimates. This voucher is illustrated in Figure 2-209.

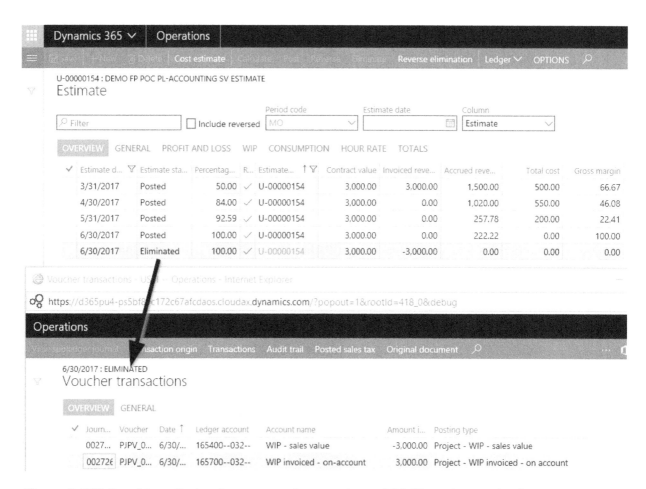

Figure 2-209 Resulting elimination transaction voucher—POC FP project with P&L accounting SV estimation

DEBIT	CREDIT	AMOUNT
END OF PROJECT		
165700 WIP invoiced on account [BalanceSheet—Project WIP invoiced on account]	165400 WIP sales value [BalanceSheet—Project WIP sales value]	$3,000

Figure 2-210 Accounting voucher elimination transaction—POC FP project with P&L accounting SV estimation

Figure 2-210 shows that the elimination voucher of the POC FP project with P&L accounting integration simply reverses the amounts that have been recorded on the WIP accounts and does consequently not affect a company's profit.

2.7.2.6.8. Summary

As for the previous project types, the following figure summarizes all vouchers that have been created for the POC FP project with P&L accounting and SV estimation.

DEBIT	CREDIT	AMOUNT
PERIOD 1		
Customer invoice		
130100 Accounts Receivable [BalanceSheet—Customer Balance]	165700 WIP Invoiced on-account [BalanceSheet—Project WIP invoiced on-account]	$3,000
Hours		
545100 Project costs [Profit&Loss—Project cost]	605100 Payroll allocation [Profit&Loss—Project payroll allocation]	$500
Estimate		
165400 WIP sales value [BalanceSheet—Project WIP sales value]	415300 Accrued revenue sales value [Profit&Loss—Project accrued revenue sales value]	$1,500
PERIOD 2		
Hours		
545100 Project costs [Profit&Loss—Project cost]	605100 Payroll allocation [Profit&Loss—Project payroll allocation]	$400
Expenses		
545100 Project costs [Profit&Loss—Project cost]	200100 Accounts Payable [BalanceSheet—Vendor balance]	$150
Estimate		
165400 WIP sales value [BalanceSheet—Project WIP sales value]	415300 Accrued revenue sales value [Profit&Loss—Project accrued revenue sales value]	$1,020

DEBIT	CREDIT	AMOUNT
PERIOD 3		
Hours		
545100 Project costs [Profit&Loss—Project cost]	605100 Payroll allocation [Profit&Loss—Project payroll allocation]	$100
Items		
545100 Project costs [Profit&Loss—Project cost]	140200 Finished Goods [BalanceSheet—Inventory issue]	$100
Estimate		
165400 WIP sales value [BalanceSheet—Project WIP sales value]	415300 Accrued revenue sales value [Profit&Loss—Project accrued revenue sales value]	$257.78
END OF PROJECT		
Final Estimate		
165400 WIP sales value [BalanceSheet—Project WIP sales value]	415300 Accrued revenue sales value [Profit&Loss—Project accrued revenue sales value]	$222.22
Elimination		
165700 WIP invoiced on account [BalanceSheet—Project WIP invoiced on account]	165400 WIP sales value [BalanceSheet—Project WIP sales value]	$3,000

Figure 2-211 Summary vouchers—POC FP project with P&L accounting SV estimation

The following graphical illustrations aim to clarify the difference that the selection of the POC versus the CC makes. Let's focus first on the POC method illustrated in Figure 2-212 that shows a continuous match of costs and revenues over the lifetime of the project.

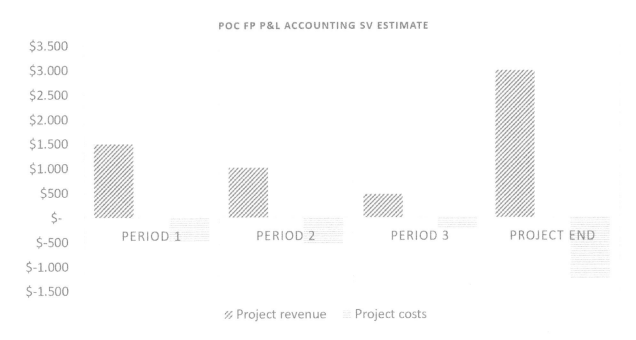

Figure 2-212 Graphical accounting summary—POC FP project with P&L accounting SV estimation

A major advantage of the periodic cost-revenue match is that it allows a contemporary and early control of the overall profit or loss of a project.

Figure 2-213 shows the same project costs and revenues for the project that makes use of the CC accounting method.

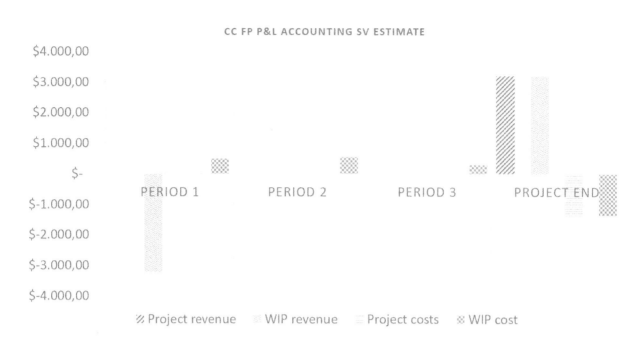

Figure 2-213 Graphical accounting summary—CC FP project with P&L accounting SV estimation

A comparison of the previous figures shows that the CC method matches costs and revenues at the end of the project whereas the POC method is doing this on a continuous basis. Project controllers thus require additional data and instruments if they apply the CC method and require a detailed control of long-term projects. Otherwise, they run the risk of identifying problems too late to take counteractive measures in case something goes wrong.

Note Even though the POC method appears to be superior to the CC method, it still suffers from the fact that the cost-revenue comparison might be distorted if actual project work is ahead or behind the planned (scheduled) work. What is missing though is a benchmark that allows a comparison of the actual project costs with a measure that indicates what those costs should be. How this deficiency can be overcome will be explained in more detail further below.

Note On first sight, the T&M project with the accrual posting setup shown in chapter 2.6.2. and the POC FP project with the P&L accounting setup seem to generate a similar outcome. There is, however, an important difference between those two project groups. That is, whereas the T&M project calculates the accruals based on the expected sales price of the transactions recorded, the FP project calculates them based on the progress of the project (POC) and the agreed upon (realized) contract value.

2.7.2.7. POC-Method—P&L Accounting—P&P Estimation

The next project group analyzed uses the same P&L accounting integration that has been used in the previous chapter but makes use of the P&P estimation principle exemplified in Figure 2-214.

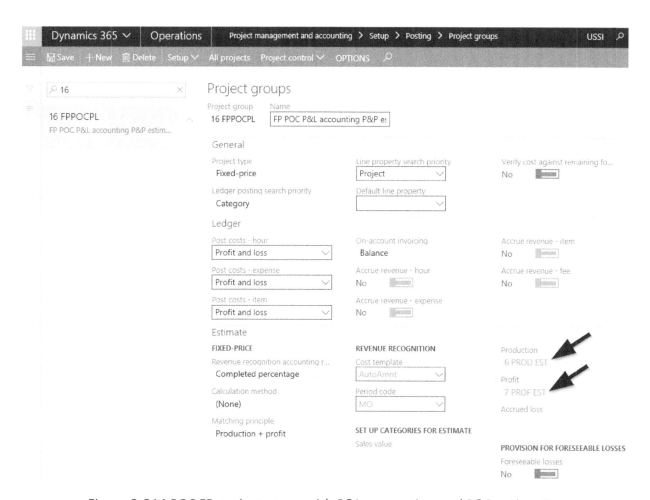

Figure 2-214 POC FP project group with P&L accounting and P&P estimation

2.7.2.7.1.   Enter Forecast Values

Identical to POC FP project with P&L accounting and SV estimation.

2.7.2.7.2.   Record and Invoice Milestones

Identical to POC FP project with P&L accounting and SV estimation.

2.7.2.7.3.   Record Hour Transactions

Identical to POC FP project with P&L accounting and SV estimation.

2.7.2.7.4.   Record Expense Transactions

Identical to POC FP project with P&L accounting and SV estimation.

2.7.2.7.5.   Record Item Transactions

Identical to POC FP project with P&L accounting and SV estimation.

2.7.2.7.6.   Project Estimates

The only major difference to what has been shown in the previous chapter for the FP POC project with a SV estimation is that the P&P estimation separates the total estimate into a production and profit part. For details, please see Figure 2-215.

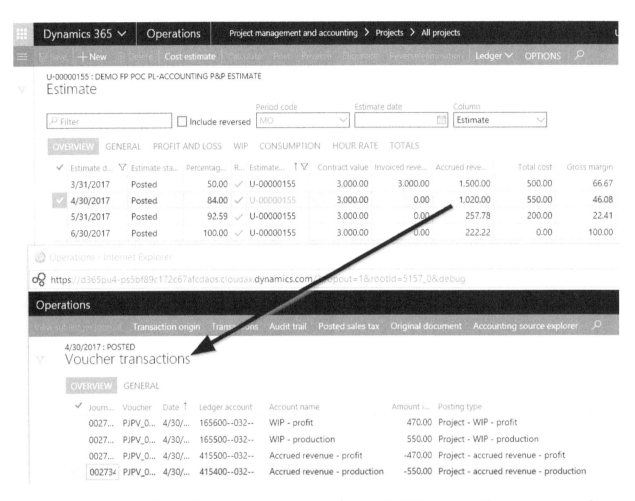

Figure 2-215 Resulting estimate transaction vouchers—POC FP project P&L accounting P&P estimation

The next accounting voucher summarizes the estimate vouchers that are generated with the posting of the project estimates.

DEBIT	CREDIT	AMOUNT
PERIOD 1		
165500 WIP production [BalanceSheet—Project WIP production]	415400 Accrued revenue production [Profit&Loss—Project accrued revenue production]	$500
165600 WIP profit [BalanceSheet—Project WIP profit]	415500 Accrued revenue profit [Profit&Loss—Project accrued revenue profit]	$1,000
PERIOD 2		
165500 WIP production [BalanceSheet—Project WIP production]	415400 Accrued revenue production [Profit&Loss—Project accrued revenue production]	$550
165600 WIP profit [BalanceSheet—Project WIP profit]	415500 Accrued revenue profit [Profit&Loss—Project accrued revenue profit]	$470
PERIOD 3		
165500 WIP production [BalanceSheet—Project WIP production]	415400 Accrued revenue production [Profit&Loss—Project accrued revenue production]	$200
165600 WIP profit [BalanceSheet—Project WIP profit]	415500 Accrued revenue profit [Profit&Loss—Project accrued revenue profit]	$57.78
FINAL PERIOD		
165500 WIP production [BalanceSheet—Project WIP production]	415400 Accrued revenue production [Profit&Loss—Project accrued revenue production]	$0
165600 WIP profit [BalanceSheet—Project WIP profit]	415500 Accrued revenue profit [Profit&Loss—Project accrued revenue profit]	$222.22

Figure 2-216 Accounting voucher estimate transaction—POC FP project P&L accounting P&P estimation

2.7.2.7.7.   Elimination of Estimates

Eliminating the project estimates results in a voucher that simply reverses the transactions posted on the company's WIP accounts. As a result, the company's profit is not affected.

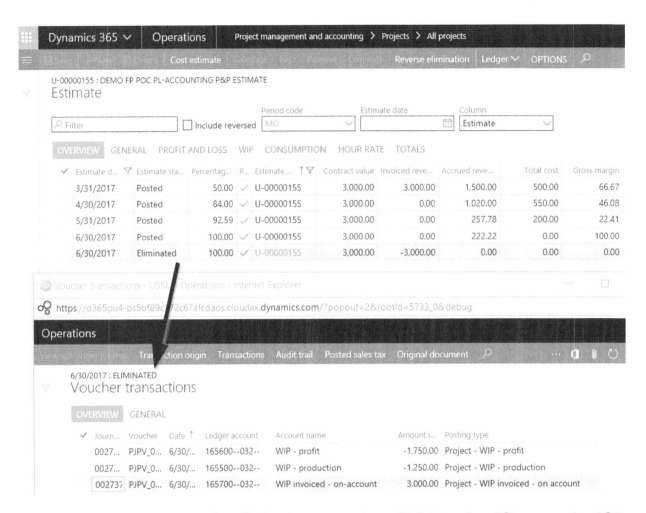

Figure 2-217 Accounting voucher elimination transaction—POC FP project P&L accounting P&P estimation

DEBIT	CREDIT	AMOUNT
END OF PROJECT		
165700 WIP invoiced on account [BalanceSheet—Project WIP invoiced on account]	165400 WIP production [BalanceSheet—Project WIP production]	$1,250
165700 WIP invoiced on account [BalanceSheet—Project WIP invoiced on account]	165500 WIP profit [BalanceSheet—Project WIP profit]	$1,750

Figure 2-218 Accounting voucher elimination transaction—POC FP project P&L accounting P&P estimation

2.7.2.7.8.   Summary

Figure 2-219 summarizes all vouchers that have been created for the POC FP project with P&L accounting and P&P estimation.

DEBIT	CREDIT	AMOUNT
PERIOD 1		
Customer invoice		
130100 Accounts Receivable [BalanceSheet—Customer Balance]	165700 WIP Invoiced on-account [BalanceSheet—Project WIP invoiced on-account]	$3,000
Hours		
545100 Project costs [Profit&Loss—Project cost]	605100 Payroll allocation [Profit&Loss—Project payroll allocation]	$500
Estimate		
165500 WIP production [BalanceSheet—Project WIP production]	415400 Accrued revenue production [Profit&Loss—Project accrued revenue production]	$500
165600 WIP profit [BalanceSheet—Project WIP profit]	415500 Accrued revenue profit [Profit&Loss—Project accrued revenue profit]	$1,000
PERIOD 2		
Hours		
545100 Project costs [Profit&Loss—Project cost]	605100 Payroll allocation [Profit&Loss—Project payroll allocation]	$400
Expenses		
545100 Project costs [Profit&Loss—Project cost]	200100 Accounts Payable [BalanceSheet—Vendor balance]	$150
Estimate		
165500 WIP production [BalanceSheet—Project WIP production]	415400 Accrued revenue production [Profit&Loss—Project accrued revenue production]	$550
165600 WIP profit [BalanceSheet—Project WIP profit]	415500 Accrued revenue profit [Profit&Loss—Project accrued revenue profit]	$470

DEBIT	CREDIT	AMOUNT
PERIOD 3		
Hours		
545100 Project costs [Profit&Loss—Project cost]	605100 Payroll allocation [Profit&Loss—Project payroll allocation]	$100
Items		
545100 Project costs [Profit&Loss—Project cost]	140200 Finished Goods [BalanceSheet—Inventory issue]	$100
Estimate		
165500 WIP production [BalanceSheet—Project WIP production]	415400 Accrued revenue production [Profit&Loss—Project accrued revenue production]	$200
165600 WIP profit [BalanceSheet—Project WIP profit]	415500 Accrued revenue profit [Profit&Loss—Project accrued revenue profit]	$57.78
END OF PROJECT		
Final Estimate		
165500 WIP production [BalanceSheet—Project WIP production]	415400 Accrued revenue production [Profit&Loss—Project accrued revenue production]	$0
165600 WIP profit [BalanceSheet—Project WIP profit]	415500 Accrued revenue profit [Profit&Loss—Project accrued revenue profit]	$222.22
Elimination		
165700 WIP invoiced on account [BalanceSheet—Project WIP invoiced on account]	165400 WIP production [BalanceSheet—Project WIP production]	$1,250
	165500 WIP profit [BalanceSheet—Project WIP profit]	$1,750

Figure 2-219 Summary vouchers—POC FP project P&L accounting SV estimation

2.7.2.8.   POC-Method—BS Accounting—SV Estimation

The third FP project group that makes use of the POC accounting method is set up with a balance sheet accounting integration and a sales-value estimate as illustrated in Figure 2-220.

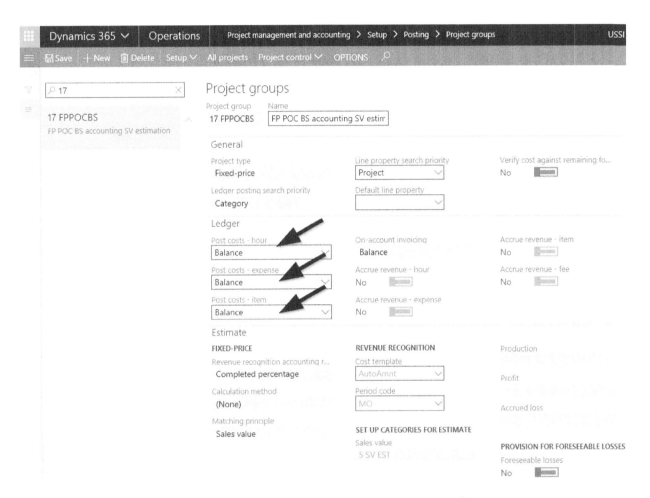

Figure 2-220 POC FP project group with BS accounting and SV estimation

Note As before, only differences to what has been said in the previous chapters will be explained in the following.

2.7.2.8.1. Enter Forecast Values

Identical to CC FP project with BS accounting and SV estimation.

2.7.2.8.2. Record and Invoice Milestones

Identical to CC FP project with BS accounting and SV estimation.

2.7.2.8.3. Record Hour Transactions

Identical to CC FP project with BS accounting and SV estimation.

2.7.2.8.4. Record Expense Transactions

Identical to CC FP project with BS accounting and SV estimation.

2.7.2.8.5. Record Item Transactions

Identical to CC FP project with BS accounting and SV estimation.

2.7.2.8.6. Project Estimates

To match project costs and revenues as the project progresses and against the background that all costs have previously been recorded on WIP accounts in the company's balance sheet, a voucher that reverses the previously WIP postings together with a revenue accrual transaction is generated when posting project estimates. This is shown in Figure 2-221.

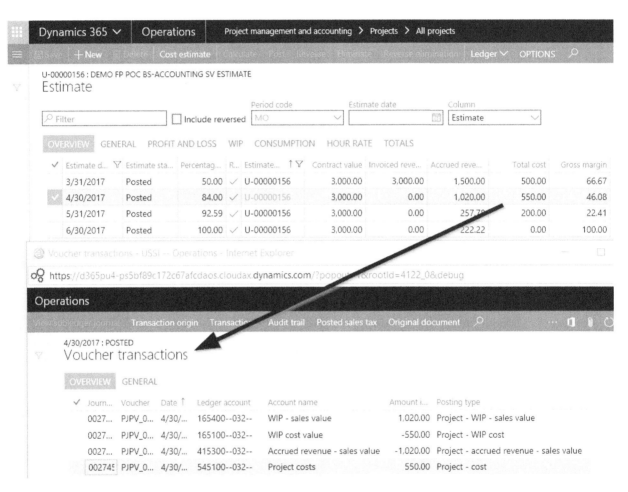

Figure 2-221 Resulting estimate transaction vouchers—POC FP project with BS accounting and SV estimation

Figure 2-222 summarizes all created estimate vouchers in an accounting-like format.

DEBIT	CREDIT	AMOUNT
PERIOD 1		
165400 WIP sales value [BalanceSheet—Project WIP sales value]	415300 Accrued revenue sales value [Profit&Loss—Project accrued revenue sales value]	$1,500
545100 Project costs [Profit&Loss—Project cost]	165100 WIP cost value [BalanceSheet—Project WIP cost]	$500
PERIOD 2		
165400 WIP sales value [BalanceSheet—Project WIP sales value]	415300 Accrued revenue sales value [Profit&Loss—Project accrued revenue sales value]	$1,020
545100 Project costs [Profit&Loss—Project cost]	165100 WIP cost value [BalanceSheet—Project WIP cost]	$550
PERIOD 3		
165400 WIP sales value [BalanceSheet—Project WIP sales value]	415300 Accrued revenue sales value [Profit&Loss—Project accrued revenue sales value]	$257.78
545100 Project costs [Profit&Loss—Project cost]	165100 WIP cost value [BalanceSheet—Project WIP cost]	$200
FINAL PERIOD		
165400 WIP sales value [BalanceSheet—Project WIP sales value]	415300 Accrued revenue sales value [Profit&Loss—Project accrued revenue sales value]	$222.22
545100 Project costs [Profit&Loss—Project cost]	165100 WIP cost value [BalanceSheet—Project WIP cost]	$0

Figure 2-222 Accounting voucher estimate transaction—POC FP project BS accounting SV estimation

2.7.2.8.7.   Elimination of Estimates

At the end of the project's lifetime when the estimates are eliminated, the following voucher is generated, which reverses the prior postings on the company's WIP accounts. For details, please see the next illustrations.

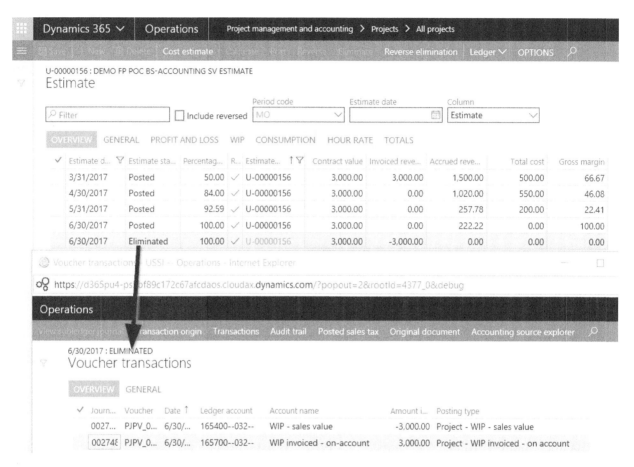

Figure 2-223 Resulting elimination transaction vouchers—POC FP project with BS accounting and SV estimation

DEBIT	CREDIT	AMOUNT
END OF PROJECT		
165700 WIP invoiced on account [BalanceSheet—Project WIP invoiced on account]	165400 WIP sales value [BalanceSheet—Project WIP sales value]	$3,000

Figure 2-224 Accounting voucher elimination transaction—POC FP project with BS accounting and SV estimation

2.7.2.8.8.   Summary

As before, the next accounting overview summarizes all vouchers generated for the POC FP project with BS accounting integration and a SV estimation.

DEBIT	CREDIT	AMOUNT
PERIOD 1		
Customer invoice		
130100 Accounts Receivable [BalanceSheet—Customer Balance]	165700 WIP Invoiced on-account [BalanceSheet—Project WIP invoiced on-account]	$3,000
Hours		
165100 WIP cost value [BalanceSheet—Project WIP cost]	605100 Payroll allocation [Profit&Loss—Project payroll allocation]	$500
Estimate		
165400 WIP sales value [BalanceSheet—Project WIP sales value]	415300 Accrued revenue sales value [Profit&Loss—Project accrued revenue sales value]	$1,500
545100 Project costs [Profit&Loss—Project cost]	165100 WIP cost value [BalanceSheet—Project WIP cost]	$500
PERIOD 2		
Hours		
165100 WIP cost value [BalanceSheet—Project WIP cost]	605100 Payroll allocation [Profit&Loss—Project payroll allocation]	$400
Expenses		
165100 WIP cost value [BalanceSheet—Project WIP cost]	200100 Accounts Payable [BalanceSheet—Vendor balance]	$150
Estimate		
165400 WIP sales value [BalanceSheet—Project WIP sales value]	415300 Accrued revenue sales value [Profit&Loss—Project accrued revenue sales value]	$1,020
545100 Project costs [Profit&Loss—Project cost]	165100 WIP cost value [BalanceSheet—Project WIP cost]	$550

DEBIT	CREDIT	AMOUNT
PERIOD 3		
Hours		
165100 WIP cost value [BalanceSheet—Project WIP cost]	605100 Payroll allocation [Profit&Loss—Project payroll allocation]	$100
Items		
545100 Project costs [Profit&Loss—Project cost]	140200 Finished goods [BalanceSheet—Inventory issue]	$100
165200 WIP cost value item [BalanceSheet—Project WIP cost item]	545200 Cost item [Profit&Loss—Project-cost item]	$100
Estimate		
165400 WIP sales value [BalanceSheet—Project WIP sales value]	415300 Accrued revenue sales value [Profit&Loss—Project accrued revenue sales value]	$257.78
545100 Project costs [Profit&Loss—Project cost]	165100 WIP cost value [BalanceSheet—Project WIP cost]	$100
545200 Cost item [Profit&Loss—Project-cost item]	165200 WIP cost value item [BalanceSheet—Project WIP cost item]	$100
END OF PROJECT		
Final Estimate		
165400 WIP sales value [BalanceSheet—Project WIP sales value]	415300 Accrued revenue sales value [Profit&Loss—Project accrued revenue sales value]	$222.22
545100 Project costs [Profit&Loss—Project cost]	165100 WIP cost value [BalanceSheet—Project WIP cost]	$0
Elimination		
165700 WIP invoiced on account [BalanceSheet—Project WIP invoiced on account]	165400 WIP sales value [BalanceSheet—Project WIP sales value]	$3,000

Figure 2-225 Summary vouchers—CC FP project BS accounting SV estimation

The previously used project groups that made use of a BS accounting setup were subject to the problem that a (temporary) profit was created through the hour-related project transactions. The underlying reason for this effect was that a WIP account was used for the debit transaction and a P&L account—the payroll allocation account—for the credit transaction. This problem does not affect the project group illustrated in this chapter, which makes use of the POC BS accounting integration because at the end of each period, posting the project estimates reversed the WIP postings and shifts all costs to P&L accounts.

2.7.2.9.   POC-Method—BS Accounting—P&P Estimation

The last project group introduced is set up with the following project-group parameters.

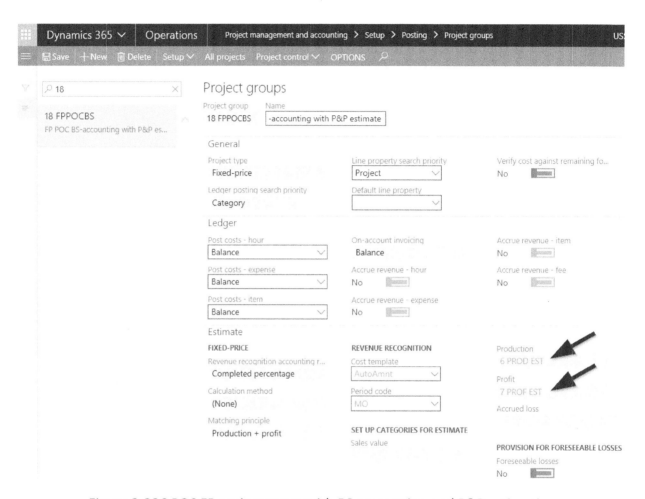

Figure 2-226 POC FP project group with BS accounting and P&P estimation

2.7.2.9.1. Enter Forecast Values

Identical to CC FP project with BS accounting and P&P estimation.

2.7.2.9.2. Record and Invoice Milestones

Identical to CC FP project with BS accounting and P&P estimation.

2.7.2.9.3. Record Hour Transactions

Identical to CC FP project with BS accounting and P&P estimation.

2.7.2.9.4. Record Expense Transactions

Identical to CC FP project with BS accounting and P&P estimation.

2.7.2.9.5. Record Item Transactions

Identical to CC FP project with BS accounting and P&P estimation.

2.7.2.9.6.   Project Estimates

Posting the project estimates results in vouchers that are similar to the ones shown in the previous chapter except for the accrued revenue postings, which are now separated into a production and profit part. Please see Figures 2-227 and 2-228 for details.

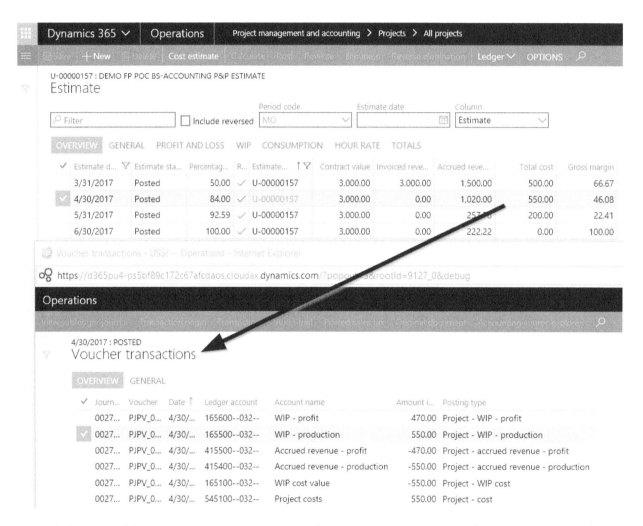

Figure 2-227 Resulting estimate transaction vouchers—POC FP project with BS accounting and P&P estimation

DEBIT	CREDIT	AMOUNT
PERIOD 1		
165500 WIP production [BalanceSheet—Project WIP production]	415400 Accrued revenue production [Profit&Loss—Project accrued revenue production]	$500
165600 WIP profit [BalanceSheet—Project WIP profit]	415500 Accrued revenue profit [Profit&Loss—Project accrued revenue profit]	$1,000
545100 Project costs [Profit&Loss—Project cost]	165100 WIP cost value [BalanceSheet—Project WIP cost]	$500
PERIOD 2		
165500 WIP production [BalanceSheet—Project WIP production]	415400 Accrued revenue production [Profit&Loss—Project accrued revenue production]	$550
165600 WIP profit [BalanceSheet—Project WIP profit]	415500 Accrued revenue profit [Profit&Loss—Project accrued revenue profit]	$470
545100 Project costs [Profit&Loss—Project cost]	165100 WIP cost value [BalanceSheet—Project WIP cost]	$550
PERIOD 3		
165500 WIP production [BalanceSheet—Project WIP production]	415400 Accrued revenue production [Profit&Loss—Project accrued revenue production]	$200
165600 WIP profit [BalanceSheet—Project WIP profit]	415500 Accrued revenue profit [Profit&Loss—Project accrued revenue profit]	$57.78
545100 Project costs [Profit&Loss—Project cost]	165100 WIP cost value [BalanceSheet—Project WIP cost]	$200

DEBIT	CREDIT	AMOUNT
FINAL PERIOD		
165500 WIP production [BalanceSheet—Project WIP production]	415400 Accrued revenue production [Profit&Loss—Project accrued revenue production]	$0
165600 WIP profit [BalanceSheet—Project WIP profit]	415500 Accrued revenue profit [Profit&Loss—Project accrued revenue profit]	$222.22
545100 Project costs [Profit&Loss—Project cost]	165100 WIP cost value [BalanceSheet—Project WIP cost]	$0

Figure 2-228 Accounting voucher estimate transaction—POC FP project BS accounting P&P estimation

2.7.2.9.7. Elimination of Estimates

At the end of the project's lifetime when the estimates are eliminated, the following voucher is generated, which reverses the prior postings on the company's WIP accounts. For details, please see Figures 2-229 and 2-230.

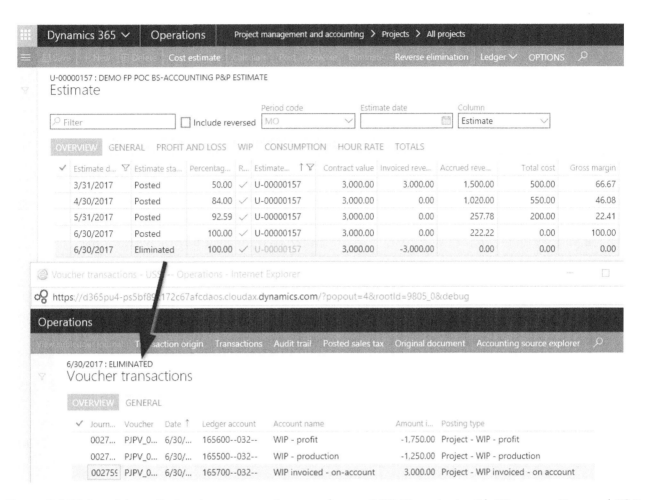

Figure 2-229 Resulting elimination transaction vouchers—POC FP project with BS accounting and P&P estimation

DEBIT	CREDIT	AMOUNT
END OF PROJECT		
165700 WIP invoiced on account [BalanceSheet—Project WIP invoiced on account]	165500 WIP production [BalanceSheet—Project WIP production]	$1,250
	165600 WIP profit [BalanceSheet—Project WIP profit]	$1,750

Figure 2-230 Accounting voucher elimination transaction—POC FP project with BS accounting and P&P estimation

2.7.2.9.8. Summary

As in the previous chapters, the next accounting overview summarizes all vouchers generated for the POC FP project with BS accounting integration and a P&P estimation.

DEBIT	CREDIT	AMOUNT
PERIOD 1		
Customer invoice		
130100 Accounts Receivable [BalanceSheet—Customer Balance]	165700 WIP Invoiced on-account [BalanceSheet—Project WIP invoiced on-account]	$3,000
Hours		
165100 WIP cost value [BalanceSheet—Project WIP cost]	605100 Payroll allocation [Profit&Loss—Project payroll allocation]	$500
Estimate		
165500 WIP production [BalanceSheet—Project WIP production]	415400 Accrued revenue production [Profit&Loss—Project accrued revenue production]	$500
165600 WIP profit [BalanceSheet—Project WIP profit]	415500 Accrued revenue profit [Profit&Loss—Project accrued revenue profit]	$1,000
545100 Project costs [Profit&Loss—Project cost]	165100 WIP cost value [BalanceSheet—Project WIP cost]	$500

DEBIT	CREDIT	AMOUNT
PERIOD 2		
Hours		
165100 WIP cost value [BalanceSheet—Project WIP cost]	605100 Payroll allocation [Profit&Loss—Project payroll allocation]	$400
Expenses		
165100 WIP cost value [BalanceSheet—Project WIP cost]	200100 Accounts Payable [BalanceSheet—Vendor balance]	$150
Estimate		
165500 WIP production [BalanceSheet—Project WIP production]	415400 Accrued revenue production [Profit&Loss—Project accrued revenue production]	$550
165600 WIP profit [BalanceSheet—Project WIP profit]	415500 Accrued revenue profit [Profit&Loss—Project accrued revenue profit]	$470
545100 Project costs [Profit&Loss—Project cost]	165100 WIP cost value [BalanceSheet—Project WIP cost]	$550

DEBIT	CREDIT	AMOUNT
PERIOD 3		
Hours		
165100 WIP cost value [BalanceSheet—Project WIP cost]	605100 Payroll allocation [Profit&Loss—Project payroll allocation]	$100
Items		
545100 Project costs [Profit&Loss—Project cost]	140200 Finished goods [BalanceSheet—Inventory issue]	$100
165200 WIP cost value item [BalanceSheet—Project WIP cost item]	545200 Cost item [Profit&Loss—Project-cost item]	$100
Estimate		
165500 WIP production [BalanceSheet—Project WIP production]	415400 Accrued revenue production [Profit&Loss—Project accrued revenue production]	$200
165600 WIP profit [BalanceSheet—Project WIP profit]	415500 Accrued revenue profit [Profit&Loss—Project accrued revenue profit]	$57.78
545100 Project costs [Profit&Loss—Project cost]	165100 WIP cost value [BalanceSheet—Project WIP cost]	$100
545200 Cost item [Profit&Loss—Project-cost item]	165200 WIP cost value item [BalanceSheet—Project WIP cost item]	$100

DEBIT	CREDIT	AMOUNT
END OF PROJECT		
Final Estimate		
165500 WIP production [BalanceSheet—Project WIP production]	415400 Accrued revenue production [Profit&Loss—Project accrued revenue production]	$0
165600 WIP profit [BalanceSheet—Project WIP profit]	415500 Accrued revenue profit [Profit&Loss—Project accrued revenue profit]	$222.22
545100 Project costs [Profit&Loss—Project cost]	165100 WIP cost value [BalanceSheet—Project WIP cost]	$0
Elimination		
165700 WIP invoiced on account [BalanceSheet—Project WIP invoiced on account]	165500 WIP production [BalanceSheet—Project WIP production]	$1,250
	165600 WIP profit [BalanceSheet—Project WIP profit]	$1,750

Figure 2-231 Summary vouchers—CC FP project BS accounting P&P estimation

2.7.2.10. Special Issues

2.7.2.10.1. Project Groups with Balance Sheet Account

An important consideration when setting up project groups relates to the posting of hour-related costs. Deciding how hour-related costs are posted at the project level is an important decision because these costs are already recorded as an expense with the monthly payroll.

For project groups with a P&L accounting setup, the posted project hour transactions can be interpreted as a cost allocation from the department of the employee to the project.

For project groups that make use of a BS accounting setup, posting-hour transactions on a project results in a temporary profit effect because a balance sheet (WIP) account is debited and an income statement account (P&L) is credited. This temporary profit effect was identified for the following project groups:

- Internal projects with BS accounting setup (see chapter 2.4.2.) until the costs were shifted to P&L accounts through the *Post costs* functionality,
- Investment projects with BS accounting setup (see chapter 2.5.3.) until the elimination of the estimates,
- T&M projects with BS accounting setup (see chapter 2.6.3.) until the project invoices are created, and
- CC fixed-price projects with BS accounting setup (see chapter 2.7.2.4 & 2.7.2.5) until the elimination of the estimates.

To avoid those temporary profit effects, which can temporarily distort the overall profitability of the company, a number of different options exist, which are explained below.

2.7.2.10.1.1. Option 1: Never Ledger Setup

The first available option is setting the *Post costs—hour* parameter to *Never ledger*, which is illustrated in Figure 2-232.

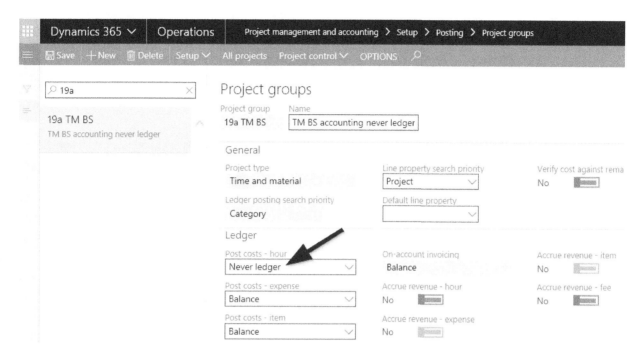

Figure 2-232 Project-group setup for hour costs (1)

A direct result of this setup is that no voucher is created when project hours are posted. Making use of the *Never ledger* setup option has thus the advantage that no temporary unrealized profit arises because no voucher is generated. However, if those allocations are required for internal analysis purposes, then one has to execute them in the cost-accounting module.

Note: The general ledger allocation rules cannot be used for this purpose because they require vouchered transactions.

Note Even though no voucher is created, the total project costs can still be analyzed at the project level through the various project control forms, provided that the project parameters that are illustrated in Figure 2-233 are turned on.

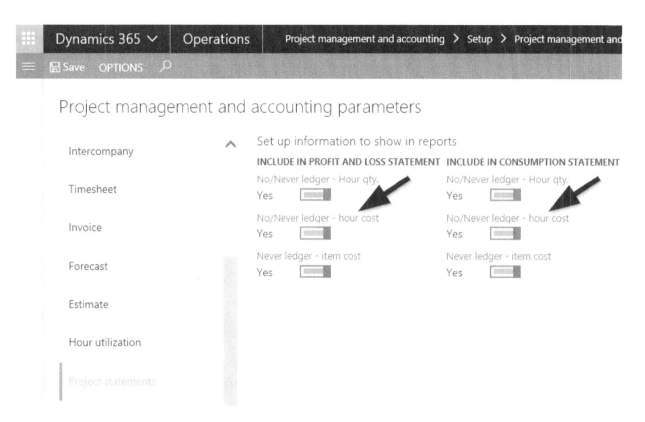

Figure 2-233 Project parameters for project statements

A major disadvantage of the *Never ledger* setup approach is that the reconciliation of project costs and general ledger transactions becomes more difficult respectively time consuming because the total project costs cannot be identified at the ledger account level. In addition, the *Never ledger* setup option will result in understated WIP ledger balances and valuation problems, which makes this option unfeasible for live environments from an external finance and accounting perspective.

2.7.2.10.1.2.   Option 2: No Ledger Setup

An alternative to the *Never ledger* setup option is the *No ledger* setup option for hour-related transactions. This setup option is illustrated in Figure 2-234 for a T&M project group.

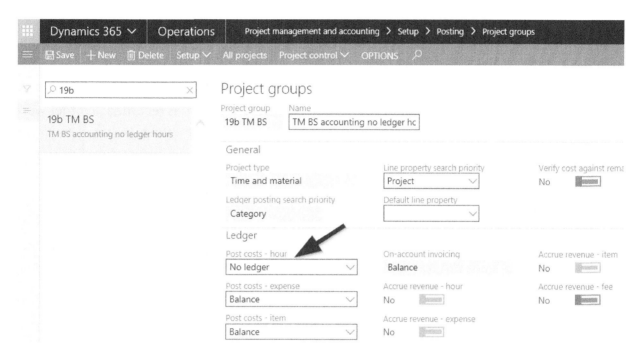

Figure 2-234 Project-group setup for hour costs (2)

Applying the *No ledger* setup option for internal projects does not result in a ledger voucher at the time hours are posted. Yet, at the time one makes use of the *Post costs* functionality, a ledger voucher is created. If the hour-related transactions are posted to balance sheet accounts (see chapter 2.4.3. for details), the same profit effect that was identified in chapter 2.4.2. materializes. Posting the hour-related costs later on to income statement accounts results—on the other hand side—in a voucher that is identical to the one that has been shown for internal projects with a P&L accounting setup. (For details, see chapter 2.4.1.1.). The temporary profit effect for internal projects with a BS accounting integration can thus be avoided by making use of the *No ledger* setup option and by posting those costs later on to P&L accounts via the *Post costs* functionality.

For T&M projects, the *No ledger* setup option similarly does not result in the creation of a ledger voucher at the time hours are posted. However, once a project invoice is created, a ledger voucher that debits the project cost account and that credits the payroll allocation account is recorded. The *No ledger* setup option can thus avoid the previously identified temporary profit effect for T&M projects with a BS accounting integration.

Also for investment projects and fixed-price projects that follow the completed contract accounting method (FP CC) and that make use of a BS ledger integration, the *No ledger* setup option does not create a voucher at the time hours are posted. However, once project estimates are created, a voucher that debits a WIP account and that credits a payroll allocation account is recorded. In other words, the *No ledger* setup option simply postpones the temporary profit effect that results from hour transactions posted to those projects.

For investment projects, this outcome might not be an issue if the elimination of the project estimates is recorded shortly after. However, for the FP CC project that makes use of a BS accounting integration, the temporary profit effect might persist and distort the overall profitability of the company, especially if the project is running over an extended period of time.

Note Investment projects that are subsequently eliminated to a fixed asset always result in an increase of the company's profit (not only for the hour-related cost amount) because costs are shifted from the income statement to the balance sheet.

2.7.2.10.1.3. Option 3: P&L Setup

While the *No ledger* accounting setup overcomes the temporary profit effect for internal, investment, and T&M projects that make use of a BS accounting integration, it does not help in the case of FP CC projects with a BS accounting integration.

For the last project group, one might consequently think of posting all hour-related costs to a P&L account, which can be achieved by the following project-group setup.

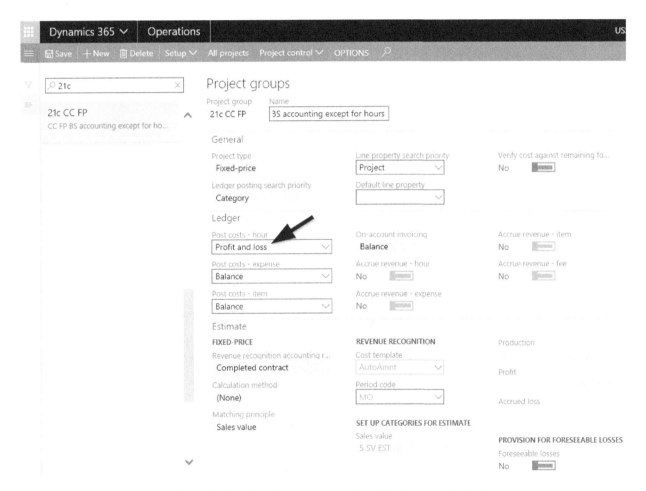

Figure 2-235 Project-group setup for hour costs (3)

Unfortunately, the project-group setup illustrated in Figure 2-235 will result in an understated WIP balance in the company's balance sheet. Problems with auditors and accounting regulators are thus likely to result.

2.7.2.10.1.4. Option 4: Offset BS Accounting Setup

As *Option 3* does not seem feasible for FP CC projects with a BS accounting integration, one might think of changing the offset payroll allocation account from a P&L to a BS account. Figure 2-236 illustrates this for the project-group *21d FPCC*.

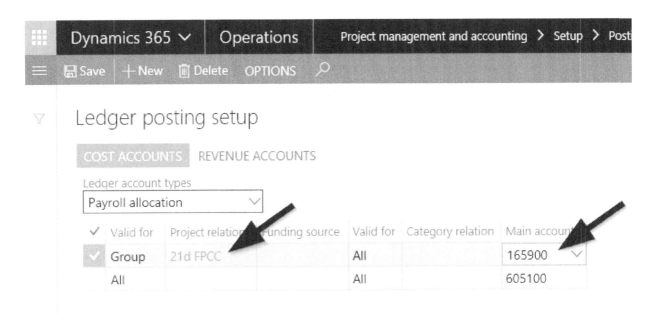

Figure 2-236 Project-group setup for hour costs (4)

A direct outcome of this setup is that the debit posting on the WIP account that is used for posting the hour transactions is offset by another WIP account—the newly set up payroll allocation WIP account no. 165900. As both, the debit and the credit side make use of balance sheet accounts no profit effect arises.

In summary, a number of different setup options exist that can help avoiding a temporary unrealized profit effect resulting from hour transactions for projects that make use of a BS accounting integration. Irrespective of the approach that is chosen, it is crucial that one is aware of this temporary profit effect in order to decide whether and what option to apply respectively not to apply.

2.7.2.10.2.   Estimate Calculation Methods

In the previous chapters on fixed-price projects, the *Calculation method* parameter that is available in the project-groups form has always been set to *None*. What difference the selection of the alternative parameter options (*Markup percent–total* and *Markup percent–estimate line*) makes will be illustrated below, based on a fixed-price project that makes use of the POC accounting method and a SV estimate. For that purpose, three identical projects respectively project groups (23a, 23b, and 23c) that differ only in the setup of the *Calculation method* parameter have been set up.

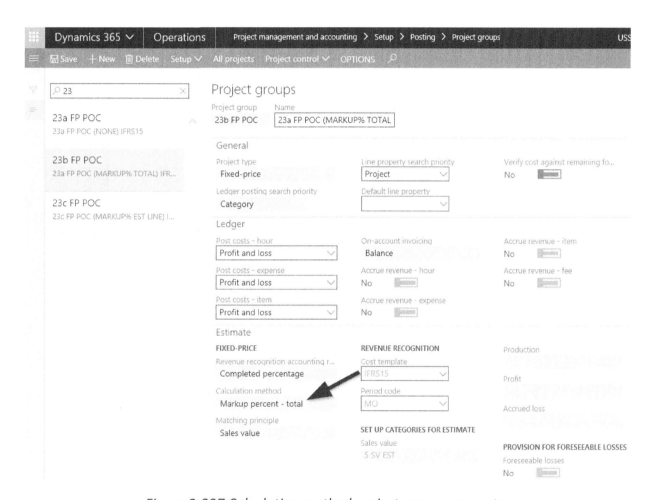

Figure 2-237 Calculation method project-group parameter

Note

Project-group 23a has been set up with the calculation method parameter *None*. Project-group 23b has been set up with the parameter *Markup percent–total* and project-group 23c with the parameter *Markup percent–estimate line*.

To identify the difference between the setup options, a slightly more complex example than the one used before is required where more than a single transaction type is posted in a given period. For that reason, the previously used example (see chapter 2.7.2.1.5.) is extended and makes use of the following plan and actual cost data.

	Period 1	Period 2	Period 3	Total
Planned cost				
Consulting Hours	5 hours ($500)		2 hours ($200)	$700
Development Hours	4 hours ($400)	9 hours ($900)		$1,300
Training Hours			4 hours ($400)	$400
Project-Management Hours	1 hour ($100)	1 hour ($100)	1 hour ($100)	$300
Travel expense	$800	$400	$300	$1,500
Other expense	$200	$100		$300
Item		5 items ($500)		$500
Total	**$2,000**	**$2,000**	**$1,000**	**$5,000**
Actual costs				
Consulting Hours	5 hours ($500)		3 hours ($300)	$800
Development Hours	4 hours ($400)	8 hours ($800)		$1,200
Training Hours			2 hours ($200)	$200
Project-Management Hours	4 hour ($400)	1 hour ($100)	1 hour ($100)	$600
Travel expense	$1,200	$1,000	$400	$2,600
Other expense		$200		$200
Item			4 items ($400)	$400
Total	**$2,500**	**$2,100**	**$1,400**	**$6,000**

Figure 2-238 Sample data estimate calculation method

Note The elements in the first column of Figure 2-238 represent different hour, expense, and item categories that are needed to illustrate the difference to the previously used setups. In addition to those data, a $10,000 milestone payment has been set up that will be invoiced to the customer at the end of the project.

A second major difference to the previously used projects relates to the project template, which classifies the different project categories used into the following cost lines.

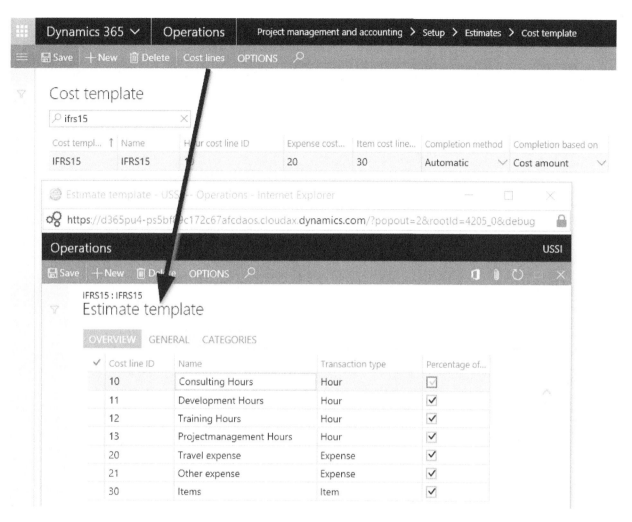

Figure 2-239 Newly setup cost template

Once all planned costs are recorded in the forecast form and the actual costs for the first period are posted, a first project estimation is run. The outcome of this estimation is identical for all projects irrespective of the estimate calculation method parameter selected and can be identified in Figure 2-240.

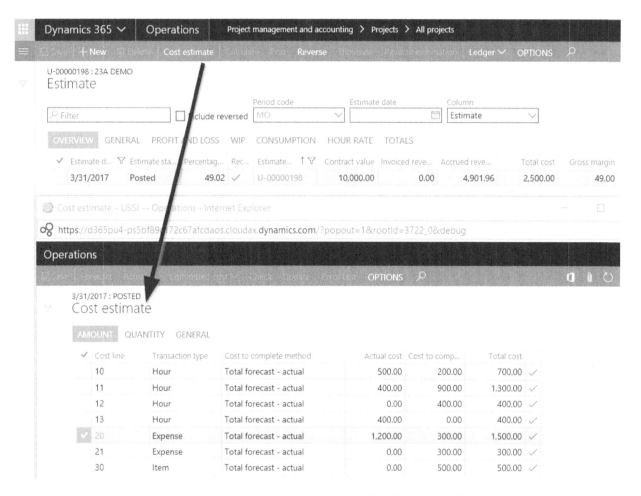

Figure 2-240 Project estimate after first period

The estimate illustrated above shows a percentage of completion (POC) of 49.02%, which is calculated as follows:

POC in % = Actual costs / (Actual costs + Cost to complete) * 100%   (10)

POC (Period 1) = $2,500 /($2,500 + $2,600) * 100% = 49.02%   (11)

2.7.2.10.2.1.   Estimate Calculation Method "None"

Posting the estimate for the first project 23a that has the *Calculation method* parameter set to *None*, results in the following voucher, that debits the WIP sales value account and credits the accrued revenue account exactly in the same way as it was shown before. See, for example, chapter 2.7.2.6.

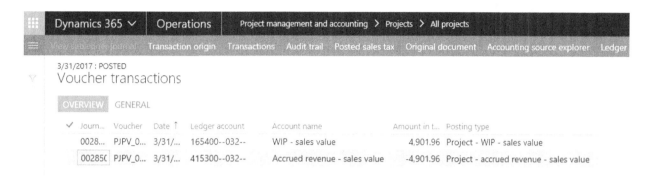

Figure 2-241 Resulting estimate transaction vouchers—POC FP project P&L accounting SV estimation—calculation method None

DEBIT	CREDIT	AMOUNT
PERIOD 1		
165400 WIP sales value [BalanceSheet—Project WIP sales value]	415300 Accrued revenue sales value [Profit&Loss—Project accrued revenue sales value]	$4,901.96

Figure 2-242 Accounting voucher estimate transaction—POC FP project P&L accounting SV estimation—calculation method None

2.7.2.10.2.2. Estimate Calculation Method *"Markup Percent-Total"*

If an identical project estimate is posted for the project 23b that has the *Calculation method* parameter set to *Markup percent–total*, the transaction and voucher result would be as shown in Figure 2-243.

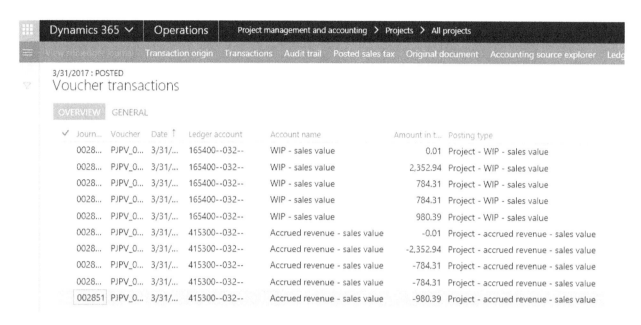

Figure 2-243 Resulting estimate transaction vouchers—POC FP project P&L accounting SV estimation—calculation method Markup percent–total

Note A prerequisite for the creation of this detailed voucher is that the project parameters do not summarize but detail the individual project postings. In other words, the financial ledger-posting parameters—not shown for reasons of brevity—needs to be set to *Line* rather than *Total*. Otherwise, the same voucher that was created for the project with the estimate calculation method *None* will be created.

The difference between the first and the second project setup in regard to the estimate voucher created can be identified from Figure 2-244 that shows how the accrued revenue amount is calculated for the different cost template lines.

Category/Cost template line	Costs	% Costs	Revenue to recognize
Consulting Hours	$500.00	20.00%	$980.39
Development Hours	$400.00	16.00%	$ 784.31
Training Hours			
Project-Management Hours	$400.00	16.00%	$784.31
Travel expense	$1,200.00	48.00%	$2,352.94
Other expense			
Item			
Total	**$2,500.00**	100.00%	**$4,901.96**

Figure 2-244 Calculation project-estimate lines with Markup percent–total setup

Rather than posting the total accrued revenue in one single amount, the *Markup percent–total* parameter calculates the fraction of each cost element on the total costs posted (*% Costs*). The calculated percentage values are then multiplied by the calculated POC amount of $4,901.96 in order to determine the accrued revenue for each of the cost template lines.

From a finance and accounting perspective, it would be better if each estimate voucher line is posted on separate ledger accounts. However, trying to split the estimate voucher based on the category that has been used for recording the actual costs—through a setup similar to the one shown in Figure 2-245—does not work because the accrued revenue posting is determined by a single sales-value estimate category for which only a single ledger account can be specified. For details, see Figure 2-237 above.

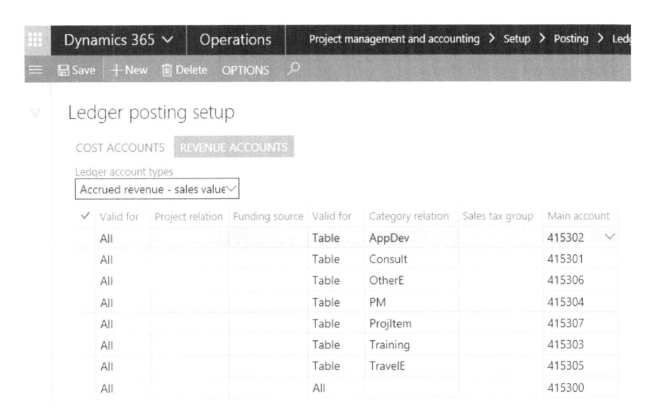

Figure 2-245 Accrued revenue ledger-posting setup

Trying to separate the estimate voucher by means of financial dimensions that are posted with the original costs does similarly not work because those financial dimensions are not inherited to the project estimate.

Because the standard reporting tools do not allow comparing the actual costs with the accrued revenue amounts for each of the cost lines, Power BI tools have to be used to make this comparison. Figure 2-246 illustrates this comparison for the sample data used in the first period.

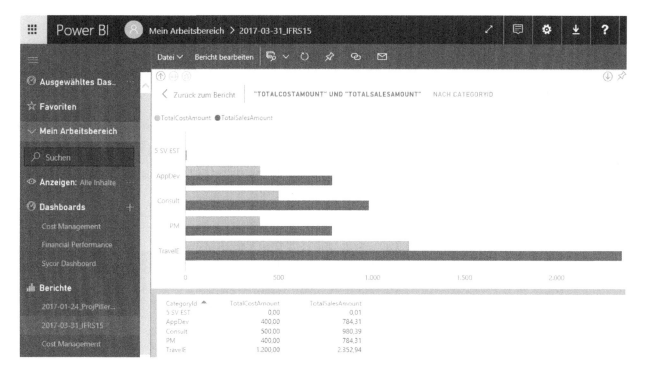

Figure 2-246 Power BI report actual costs versus accrued revenue by category

As one can identify from Figure 2-246, making use of the *Markup percent–total* parameter allows a comparison of the actual cost and accrued revenue data at the project category or cost template line level. Stated differently, the use of the *Markup percent–total* parameter has the advantage that it does not only allow comparing actual costs and accrued revenue amounts at the overall project level but at the project category or cost template line level. It thus provides users with an early and deep insight into those project elements that generate money for the company and those that do not. A knowledge of this relationship can help identifying potential project tasks that might, for example, be outsourced or that might need a new price negotiation with the customer to avoid an overall loss.

2.7.2.10.2.3. Estimate Calculation Method *"Markup Percent–Estimate Line"*

For the last project that makes use of the *Markup percent–estimate line* parameter, the project estimate shows the same POC figure that has been calculated for the projects with the other calculation method parameter setups. Trying to post the estimate for the project with the *Markup percent–estimate line* parameter does, however, result in an error message that disappears only after the total contract value has manually been allocated to the different estimate lines. This is illustrated in Figure 2-247.

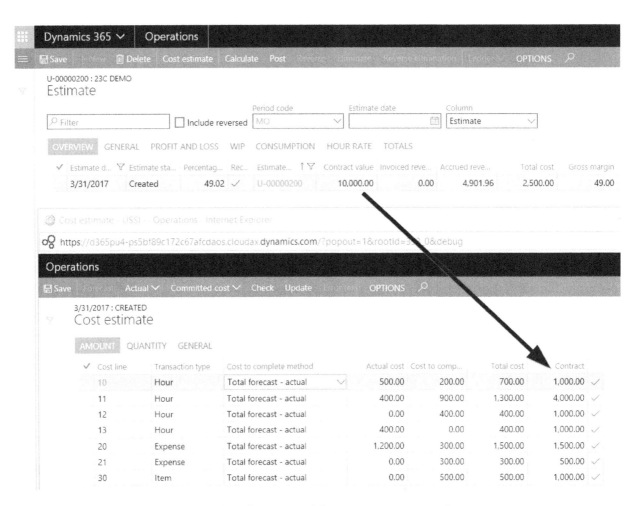

Figure 2-247 Project estimate after first period for project setup with cost-estimate-parameter Markup percent–estimate line

Once the allocation of the contract value to the different estimate lines has been made, the estimate can be posted. The resulting accounting voucher shows accrual postings that differ from the ones that have been shown previously. That is because the *Markup percent–estimate line* parameter setting calculates the accrued revenue slightly different, as illustrated in Figures 2-248 to 2-252.

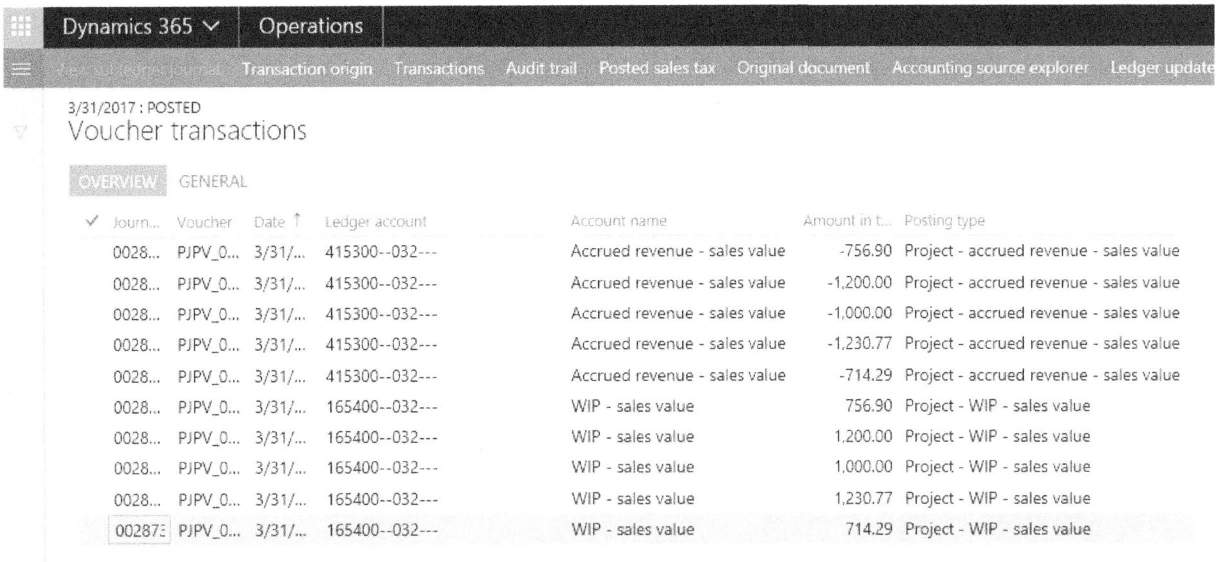

Journ...	Voucher	Date	Ledger account	Account name	Amount in t...	Posting type
0028...	PJPV_0...	3/31/...	415300--032---	Accrued revenue - sales value	-756.90	Project - accrued revenue - sales value
0028...	PJPV_0...	3/31/...	415300--032---	Accrued revenue - sales value	-1,200.00	Project - accrued revenue - sales value
0028...	PJPV_0...	3/31/...	415300--032---	Accrued revenue - sales value	-1,000.00	Project - accrued revenue - sales value
0028...	PJPV_0...	3/31/...	415300--032---	Accrued revenue - sales value	-1,230.77	Project - accrued revenue - sales value
0028...	PJPV_0...	3/31/...	415300--032---	Accrued revenue - sales value	-714.29	Project - accrued revenue - sales value
0028...	PJPV_0...	3/31/...	165400--032---	WIP - sales value	756.90	Project - WIP - sales value
0028...	PJPV_0...	3/31/...	165400--032---	WIP - sales value	1,200.00	Project - WIP - sales value
0028...	PJPV_0...	3/31/...	165400--032---	WIP - sales value	1,000.00	Project - WIP - sales value
0028...	PJPV_0...	3/31/...	165400--032---	WIP - sales value	1,230.77	Project - WIP - sales value
00287:	PJPV_0...	3/31/...	165400--032---	WIP - sales value	714.29	Project - WIP - sales value

Figure 2-248 Resulting estimate transaction vouchers—POC FP project P&L accounting SV estimation—calculation method Markup percent–estimate line

In a first step, the POC for each estimate line is calculated by comparing actual costs with the costs to complete. For details, please see formula (10) above.

Step 1			
Category/Cost template line	***Costs***	***Cost to complete***	***POC***
Consulting Hours	$500.00	$200.00	71.43%
Development Hours	$400.00	$900.00	30.77%
Training Hours		$400.00	
Project-Management Hours	$400.00	$0.00	100.00%
Travel expense	$1,200.00	$300.00	80.00%
Other expense		$300.00	
Item		$500.00	
Total	***$2,500.00***	***$2,600.00***	

Figure 2-249 Accrued revenue calculation Markup percent–estimate line (1)

Provided that the contract value has been assigned to the different cost estimate lines as shown in Figure 2-250...

Category/Cost template line	Costs	Cost to complete	POC	Manually allocated contract value
Step 2				
Consulting Hours	$500.00	$200.00	71.43%	$1,000.00
Development Hours	$400.00	$900.00	30.77%	$4,000.00
Training Hours		$400.00		$1,000.00
Project-Management Hours	$400.00	$0.00	100.00%	$1,000.00
Travel expense	$1,200.00	$300.00	80.00%	$1,500.00
Other expense		$300.00		$500.00
Item		$500.00		$1,000.00
Total	**$2,500.00**	**$2,600.00**		**$10,000.00**

Figure 2-250 Accrued revenue calculation Markup percent–estimate line (2)

...the calculated POC figures are multiplied by the assigned contract value in order to arrive at the revenue amount that is accrued.

Step 3					
Category/Cost template line	Costs	Total Forecast	POC	Manually allocated contract value	Revenue to recognize
Consulting Hours	$500.00	$200.00	71.43%	$1,000.00	$714.29
Development Hours	$400.00	$900.00	30.77%	$4,000.00	$1,230.77
Training Hours		$400.00	0.00%	$1,000.00	$0.00
Project-Management Hours	$400.00	$0.00	100.00%	$1,000.00	$1,000.00
Travel expense	$1,200.00	$300.00	80.00%	$1,500.00	$1,200.00
Other expense		$300.00	0.00%	$500.00	$0.00
Item		$500.00	0.00%	$1,000.00	$0.00
Total	**$2,500.00**	**$2,600.00**		**$10,000.00**	**$4,145.06**
				Estimated revenue to recognize	**$4,901.96**
				Adjustment position	**$756.90**

Figure 2-251 Accrued revenue calculation Markup percent–estimate line (3)

If the sum of the calculated revenue to recognize ($4,145.06) differs from the POC amount that has been calculated for the whole estimate ($4,901.96), an adjustment position is created and included in the accrued revenue voucher that is shown in Figure 2-248.

207

Figure 2-252 summarizes and compares the accrued revenue amounts that have been posted for the three projects with the different cost-estimate-parameter setups.

	Revenue to recognize		
	Setup "None"	Setup "Markup percent total"	Setup "Markup estimate line"
Consulting Hours		$980.39	$714.29
Development Hours		$784.31	$1,230.77
Training Hours			
Project-Management Hours		$784.31	$1,000.00
Travel expense		$2,352.94	$1,200.00
Other expense			
Item			
Adjustment Position			756.90
Total	$4,901.96	$,4901.96	$4,901.96

Figure 2-252 Comparison revenue recognition

As one can identify, the total recognized revenue is identical for all of the projects with the different cost-estimate-parameter setups. The level of detail and the breakdown of the accrued revenue amounts differ, however, significantly. Whereas the first project does not provide an information on the accrued revenue for each of the estimate lines, the projects with the *Markup parameter* setup show this detail, even though—because of the different calculation methods applied—differently.

2.7.2.10.2.4.   Calculation Method Application

After having analyzed the differences in the cost-estimate-parameter setup options, one might ask when, that is under which circumstances, the *Markup-total* and *Markup-estimate line* parameters might be applied.

This question can be answered by the forthcoming accounting regulation changes of IFRS15 and ASC606. Those accounting regulations deal with the question when and how companies have to recognize revenue. In order to stipulate the time and revenue amount that has to be recognized, the accounting regulations make use of the following five-step model framework.

Step 1: Identify the contract with the customers

Identifying the contract with the customer is not an issue that is directly related to the ERP system but a task that requires a judgment—

   a) whether the contract has been approved by the parties to the contract,
   b) whether each party's rights can be identified,
   c) whether the payment terms can be identified, and
   d) whether the contract has commercial substance.

For additional information, reference is made to the aforementioned accounting standards.

Step 2: Identify the performance obligations in the contract

After a contract has been identified, one has to assess the goods and services that have been promised to the customer in order to identify the performance obligations. Those performance obligations can consist of a distinct good or service or a series of distinct goods or services. D365 supports this identification process in two ways. First, through the cost template, where users can set up different cost template lines that represent different performance obligations. (Please see Figure 2-253 for an example.)

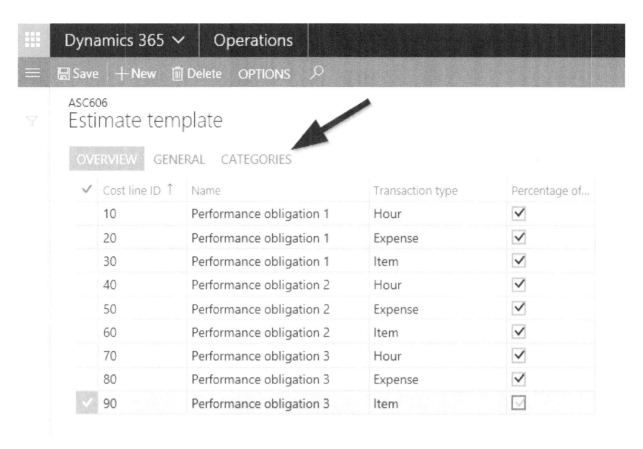

Figure 2-253 Cost template with template lines that represent performance obligations

Note A prerequisite for using the cost template for incorporating contractual performance obligations is that distinct project categories exist that can clearly be assigned to those performance obligations.

If this is not the case, that is, if a project category cannot clearly be assigned to one of those cost template lines, one can alternatively make use of main- and subprojects to differentiate performance obligations that have been determined in the contract with the customer.

Step 3: Determine the transaction price

Determining the transaction price is—once again—primarily not an ERP-system-related issue but supported by the various milestone and billing rule functionalities in D365. (See, for example, Figure 2-168.)

Step 4: Allocate the transaction price to the performance obligations in the contracts

Once the total transaction price for the contract has been identified, it needs to be allocated to the different performance obligations, which can, for example, be achieved by assigning the total contract value to the different lines of the cost template, as illustrated in Figure 2-247 above.

If one cannot clearly differentiate and assign the various project categories to the cost template lines, this allocation can be realized by assigning the different transaction prices for the performance obligations to the main projects and subprojects used.

Step 5: Recognize revenue when or as the entity satisfies a performance obligation

The last process step finally consists of recognizing the revenue, which can—depending on the project type used—be realized by creating and posting project estimates or by creating project invoices.

Provided that one does not have to follow IFRS or US-GAAP accounting rules, making use of the *Markup percent–total* parameter seems preferable over selecting the *None* parameter setting. That is because the *Markup percent–total* parameter provides users with a detailed breakdown of the accrued revenue by cost template lines that allows getting a much deeper insight into their cost and value drivers that cannot be achieved with a *None* parameter setup.

2.8. Summary Project-Group Setup

After having analyzed the various project-group and accounting setups and the resulting ledger vouchers, let's have a look at Figure 2-254, which illustrates a decision tree that helps deciding which project type and accounting setup to use.

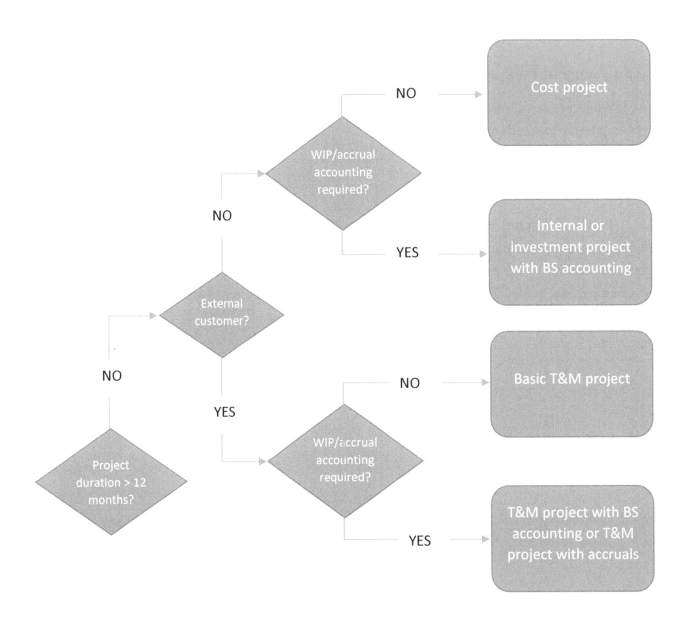

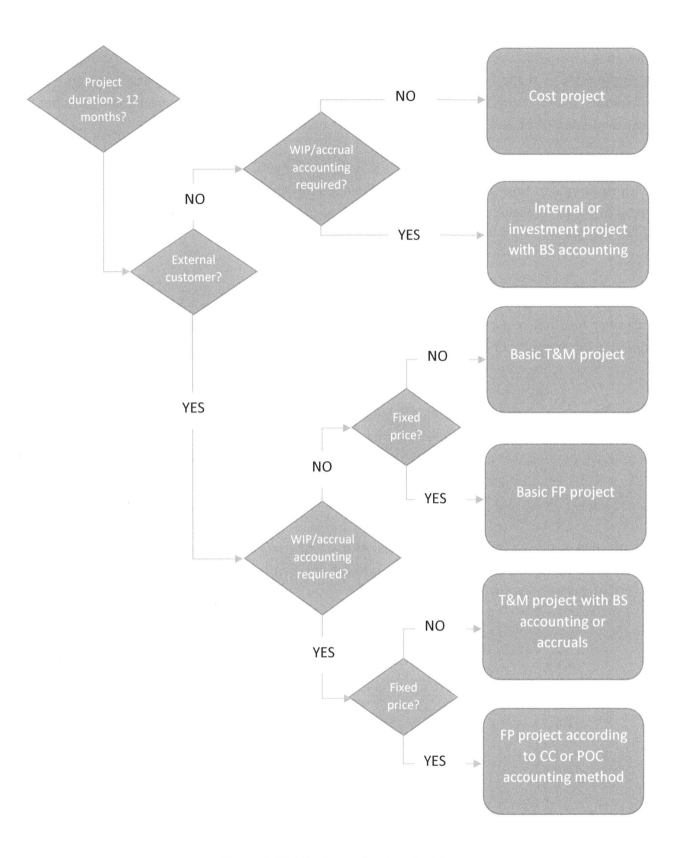

Figure 2-254 Project selection decision tree

The decision tree starts with making a first differentiation between short-term (duration < 12 months) and long-term (duration > 12 months) projects. Based on this first differentiation, a second differentiation is made based on the fact whether the project has a relationship to an external customer—for which invoices need to be created—or not. The third level finally differentiates projects that require a WIP or accrual accounting and those that don't.

With those major three decision layers, one can identify the preferable project type and accounting setup to select. Please note that the decision tree illustrated above does not always result in a definite project to select.

Take—as an example—the short-term project that does not have an association to an external customer but that requires a WIP or accrual accounting. Depending on the underlying purpose of initiating this project, either an internal or an investment project with BS accounting might be used.

Something similar can be identified for long-term projects that have an association to an external customer and which require a WIP or accrual accounting with a fixed-price setup. Depending on the accounting method that is allowed to be applied (POC vs. CC accounting), either a FP project with a POC or a CC method might be used.

Irrespective of those shortcomings and against the background that no fully comprehensive decision tree can be set up, it is believed that the project decision tree illustrated in Figure 2-254 provides sufficient guidance to select the right project.

3. Project Reporting and Analysis

This third and final chapter focuses on different tools one can use for analyzing project costs, revenues, and the overall profitability of a company's projects.

3.1. Standard Reporting Tools

3.1.1. Project-Specific Inquiry Forms

Let's start by having a look at the tools that are available for analyzing individual projects. This analysis will be executed for a fixed-price project that makes use of a WIP accounting setup because analyzing project WIP is often a major issue in practice. The actual and planned data that will be used in the following are the ones illustrated in Figure 2-238.

For the following analysis, four major control forms will be examined in regard to their ability to control the progress of the project.

Figure 3-1 Project-specific control forms

3.1.1.1.   Cost Control Form

The cost control form makes a simple actual-budget comparison, which allows identifying those costs that exceed their budget amounts. Additional details of the actual and budget data can be obtained through the forecast and transaction buttons available on top of the cost control form. Please note that the *Show by* field allows users grouping the cost data by cost template, categories, or transaction type, which has the advantage that users can investigate their actual and budget data from different angles.

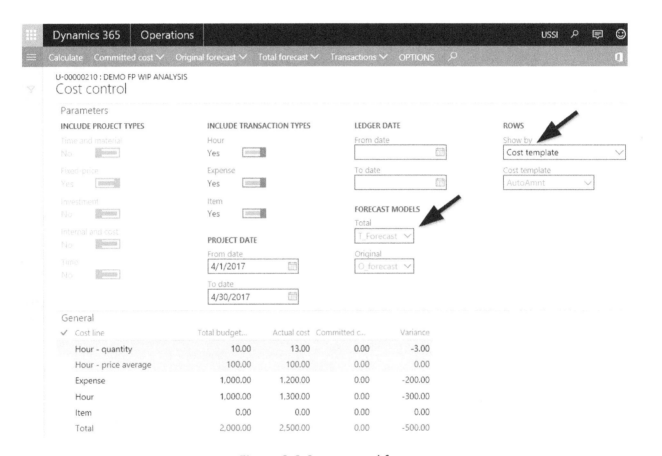

Figure 3-2 Cost control form

Note
The Pivot-Excel export functionality that was available in prior system versions has been removed from the cost control form and is no longer available.

3.1.1.2.   Project Budget Balances Form

Provided that a project budget has been established, the project budget balance control form can be used for controlling purposes. Compared to the cost control form, the project budget balances form provides more details of the original, approved, consumed...budget amounts. One can thus gain a deeper insight into the progress of a project.

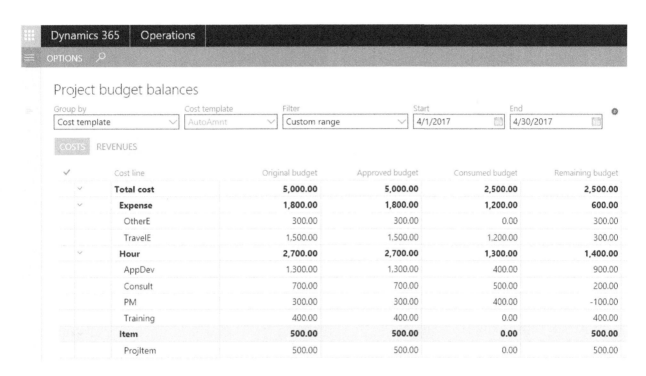

Figure 3-3 Project budget balances control form

Irrespective of the advantages of the project budget balances form, the form suffers from two major shortcomings. First, the fact that budget balances are not separated by date ranges (which seems to be a current system bug in the author's application).

A second major shortcoming of the project budget balances form is that an actual-budget comparison requires a detailed planning and posting of costs with the correct project category. As an example, if costs are budgeted with the travel expense (TravelE) category but later on recorded with the other expense (OtherE) category, the data shown in the budget balances form are misleading.

3.1.1.3. Project Statement Form

The third control form that can be started directly from the project is the project statement form that is shown in Figure 3-4.

Project statements

GENERAL   PROFIT AND LOSS   WIP   CONSUMPTION   INVOICE   HOUR RATE

	ACTUAL
	WIP cost price
WIP - COST VALUE - HOUR	1,300.00
WIP - COST VALUE - EXPENSE	1,200.00
WIP - COST VALUE - ITEM	0.00
WIP - ACCRUED LOSS	0.00
TOTAL WIP COST	2,500.00
	WIP sales price
WIP - SALES VALUE	0.00
WIP - PRODUCTION	0.00
WIP - PROFIT	0.00
WIP - SUBSCRIPTION	0.00
TOTAL WIP SALES	0.00
	WIP total
GROSS WIP	2,500.00
WIP - INVOICED - ON-ACCOUNT	0.00
NET WIP	2,500.00

Figure 3-4 Project statement control form

As the project form simply summarizes actual cost and revenue data from an accounting perspective, it is not suitable for a detailed project analysis.

3.1.1.4. Project-Cost-Tracking Form

The last and from the author's perspective most suitable form for project-controlling purposes is the project-cost-tracking form, which is exemplified in Figure 3-5.

Figure 3-5 Project-cost-tracking form

The main reason why the cost-tracking form appears to be the most suitable control form is because it does not only provide users with a comparison of actual and budgeted cost data but also provides an indication of the forthcoming costs and the overall prospective costs of the project.

Please note that the use of the cost-tracking form requires the use of the work breakdown structure (WBS). For details, please see the first part of the book.

3.1.2.   General Inquiry Forms and Reports

Even though the previously shown cost control and project statement form can be used for analyzing main projects and subprojects, the budget balance and project-tracking form are not made for a cross-project control analysis. For that purpose, one can make use of the various project inquiries and reports.

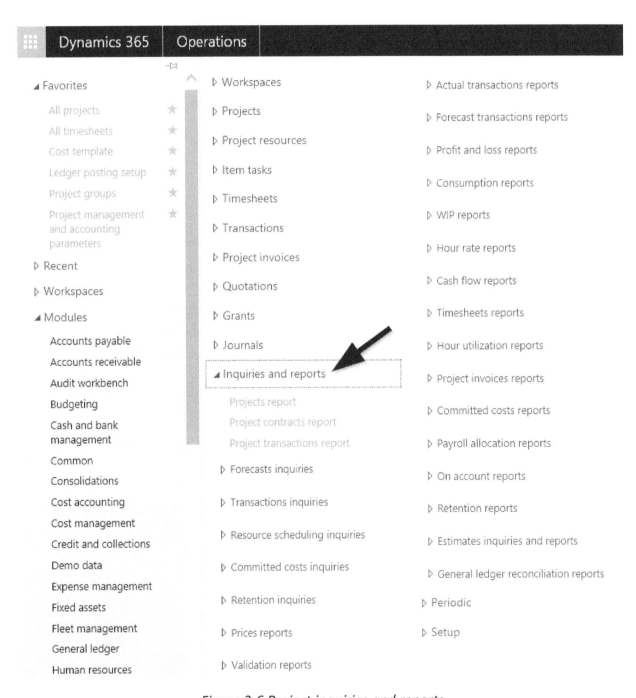

Figure 3-6 Project inquiries and reports

Especially the WIP and profit and loss reports provide the possibility of analyzing costs, revenues, and WIP amounts across projects. Figures 3-7 and 3-8 exemplify a sample *WIP* and *profit and loss report* and the information they provide.

Project WIP

Go to ∨ |◁ ◁ ▷ ▷| Find ∨   Zoom ∨ ◌   Export ∨ 🖶

Project - WIP
Contoso Consulting USA

4/10/2017
1:37 PM

Project date from 4/1/2017 to 4/30/2017
Actual

Project	Name	Quantity	Total WIP cost	Total WIP sales	Gross WIP	WIP - Invoiced - on-account	Net WIP
U-00000200	23c DEMO	0.00	0.00	0.00	0.00	0.00	0.00
U-00000201	23b DEMO Alternative Setup	0.00	0.00	0.00	0.00	0.00	0.00
U-00000205	Demo FP POC	0.00	0.00	0.00	0.00	0.00	0.00
U-00000206	Demo FP POC PL	13.00	0.00	4,901.96	4,901.96	0.00	4,901.96
U-00000208	Demo FP POC WIP	0.00	0.00	0.00	0.00	0.00	0.00
U-00000209	DEMO FP P&L ACC	0.00	0.00	0.00	0.00	0.00	0.00
U-00000210	DEMO FP WIP ANALYSIS	13.00	2,500.00	0.00	2,500.00	0.00	2,500.00
Total		**26.00**	**2,500.00**	**4,901.96**	**7,401.96**	**0.00**	**7,401.96**

Figure 3-7 Sample Project-WIP report

Project profit and loss

Go to ∨ |◁ ◁ ▷ ▷| Find ∨   Zoom ∨ ◌   Export ∨ 🖶

Project - profit and loss
Contoso Consulting USA

Ledger date from to
Actual

Project	Name	Hour - quantity	Cost - hour	Cost - expense	Cost - item	Total cost	Revenue	Value-added	Gross margin
U-00000200	23c DEMO	13.00	1,300.00	1,200.00	0.00	2,500.00	4,145.06	2,945.1	1,645.1
U-00000201	23b DEMO Alternative Setup	13.00	1,300.00	1,200.00	0.00	2,500.00	4,901.95	3,702.0	2,402.0
U-00000203	Building of Stadium	1,163.00	111,745.00	0.00	0.00	111,745.00	0.00	0.0	-111,745.0
U-00000204	Demo T&M	0.00	0.00	0.00	0.00	0.00	0.00	0.0	0.0
U-00000205	Demo FP POC	13.00	1,300.00	1,200.00	0.00	2,500.00	0.00	-1,200.0	-2,500.0
U-00000206	Demo FP POC PL	13.00	1,300.00	1,200.00	0.00	2,500.00	4,901.95	3,702.0	2,402.0
U-00000207	X	0.00	0.00	0.00	0.00	0.00	0.00	0.0	0.0
U-00000208	Demo FP POC WIP	0.00	0.00	0.00	0.00	0.00	0.00	0.0	0.0
U-00000209	DEMO FP P&L ACC	13.00	1,300.00	1,200.00	0.00	2,500.00	0.00	-1,200.0	-2,500.0
U-00000210	DEMO FP WIP ANALYSIS	0.00	0.00	0.00	0.00	0.00	0.00	0.0	0.0
Total		**1,228.00**	**118,245.00**	**6,000.00**	**0.00**	**124,245.00**	**13,948.96**	**7,949.0**	**-110,296.0**

Figure 3-8 Sample Project-Profit and loss report

It is not possible to describe each inquiry form and report that can be used for cross-project control and analysis purposes. From the author's perspective, the *WIP and Profit and loss* reports are the ones that are suited best for analyzing projects. However, before going live with the project-management and accounting module, it is recommendable to verify whether those standard reports and inquiry forms provide all necessary information that project managers and controllers require.

3.1.3. Financial Accounts and Dimensions

Many times one is confronted with the fact that project controllers or management accountants are the ones responsible for analyzing projects. Because of their accounting background, these people regularly prefer to analyze projects based on ledger accounts and financial dimensions. Making the project analysis this way necessitates that projects are set up with their own project financial dimension value, which is exemplified in Figure 3-9.

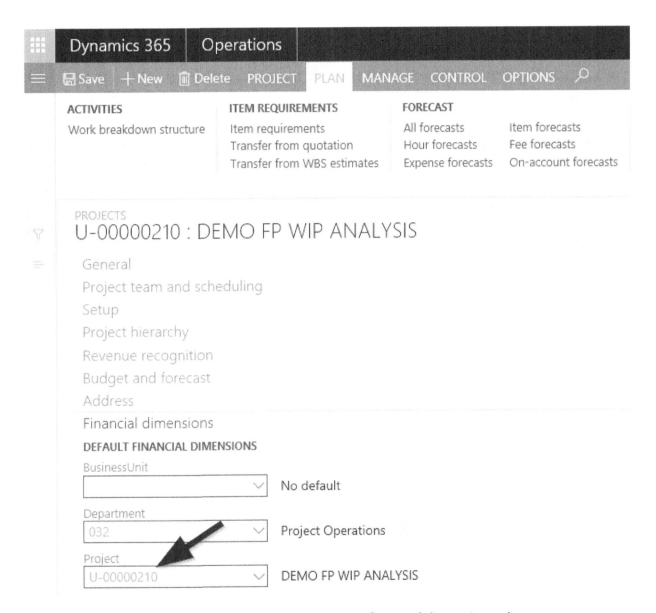

Figure 3-9 Project setup with project financial dimension value

Linking a project to its own financial dimension is a best practice setup, not only because financial dimensions offer an additional analysis tool but also because they help reconciling the project-management and accounting module with the general ledger module.

The standard application does not automatically fill the project financial dimension but rather requires that users assign this financial dimension manually.

For a detailed project analysis, which makes use of financial accounts and dimensions, the set up and use of financial dimensions is not sufficient. What is required in addition is a detailed ledger accounting setup that differentiates—at a minimum—between the different project categories. Such a setup is illustrated in Figure 3-10.

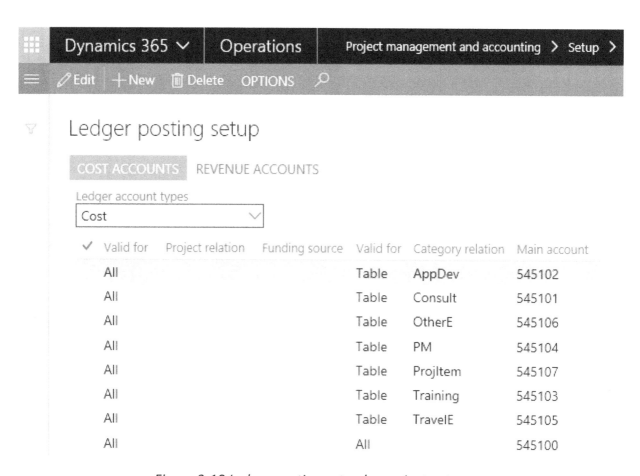

✓	Valid for	Project relation	Funding source	Valid for	Category relation	Main account
	All			Table	AppDev	545102
	All			Table	Consult	545101
	All			Table	OtherE	545106
	All			Table	PM	545104
	All			Table	ProjItem	545107
	All			Table	Training	545103
	All			Table	TravelE	545105
	All			All		545100

Figure 3-10 Ledger-posting setup by project category

Note The last ledger-posting setup line shown in Figure 3-10 applies to all projects and categories, which is something that should be avoided in live environments if a detailed project analysis needs to be executed on a ledger account-financial dimension basis.

Once financial dimensions and ledger accounts have been set up, one can use the management reporter for a detailed project analysis. This can be achieved by setting up reports that make use of main account-financial dimension combinations, as illustrated in Figure 3-11.

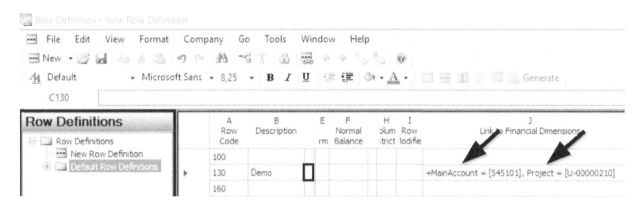

Figure 3-11 Management reporter setup for project analysis purposes

Note Setting up a detailed MR report for analyzing projects is left as an exercise for the reader. An example of such a report can be found further below.

Alternatively, one can make use of a financial dimension set that includes the main account and the project financial dimension in order to analyze the project data through the trial balance form. For an example, please see Figure 3-12.

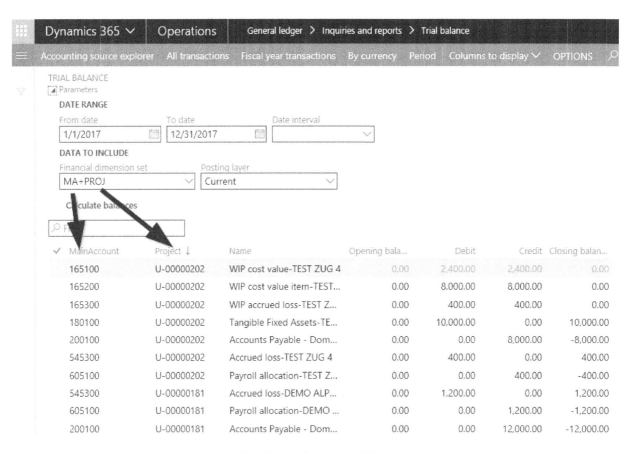

Figure 3-12 Trial balance form used for project analysis

Note

Using financial dimensions and ledger accounts for analyzing projects has two major disadvantages: The first disadvantage is that only financial data but no quantities can be analyzed. The second disadvantage—that applies only to the project analysis in the trial balance form—is that no actual versus budget data comparison can be made. For those reasons, a financial dimension and account-based analysis can only be considered a second best project analysis instrument.

3.1.4. BI Tools

The last standard reporting tools examined in this section are the business intelligence (BI) tools that allow a detailed analysis of cost-, revenue-, budget-, and quantity-related project data through predefined reports and measures.

The only thing required to make use of those tools is to deploy them; in older system versions by deploying the project accounting cube and in newer system versions by making the standard Power BI content packs available. The latter is exemplified in Figures 3-13.

Figure 3-13 Practice Manager Power BI standard content pack (1)

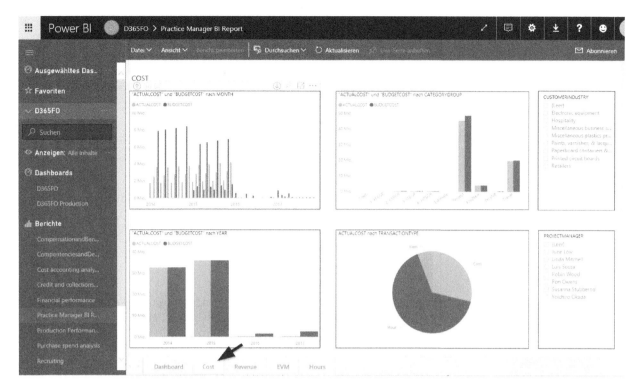

Figure 3-14 Practice Manager Power BI standard content pack (2)

Major advantages of making use of the standard BI tools comprise the ability to drill down into transaction details that make up the illustrated data. BI tools provide thus more flexibility when it comes to analyzing project-related data from different perspectives. The downside of using those predefined dashboards or cubes is that they might not exactly fit the reporting and analysis requirements of the company and thus require some adjustment.

3.2. Earned Value Analysis (EVA)

For long-term projects, a simple actual versus budget comparison, such as the one shown in previous chapters might not be sufficient in order to control whether projects are still on time and within budget. That is because budget overruns can simply be caused by the fact that project work is executed faster or slower than originally planned. Figures 3-15 to 3-18 illustrate the issue of a missing time perspective in traditional actual versus budget comparisons.

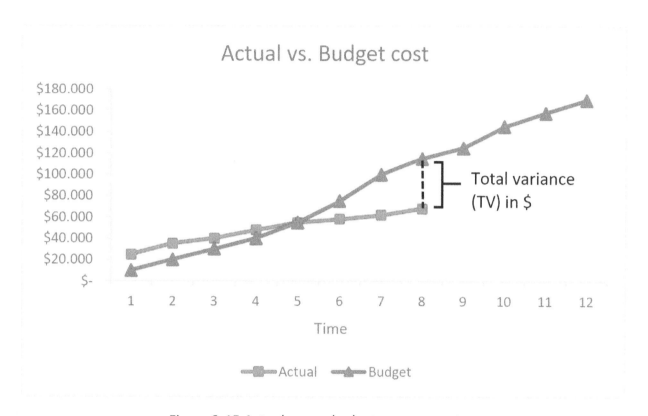

Figure 3-15 Actual versus budget cost comparison

Let's start with the simple actual-budget comparison in Figure 3-15 that illustrates a total variance (TV) between the actual and budgeted costs. The TV that is shown in Figure 3-15 indicates that the actual costs are below the budgeted ones, which—on first sight—is a good sign.

The positive variance between the actual and budget costs might, however, simply be caused by the fact that people work slower than expected. What is missing though is a measure that incorporates the project work that has been accomplished so far.

This measure is the so-called earned value (EV), which allows separating the TV into a schedule variance (SV)—that measures whether project work progresses faster or slower than expected—and a cost variance (CV)—that measures whether the actual costs are above or below the budget given the current progress of the project.

Figures 3-16 to 3-18 exemplify those measures and variances as well as the overall project EV control diagram, which combines all three measures that are required for a detailed project controlling.

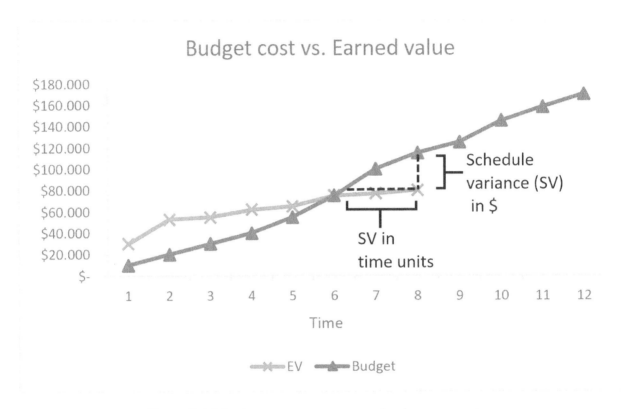

Figure 3-16 Budget cost versus earned value comparison

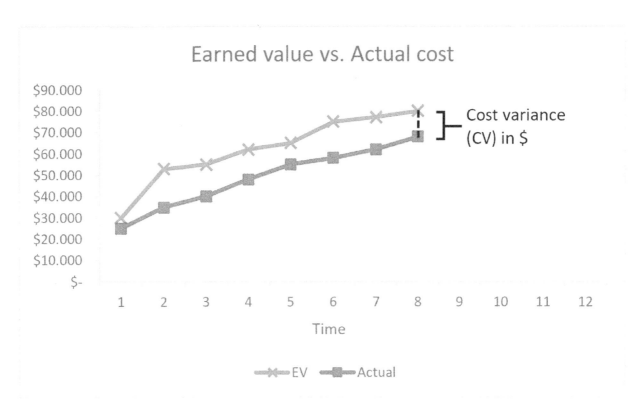

Figure 3-17 Earned value versus actual cost comparison

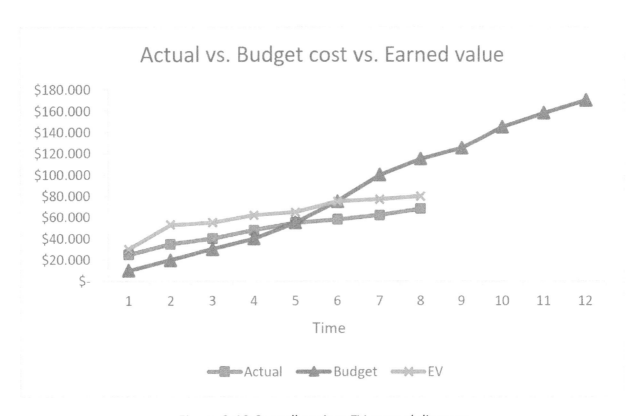

Figure 3-18 Overall project EV control diagram

3.2.1. Sample Data

After having analyzed the theoretical background of the EVA technique, let's take a look at how it can be incorporated into D365. This incorporation will be exemplified based on the following example for the construction of a building.

Invoicing	Jan 17	$1,000,000
plan	Jan 18	$1,000,000
	Jan 19	$1,000,000

Project stage	Start	End	Project category	Type	Budget			Actual		
					Qty	Cost price	Value	Qty	Cost price	Value
1. Excavation	Jan 17	May 17	100 Digger	Expense	800 hrs	$250	$200,000	1,000 hrs	$250	$250000
			110 Excavation worker	Hour	700 hrs	$80	$56,000	950 hrs	$80	$76,000
				Subtotal			*$256,000*			*$326,000*
2. Structural work	Jun 17	Dec 17	101 Building crane	Expense	1,500 hrs	$200	$300,000	1,900 hrs	$220	$418,000
			111 Construction worker	Hour	1,200 hrs	$50	$60,000	1,800 hrs	$60	$108,000
			121 Concrete	Item	500 to	$1,000	$500,000	550 to	$1,000	$550,000
				Subtotal			*$860,000*			*$1,076,000*
3. Interior fittings	Jan 18	Dec 18	102 Tools	Expense	3,000 hrs	$80	$240,000	3,600 hrs	$75	$270,000
			112 Carpenter	Hour	2,750 hrs	$60	$165,000	3,400 hrs	$50	$170,000
			122 Wooden panels	Item	950 pcs	$40	$38,000	1,200 pcs	$50	$48,000
				Subtotal			*$443,000*			*$488,000*
4 Gardening	Mar 19	Jun 19	103 Gardening equipment	Expense	1,000 hrs	$60	$60,000	800 hrs	$65	$52,000
			113 Gardener	Hour	800 hrs	$40	$32,000	750 hrs	$40	$30,000
			123 Plants	Item	500 pcs	$25	$12,500	600 pcs	$25	$15,000
				Subtotal			*$104,500*			*$97,000*
5 Additions (not planned)	Jul 19	Jul 19	104 Repair equipment	Expense				100 hrs	$50	$5,000
			114 Service worker	Hour				80 hrs	$100	$8,000
				Subtotal						*$13,000*
				Total			$1,663,500			$2,000,000

Figure 3-19 Sample data EVM analysis

The construction of the building is separated into five different stages and starts with the excavation of the ground. Thereafter, the structural works and interior fittings are done before the project work closes with the gardening work. The last project stage represents unplanned additional work that is required to finish the project.

The second and third columns in Figure 3-19 show the start and end periods for each stage. The project category and transaction-type columns follow those. Finally, the budget and actual columns show the planned (budgeted) and realized (actual) quantities and values for each of the project stages. Based on the sample data, total costs of $1,663,500 are expected. However, at the end of the project total costs of $2,000,000 are realized.

Within the following, different EV calculation methods will be presented that demonstrate how and at which stage one could have identified the realized cost overruns in order to take counteractive measures. A major aim of the following illustrations is highlighting the strength and weaknesses of each of those methods in order to allow the reader making an assessment what might fit best in a specific company environment.

Irrespective of the planned and realized costs, a fixed sales price of $3,000,000 has been agreed upon with the customer, which needs to be paid in three installments that are shown in the upper part of Figure 3-19.

3.2.2. Setup

3.2.2.1. Project Group and Cost Template

The following illustration of the EVA makes use of a project group that posts all costs to P&L accounts and which uses a cost template that has the *work progress percentage* completion method set up. Figures 3-20 and 3-21 illustrate this setup.

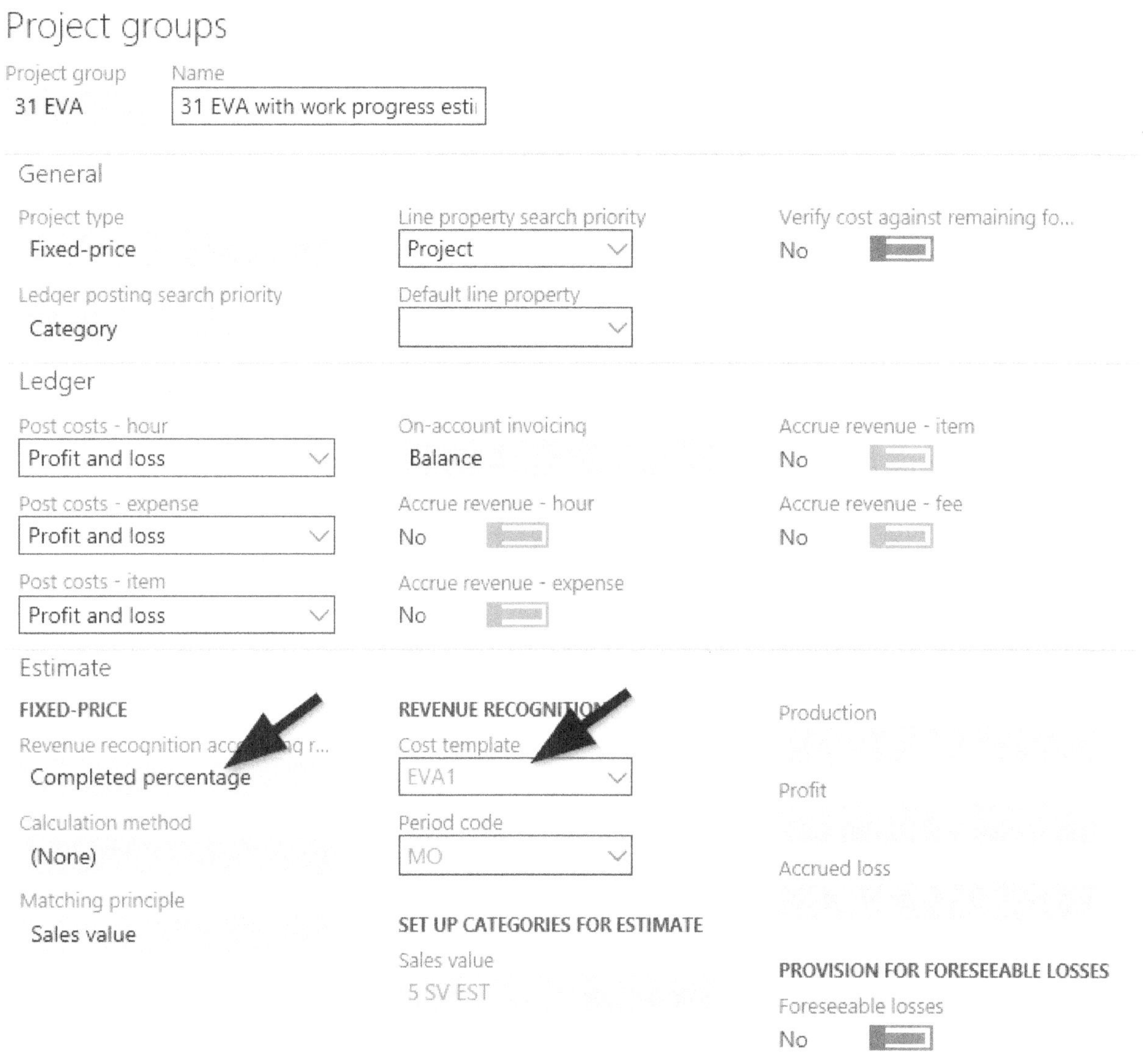

Figure 3-20 Project group used for EVA

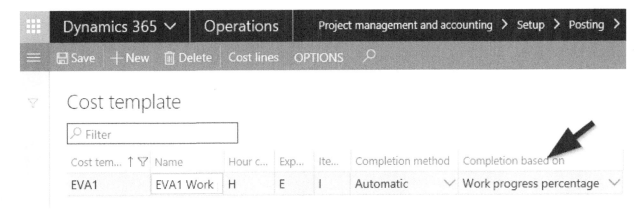

Figure 3-21 Cost template used for EVA

3.2.2.2.   WBS

Once the project and the cost template have been established, a new fixed-price (FP) project is created. The first project step consists then of transferring the budget data that are shown in Figure 3-19 into the WBS form. Details of this transfer can be found in Figures 3-22 and 3-23.

Figure 3-22 WBS schedule planning

Work breakdown structure

U-00000228: DEMO 31

Currently published

SCHEDULE PLANNING ESTIMATED COSTS AND REVENUE

Filter

New   Save   Delete   Refresh   Expand to   Rename auto style   Position dimension

✓	WBS ID	Task	Transaction ty...	Description	Category	R...	Quantity	Unit cost price	Unit sales price	Total cost price
		U-00000228								1,663,500.00
	1	1. Excavation								256,000.00
			Expense	100 Digger	100 Digger		800	250.00	287.50	200,000.00
			Hour	110 Excavation worker	110 Exc worker		700	80.00	300.00	56,000.00
	2	2. Structural work								860,000.00
			Expense	101 Building crane	101 Build crane		1500	200.00	230.00	300,000.00
			Item	121 Concrete	121 Concrete		500	1,000.00	2,000.00	500,000.00
			Hour	111 Construction wo...	111 Const worker		1200	50.00	300.00	60,000.00
	3	3. Interior fittings								443,000.00
			Expense	102 Tools	102 Tools		3000	80.00	92.00	240,000.00
			Item	122 Wooden panels	122 Wooden panels		950	40.00	100.00	38,000.00
			Hour	112 Carpenter	112 Carpenter		2750	60.00	300.00	165,000.00
	4	4. Gardening								104,500.00
			Expense	103 Gardening equip...	103 Gardening equip		1000	60.00	69.00	60,000.00
			Item	123 Plants	123 Plants		500	25.00	80.00	12,500.00
			Hour	113 Gardener	113 Gardener		800	40.00	300.00	32,000.00
	5	5. Additions								0.00
			Hour	114 Service worker	114 Service worker			100.00	300.00	0.00

Figure 3-23 WBS estimated costs and revenue

3.2.2.3. Forecast

Because FP projects require forecast data for the calculation of the project estimates, all WBS budget data are transferred into the forecast forms by making use of the *transfer from WBS* functionality.

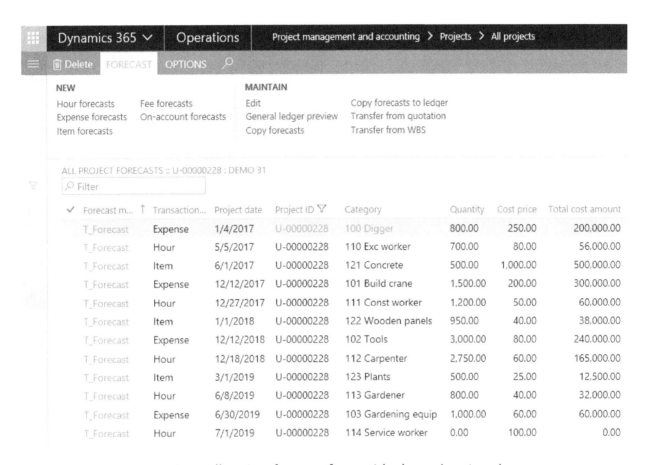

Figure 3-24 All project forecast form with planned project data

Note For reasons of brevity, the WBS planning data are not transferred into the project budget form because this is not required for the EV calculations, which are shown next.

Note Transferring WBS budget data to the forecast forms is not required for estimates that make use of the work progress percentage estimate. All other estimate types require this transfer.

3.2.2.4. On-account

A considerable difference to the previously used setups can be found in the on-account form, which is filled with the planned costs of the project rather than the amounts that are invoiced to the customer.

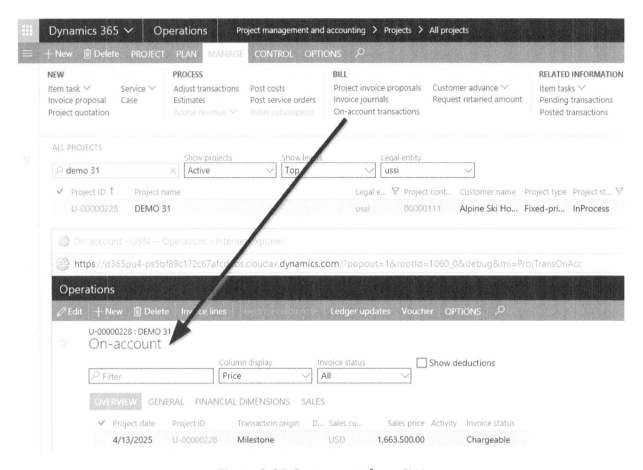

Figure 3-25 On-account form EVA

The underlying reason for recording the planned costs in the on-account form is the necessity to calculate the EV, which will be realized by making use of the project-estimate functionality.

Note

In order to avoid that the on-account budget amount will ever be invoiced to a customer, a project date that lies far in the future has been entered in the project date field.

3.2.2.5. Subproject For Invoicing

As the on-account milestone function cannot be used for invoicing the customer, a separate T&M project has been set up for this purpose. Later on, fee transactions will be recorded and invoiced through this subproject. In other words, the FP project will be used for tracking project costs only, while the T&M subproject will be used for tracking the project revenues.

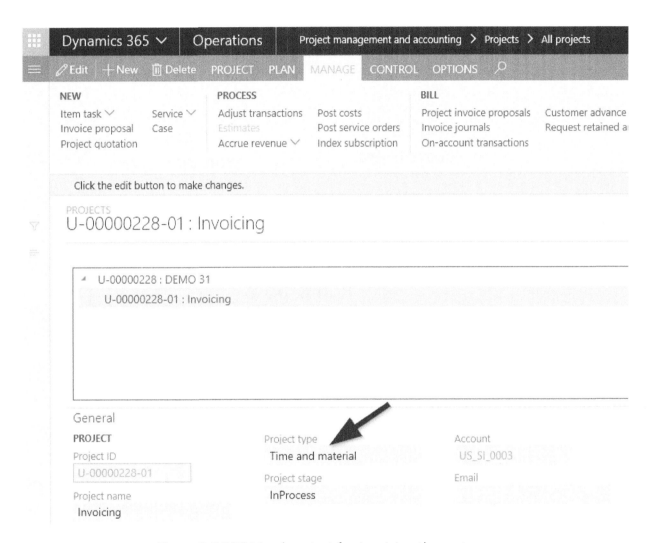

Figure 3-26 T&M subproject for invoicing the customer

Note: Numerous tests—not shown here for reasons of brevity—demonstrated that only the use of a separate subproject ensures a clear separation of costs and revenues that is required for the EVA. Billing rules that can also be associated with FP projects cannot achieve this because they influence and distort the amounts recorded in the on-account form.

3.2.3. Process and Analysis

With those setups in place, the EVA project cycle starts with recording actual project transactions that are compared with the budgeted data in the estimate form in order to calculate the EV. The cycle continues with the creation of customer invoices through the subproject before additional transactions are recorded at the main project level.

Figure 3-27 Project process cycle

For reasons of brevity, no details of the recorded transactions will be presented in the following because this has already been done extensively in the previous chapters. Rather than that, a focus is made on the results and analysis.

After all transactions for a specific project stage have been recorded, three different forms are available for analyzing the project, the cost-tracking form, the effort-tracking form, and the estimate form. Please note that only the last one is used for calculating the POC and the EV. The other forms are presented here in addition because they provide supplementary insights into the overall progress of the project from a different perspective.

3.2.3.1.　　Analysis Cost-Tracking Form

After the hour and expense transaction for the first project stage have been recorded, the cost-tracking form shows a so-called cost percentage of 18.81%, which indicates that 18.81% of the total costs of the project have been consumed at the end of the first project stage.

TRACKING VIEWS
U-00000229: DEMO 31 STEP 1
Cost tracking view

WBS ID	Task	Cost percent	Actual cost	Remaining cost	Cost at complete	Planned cost	Cost variance
	U-00000229	18.81	326,000.00	1,407,500.00	1,733,500.00	1,663,500.00	-70,000.00 ✗
1	1. Excavation	100.00	326,000.00	0.00	326,000.00	256,000.00	-70,000.00 ✗
2	2. Structural work	0.00	0.00	860,000.00	860,000.00	860,000.00	0.00 ✓
3	3. Interior fittings	0.00	0.00	443,000.00	443,000.00	443,000.00	0.00 ✓
4	4. Gardening	0.00	0.00	104,500.00	104,500.00	104,500.00	0.00 ✓
5	5. Additions	0.00	0.00	0.00	0.00	0.00	0.00 ✓

Figure 3-28 Cost-tracking form after finalizing the first project stage

The following formulas exemplify how this percentage is calculated:

Cost percent = Actual costs / (Actual costs + Remaining cost) * 100%　　　　　(12)

Cost percent (Stage 1) = $326,000 / ($326,000 + $860,000 + $443,000 + $104,500)

* 100% = 18.81%　　　　　(13)

Note At the end of the second project stage, a cost percentage of 71.92% is calculated. Thereafter, a cost percentage of 94.76% could be identified before the cost percentage jumps to 100% at the end of the fourth project stage. Those data indicate that the project budget has almost completely been consumed already at the end of the third project stage.

3.2.3.2. Analysis Effort-Tracking Form

The effort-tracking form, which focuses on the effort—that is, the hours—only, shows a slightly lower progress percentage at the end of the first project stage. It is calculated as illustrated in formula 15 below.

Figure 3-29 Effort-tracking form after finalizing the first project stage

Progress percent = Actual effort / (Actual effort + Remaining effort) * 100%   (14)

Cost percent (Stage 1) = 950 hours / (950 hours + 1,200 hours + 2,750 hours

+ 800 hours) *100%   (15)

= 16.67%

Note The progress percentage figures at the end of the project stages two, three, and four are 43.65%, 88.49%, and 100%, respectively. The next table compares the cost and progress percentage figures at the end of each project stage.

Project stage	Cost percentage	Effort percentage
1. Excavation	18.81%	16.67%
2. Structural work	71.92%	43.65%
3. Interior fittings	94.76%	88.49%
4 Gardening	100.00%	100.00%
5 Additions (not planned)	100.00%	100.00%

Figure 3-30 Cost and progress percentage at the end of each project stage

A comparison of the cost and progress percentage figures shows that the cost percentage has always been higher than the progress percentage over the first three project stages. Even though no EV and variances have been calculated so far, this outcome can be taken as an early warning indicator that something is not running well with the project from a cost perspective.

Before making additional interpretations, let's have a look at the percentage of completion (POC) calculation in the estimate form that is required for calculating the EV.

3.2.3.3. Analysis Estimate Form

As mentioned before, the POC of the project is calculated in the estimate form based on the following formula.

POC based on work progress % calculation = Actual effort / Planned effort * 100%   (16)

Please note that the POC—which is calculated based on the work progress percentage that has been specified in the cost template—only takes the effort, that is, the hours worked into account to measure the progress of the project. The next formula shows this for the POC calculated for the first project stage.

POC (Stage 1) = 950 hrs / (700 + 1,200 + 2,750 + 800) hrs *100% = 17.43%   (17)

The previously calculated progress percentage and the POC differ only in the denominator. That is, the progress percentage takes the actual and the (prospective) remaining effort into account, while the POC simply compares the actual with the originally planned effort.

With a POC of 17.43% at the end of the first project stage and a total budget of $1,663,500, an EV of $289,967.89 is calculated. Based on this EV measure, a cost variance of $36,032.11 and a schedule variance of $33,967.89 result, which add up to the TV of $70,000 between the actual and budgeted costs.

Figure 3-31 shows the estimate form and the EV calculation that result at the end of the first project stage. Please note that the schedule variance cannot directly be identified from the estimate form but rather needs to be calculated, for example, in a Management Reporter (MR) or Power BI report.

Figure 3-31 POC, EV, and CV after finalizing the first project stage

Figure 3-32 shows the EV calculation results at the end of the other project stages.

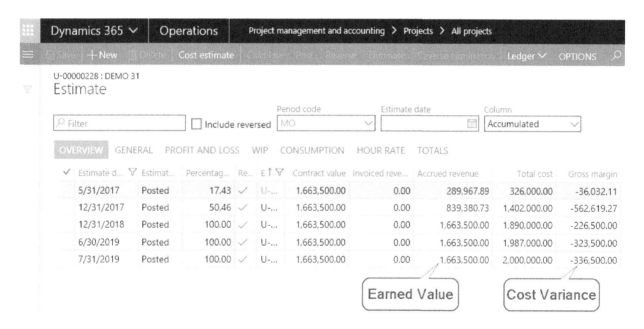

Figure 3-32 POC, EV, and CV at the end of the project

The POC percentages for the other project stages are calculated as follows:

POC (Stage 2) = (950 + 1,800) hrs / (700 + 1,200 + 2,750 + 800) hrs *100%

= 50.46%

(18)

POC (Stage 3) = (950 + 1,800 + 3,400) hrs / (700 + 1,200 + 2,750 + 800) hrs

*100% = 112.84% (max. 100%)

(19)

POC (Stage 4) = (950 + 1,800 + 3,400 + 750) hrs / (700 + 1,200 + 2,750 +

+ 800) hrs * 100% = 126.61% (max. 100%)

(20)

As one can identify from Figure 3-32, the POC measure already reaches its maximum of 100% in December 2018, which indicates that all or more than the originally planned work—in hour terms—has been consumed at the end of the third project stage. For that reason, additional work that is executed will result in an overall cost overrun. Figure 3-33 illustrates the previously mentioned graphically.

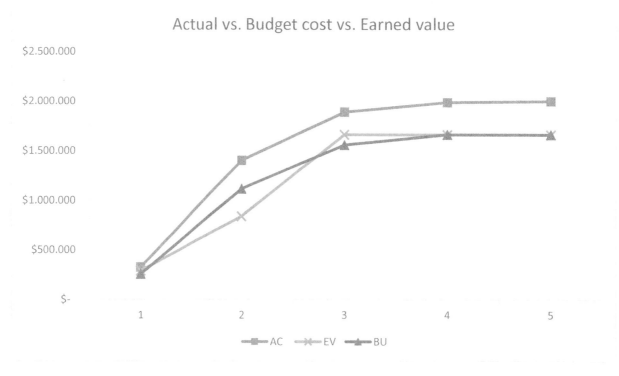

Figure 3-33 Actual versus budget cost versus earned value sample project

The resulting total, schedule, and cost variance figures together with the POC measure are illustrated in Figure 3-34. From there, one can identify the negative SV in the second period, which supports the previous interpretations.

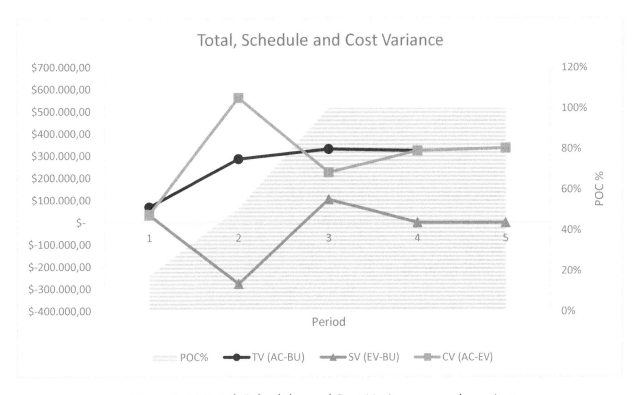

Figure 3-34 Total, Schedule, and Cost Variance sample project

Note From an analytical perspective, the progress percentage seems to be better suited for measuring the progress of the project than the POC measure shown above because the progress percentage takes modifications of the original plan into account. Both measures suffer, however, from the problem that only hour-related transactions are taken into account when it comes to measuring the progress of the project. This fact can result in very misleading progress or POC figures where hour-related transactions account only for a small part of the overall project costs as in the sample project, where hour-related costs account for less than 20% of the overall budgeted costs. How this disadvantage can be overcome will be shown in the following chapters.

Irrespective of the limitations of the chosen POC estimate, the calculated EV is finally posted on the ledger accounts that have been set up in the project ledger-posting setup form. (Details of this setup can be found in chapter 2.1.) Figure 3-35 summarizes all the vouchers that have been created for the sample project used.

DEBIT	CREDIT	AMOUNT
PROJECT STAGE 1 (Excavation)		
Customer invoice		
130100 Accounts Receivable [BalanceSheet—Customer Balance]	415100 Invoiced revenue [Profit&Loss—Project invoiced revenue]	$1,000,000
Expense		
545100 Project costs [Profit&Loss—Project cost]	200100 Accounts Payable [BalanceSheet—Vendor balance]	$250,000
Hours		
545100 Project costs [Profit&Loss—Project cost]	605100 Payroll allocation [Profit&Loss—Project payroll allocation]	$76,000
Estimate		
165400 WIP sales value [BalanceSheet—Project WIP sales value]	415300 Accrued revenue sales value [Profit&Loss—Project accrued revenue sales value]	$289,968
PROJECT STAGE 2 (Structural work)		
Expense		
545100 Project costs [Profit&Loss—Project cost]	200100 Accounts Payable [BalanceSheet—Vendor balance]	$418,000
Hours		
545100 Project costs [Profit&Loss—Project cost]	605100 Payroll allocation [Profit&Loss—Project payroll allocation]	$108,000
Item		
545100 Project costs [Profit&Loss—Project cost]	140200 Finished Goods [BalanceSheet—Inventory issue]	$550,000
Estimate		
165400 WIP sales value [BalanceSheet—Project WIP sales value]	415300 Accrued revenue sales value [Profit&Loss—Project accrued revenue sales value]	$549,413

DEBIT	CREDIT	AMOUNT
PROJECT STAGE 3 (Interior fittings)		
Customer invoice		
130100 Accounts Receivable [BalanceSheet—Customer Balance]	415100 Invoiced revenue [Profit&Loss—Project invoiced revenue]	$1,000,000
Expense		
545100 Project costs [Profit&Loss—Project cost]	200100 Accounts Payable [BalanceSheet—Vendor balance]	$270,000
Hours		
545100 Project costs [Profit&Loss—Project cost]	605100 Payroll allocation [Profit&Loss—Project payroll allocation]	$170,000
Item		
545100 Project costs [Profit&Loss—Project cost]	140200 Finished Goods [BalanceSheet—Inventory issue]	$48,000
Estimate		
165400 WIP sales value [BalanceSheet—Project WIP sales value]	415300 Accrued revenue sales value [Profit&Loss—Project accrued revenue sales value]	$824,119
PROJECT STAGE 4 (Gardening)		
Customer invoice		
130100 Accounts Receivable [BalanceSheet—Customer Balance]	415100 Invoiced revenue [Profit&Loss—Project invoiced revenue]	$1,000,000
Expense		
545100 Project costs [Profit&Loss—Project cost]	200100 Accounts Payable [BalanceSheet—Vendor balance]	$52,000
Hours		
545100 Project costs [Profit&Loss—Project cost]	605100 Payroll allocation [Profit&Loss—Project payroll allocation]	$30,000
Item		
545100 Project costs [Profit&Loss—Project cost]	140200 Finished Goods [BalanceSheet—Inventory issue]	$15,000
Estimate		
No voucher generated		

DEBIT	CREDIT	AMOUNT
PROJECT STAGE 5 (Additions not planned)		
Expense		
545100 Project costs [Profit&Loss—Project cost]	200100 Accounts Payable [BalanceSheet—Vendor balance]	$5,000
Hours		
545100 Project costs [Profit&Loss—Project cost]	605100 Payroll allocation [Profit&Loss—Project payroll allocation]	$8,000
Estimate		
No voucher generated		

Figure 3-35 Vouchers created EVA project

As no invoice has been created for the fixed-price project, the created estimates cannot be eliminated because the elimination button in the estimate form only becomes available after all on-account transactions have been invoiced. This fact results in a situation where too much revenue has been recorded on the P&L accounts 415100 and 415300. For details, please see the gray-highlighted cells in Figure 3-35.

To overcome this issue, a dummy invoice for the total project budget amount could be created in order to eliminate the revenue postings that have been recorded on the accrued sales revenue account no. 415300. The issue with this approach is that the overstated revenue will only be corrected at the end of the project and therefore too late.

For that reason, an alternative approach is used that makes use of the statistical ledger accounts 165401 and 165402, which are not included in the company's balance sheet and income statement but allow tracking the earned values in the general ledger. This modified accounting setup can be observed from Figure 3-36 and will be used for the following modifications of the EV calculation.

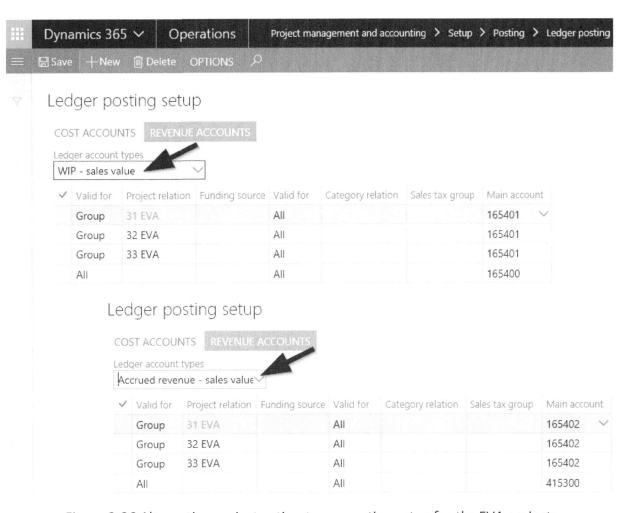

Figure 3-36 Alternative project-estimate-accounting setup for the EVA projects

3.2.4. Special Issues

Before, it was mentioned that the POC that was calculated in the previous chapter might not be correct because it incorporates hour-related transactions only that might not be a good measure of the project's overall progress if hours only account for a small part of the overall project cost and effort. For that reason, let's have a look at some alternative setups and the resulting POC, EV, and variance measures.

3.2.4.1. Alternative Project-Group Setup with Estimate Based on Cost Amount

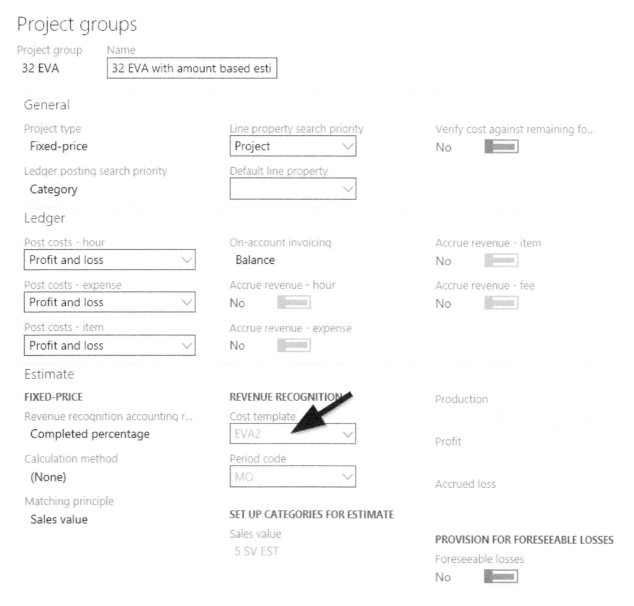

Figure 3-37 Alternative project group used for EVA (1)

The first alternative setup differs from the previously used one in the way how the cost template is set up. That is, the alternative cost template *EVA2* makes use of a completion method that is based on the cost amount rather than the work progress percentage.

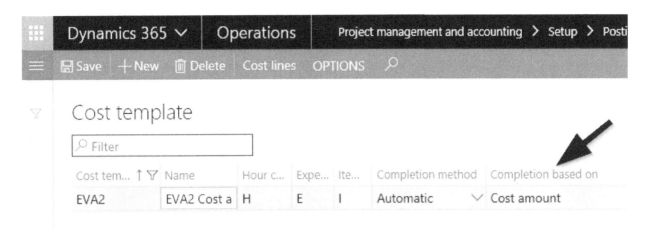

Figure 3-38 Alternative cost template used for EVA (1)

After posting all transactions and posting all project estimates, the following POC, EV, and cost variance data can be observed from the project-estimate form.

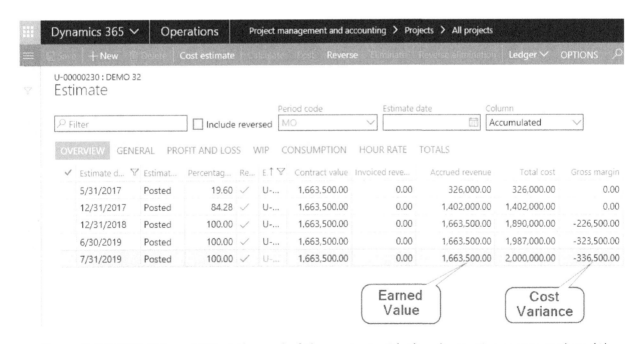

Figure 3-39 POC, EV, and CV at the end of the project with the alternative cost template (1)

Please note that the cost and progress percentage figures in the project-tracking forms—not shown here for reasons of brevity—are identical to the ones that have been illustrated in the previous chapter and are not influenced by the cost template setup.

The next formulas show the POC calculation for the project with the alternative cost template setup.

POC based on cost amount = Actual costs / (Actual costs + Remaining planned costs) * 100%   (21)

POC (Period 1) = $326,000 / ($326,000 + $1,337,500) *100% = 19.60%   (22)

POC (Period 2) = $1,402,000 / ($1,402,000 + $261,500) *100% = 84.28%   (23)

POC (Period 3) = $1,890,000 / $1,890,000 *100% = 100%   (24)

POC (Period 4) = $1,987,000 / $1,987,000 *100% = 100%   (25)

POC (Period 5) = $2,000,000 / $2,000,000 *100% = 100%   (26)

Figure 3-39 shows that no cost variance can be identified in the first two periods. A comparison of this outcome with the sample data shown in Figure 3-19 shows that this can't be right because the actual cost prices of the building crane and the construction workers are higher than the planned cost prices for those categories, which should give raise to a cost variance.

Based on this finding, it can be concluded that a major problem of the cost-amount-based estimate method is that rising cost prices—that are, for example, caused by inflation—automatically result in higher actual costs and consequently in higher and potentially misleading POC and EV measures.

Even though the alternative cost template seemingly leads to incorrect POC, EV, and variance measures, it was included here to illustrate the sensitivity of the EVA analysis and the interpretation of the variance measures, which highly depends on a correctly calculated POC.

3.2.4.2. Alternative Project-Group Setup with Estimate Based on Quantity

As the cost-based estimate that has been used in the previous chapter does not seem to be a good measure for the overall progress of the project, another project-group with a quantity-based cost estimate will be used as an alternative in this subchapter to identify whether it makes a difference to the calculated POC, EV, and variance measures. For that reason, the following project-group with the cost template *EVA3* has been set up.

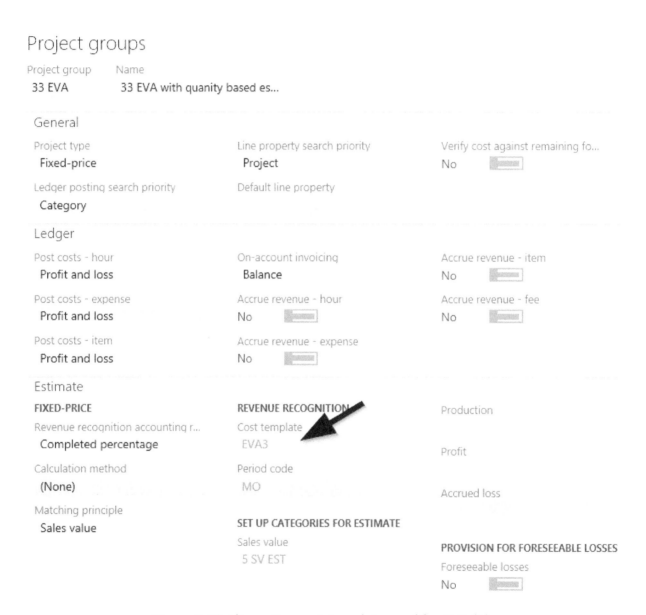

Figure 3-40 Alternative cost template used for EVA (2)

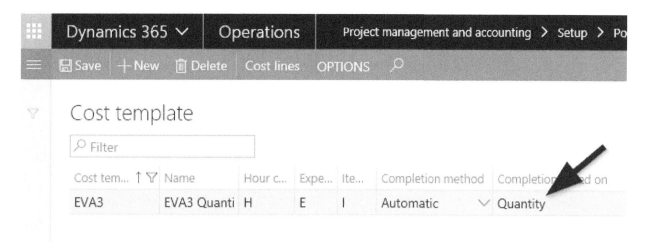

Figure 3-41 Alternative cost template used for EVA (2)

Recording the same transactions as before results in the following POC, EV, and cost variance measures for the five project stages.

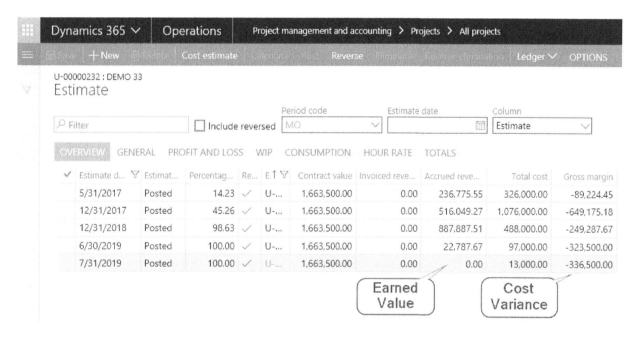

Figure 3-42 POC, EV, and CV at the end of the project with the alternative cost template (2)

Different from before, the POC is now calculated based on all quantities, as illustrated in the following formula.

POC based on quantity = Actual Quantity / (Actual + Remaining planned quantity) * 100%   (27)

Similar to what has been shown in the previous chapter, the next formulas demonstrate how the POC for the different project stages is calculated.

$$\text{POC (Period 1)} = 1{,}950 / (1{,}950 + 11{,}750) * 100\% = 14.23\% \tag{28}$$

$$\text{POC (Period 2)} = 6{,}200 / (6{,}200 + 7{,}500) * 100\% = 45{,}26\% \tag{29}$$

$$\text{POC (Period 3)} = 14{,}400 / (14{,}400 + 200) * 100\% = 98{,}63\% \tag{30}$$

$$\text{POC (Period 4)} = 16{,}550 / 16{,}550 * 100\% = 100\% \tag{31}$$

$$\text{POC (Period 5)} = 16{,}730 / 16{,}730 * 100\% = 100\% \tag{32}$$

As one can identify from the previous formulas and the sample data in Figure 3-19, the quantity-based POC measure simply adds up different units (hrs, to, pcs) for the calculation of the POC. Even though the calculated measures look plausible on first sight, they do not make sense from a mathematical point of view because all quantities get the same weight and importance in the POC calculation. Expressed hyperbolically, the consumption of a single screw and a ton of concrete have the same influence on the POC, that is, the measured progress of the project, which is in contrast to common sense.

Another problem of all POC calculations used so far is related to the POC measure in general, which reaches 100% far before the project work is finished. As an example, in the POC calculation that makes use of the work progress calculation (please see chapter 3.2.3.3.), the POC already reaches 100% at the end of the third project stage. The same outcome was identified for the POC measure that was calculated based on the cost amount in chapter 3.2.4.1. and the POC measure calculated in this chapter. A direct result of those calculations is that the remaining project stages do not create value anymore and simply result in a higher cost variance. An investigation of the budgeted and actual cost in the fourth project stage (please see Figure 3-19) shows that this cannot be correct, as the actual costs are below the budgeted ones for this stage.

3.2.4.3.   EVA—Best Practice Approach

The former illustrations and POC calculations showed that all of the previously used POC calculations had some problems and seemingly did not result in a POC that captures the correct progress of the project.

As an example, the work-progress-based estimate used in chapter 3.2.3.3. only took hour-related transactions into account, the cost-based estimate that was used in chapter 3.2.4.1. suffered from inflated cost price measures and the quantity-based estimate that was used in chapter 3.2.4.2. simply put the same weight to all project transactions irrespective of their ability to measure the progress of the project.

What is more, all POC measures used in the previous chapters reached 100% far before the project work was finished, which results in wrong cost and schedule variance figures in the latter stages of the project.

Finally, the standard ledger-posting setup was found to result in overstated revenue figures.

To overcome those issues, the following modifications are made to the previously used setups.

1. Cost template

In an idealized world, a single cost or progress driver can be identified that reliably measures the overall progress of the project. In chapter 3.2.3.3., the recorded hour transactions were used for this purpose. Unfortunately, it was found that the hour transactions are not a good measure for the overall progress of the sample project because they account only for a small part of the total project cost and effort and consequently result in a misleading POC measure.

As the recorded hour transactions did not provide a good measure for the progress of the project, alternative categories or transaction types could be used for this purpose. Using alternative categories or transaction types necessitates two things for a reliable measurement of a project's progress. First that those alternative categories or transaction types are used in all project stages and second that the cost template refers to those categories or transaction types.

The second prerequisite can be realized by setting up a cost template that makes use of a quantity-based estimate and that has only those categories assigned to specific cost template lines that will be considered in the POC calculation. Figure 3-43 exemplifies such a setup.

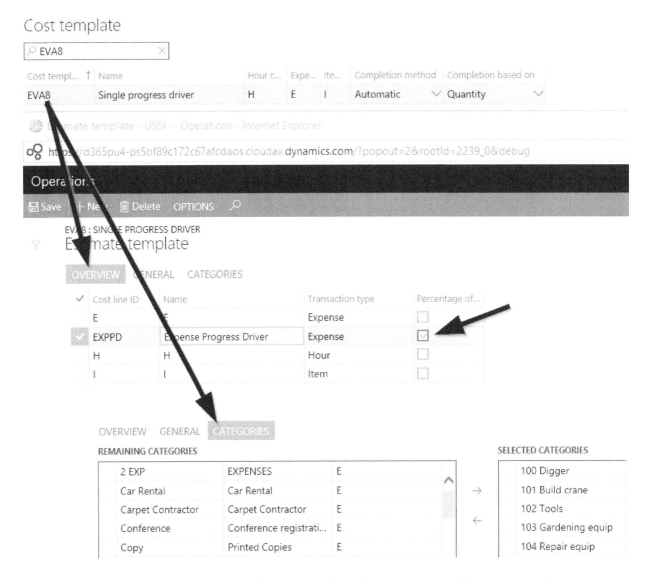

Figure 3-43 Cost template with quantity-based measurement for progress drivers

Note In Figure 3-43 all five expense categories that are used in the sample project are selected for measuring the overall progress of the project. Technically this is not exactly in line with what has been described before. However, as there is no single category available that is used in all project stages and that is able to reliably measure the progress of the project, a combined progress driver is used.

If no single or combined cost driver can be identified that can be used for measuring the overall progress of the project, heuristic estimation methods must be applied. In other words, the POC must be determined manually.

2. Adjustment of remaining effort

Previously it was identified that the POC reached 100% before the project work was finished. This outcome can regularly be identified in situations where more costs or effort are consumed than originally planned. To avoid this outcome and the related incorrect variance measures, a regular review of the budgeted values is required.

If one makes use of the work progress estimation method, the review of the budgeted values must be made in the WBS form. In all other cases, it must be made through an adjustment of the forecast forms. An example how such adjustments can be made is provided further below.

3. Ledger-posting setup

The last previously identified pain point relates to the ledger-posting setup, which has been modified as described in chapter 3.2.3.3. to avoid a double counting of project revenues.

The next illustrations show the effect that those modifications have on the analysis of the sample project.

A first major difference to what has been shown previously is that only the expense-related categories that were identified as the progress drivers are transferred from the WBS form into the forecast form. That is because of the changed cost template, which only considers those categories for the determination of the POC.

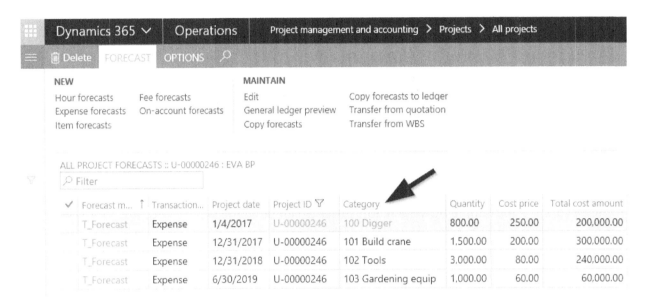

Figure 3-44 All project forecasts form

Note From a technical or POC calculation perspective, the categories that have been selected in the cost template determine the numerator of the POC calculation. The denominator is specified in the forecast form. In order to avoid comparing apples with oranges, one has to ensure that only those categories that are considered in the POC calculation do have forecast values setup.

A second major difference in processing the project relates to adjustments of the forecast values, which is required in order to avoid that outdated budget values result in a POC of 100% before the project finishes. Figure 3-45 shows such an adjustment where the original forecast values that are recorded with the *T_Forecast* model are copied and adjusted in the *S1* model based on new or better information that have been obtained during the execution of the first project stage.

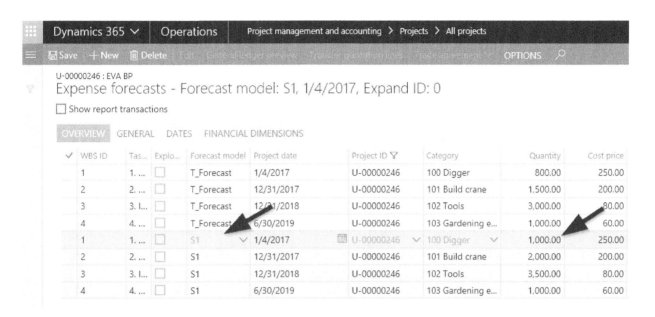

Figure 3-45 Modification of the original forecast at the end of the first project stage

Note Please note that the forecast modifications are made in a separate forecast model, which has the advantage that the original values can be identified and be used for analysis purposes.

At the end of the next project stage, the realized transactions are consequently compared against the updated forecast, as illustrated in Figure 3-46.

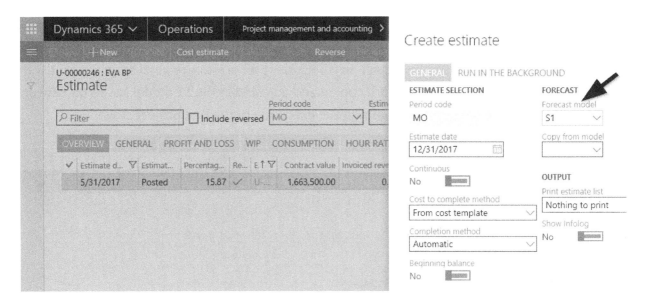

Figure 3-46 Estimate creation at the end of the second project stage

Once the second project stage is finished and new information in regard to the overall progress of the project have been obtained, a second forecast adjustment is made to incorporate the new information. Those changes are once again made in a separate forecast model (*S2*).

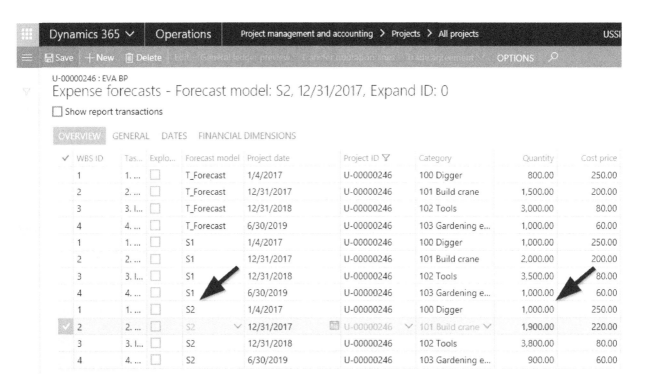

Figure 3-47 Modification of the original forecast at the end of the second project stage

After the third project stage, the realized transactions are once again compared with the latest forecast. For details, please see Figure 3-48.

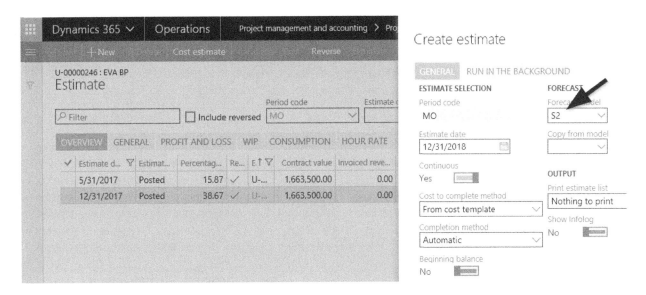

Figure 3-48 Estimate creation at the end of the third project stage

For the sample project, no further adjustments are made until the end of the project where the *Set costs to complete to zero* completion method is selected in order to ensure that a POC of 100% is reached.

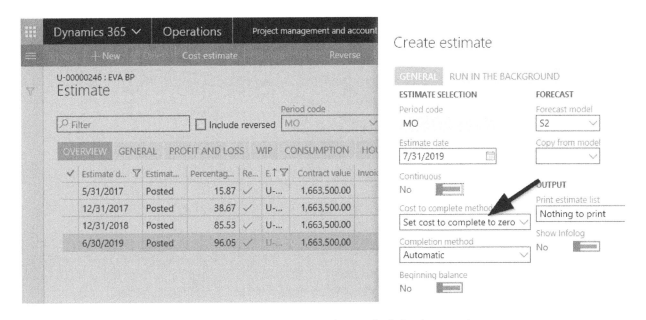

Figure 3-49 Estimate creation at the end of the last project stage

Figures 3-50 to 3-52 summarize the resulting POC, EV, and variance measures that can be identified at the end of the project.

Figure 3-50 POC, EV, and CV at the end of the project

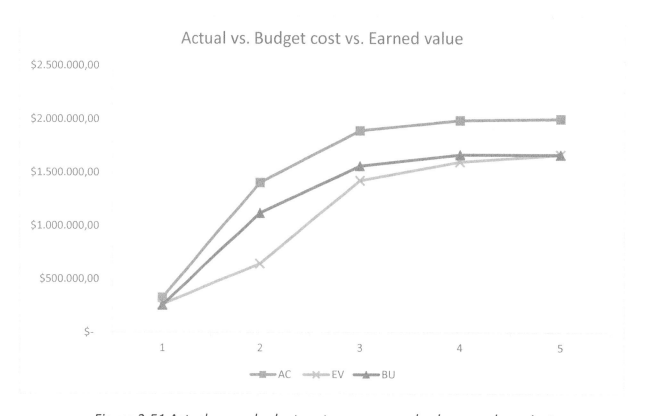

Figure 3-51 Actual versus budget cost versus earned value sample project

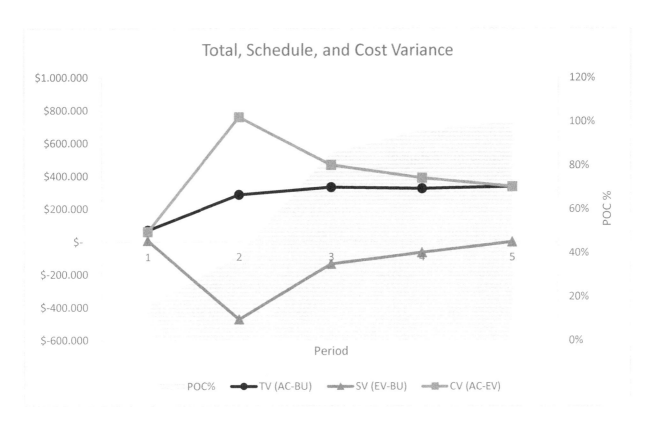

Figure 3-52 Total, Schedule, and Cost Variance sample project

A comparison of those figures with the ones that have been included in chapter 3.2.3.3. indicates some considerable differences, especially in the cost variance measure. In other words, the previously used estimation methods illustrated the cost problem comparatively too late.

After analyzing the EV, POC, and variance measures, let's have a look at the accounting entries that are generated for the sample project with the modified setup that has been used in this section. Those vouchers are summarized in Figure 3-53.

DEBIT	CREDIT	AMOUNT
PROJECT STAGE 1 (Excavation)		
Customer invoice		
130100 Accounts Receivable [BalanceSheet—Customer Balance]	415100 Invoiced revenue [Profit&Loss—Project invoiced revenue]	$1,000,000
Expense		
545100 Project costs [Profit&Loss—Project cost]	200100 Accounts Payable [BalanceSheet—Vendor balance]	$250,000
Hours		
545100 Project costs [Profit&Loss—Project cost]	605100 Payroll allocation [Profit&Loss—Project payroll allocation]	$76,000
Estimate		
165401 Earned Value Estimate [BalanceSheet—Project WIP sales value]	165402 Earned Value Estimate Offset [BalanceSheet—Project accrued revenue sales value]	$264,048
PROJECT STAGE 2 (Structural work)		
Expense		
545100 Project costs [Profit&Loss—Project cost]	200100 Accounts Payable [BalanceSheet—Vendor balance]	$418,000
Hours		
545100 Project costs [Profit&Loss—Project cost]	605100 Payroll allocation [Profit&Loss—Project payroll allocation]	$108,000
Item		
545100 Project costs [Profit&Loss—Project cost]	140200 Finished Goods [BalanceSheet—Inventory issue]	$550,000
Estimate		
165401 Earned Value Estimate [BalanceSheet—Project WIP sales value]	165402 Earned Value Estimate Offset [BalanceSheet—Project accrued revenue sales value]	$379,172

DEBIT	CREDIT	AMOUNT
PROJECT STAGE 3 (Interior fittings)		
Customer invoice		
130100 Accounts Receivable [BalanceSheet—Customer Balance]	415100 Invoiced revenue [Profit&Loss—Project invoiced revenue]	$1,000,000
Expense		
545100 Project costs [Profit&Loss—Project cost]	200100 Accounts Payable [BalanceSheet—Vendor balance]	$270,000
Hours		
545100 Project costs [Profit&Loss—Project cost]	605100 Payroll allocation [Profit&Loss—Project payroll allocation]	$170,000
Item		
545100 Project costs [Profit&Loss—Project cost]	140200 Finished Goods [BalanceSheet—Inventory issue]	$48,000
Estimate		
165401 Earned Value Estimate [BalanceSheet—Project WIP sales value]	165402 Earned Value Estimate Offset [BalanceSheet—Project accrued revenue sales value]	$779,510
PROJECT STAGE 4 (Gardening)		
Customer invoice		
130100 Accounts Receivable [BalanceSheet—Customer Balance]	415100 Invoiced revenue [Profit&Loss—Project invoiced revenue]	$1,000,000
Expense		
545100 Project costs [Profit&Loss—Project cost]	200100 Accounts Payable [BalanceSheet—Vendor balance]	$52,000
Hours		
545100 Project costs [Profit&Loss—Project cost]	605100 Payroll allocation [Profit&Loss—Project payroll allocation]	$30,000
Item		
545100 Project costs [Profit&Loss—Project cost]	140200 Finished Goods [BalanceSheet—Inventory issue]	$15,000
Estimate		
165401 Earned Value Estimate [BalanceSheet—Project WIP sales value]	165402 Earned Value Estimate Offset [BalanceSheet—Project accrued revenue sales value]	$175,105

DEBIT	CREDIT	AMOUNT
PROJECT STAGE 5 (Additions not planned)		
Expense		
545100 Project costs [Profit&Loss—Project cost]	200100 Accounts Payable [BalanceSheet—Vendor balance]	$5,000
Hours		
545100 Project costs [Profit&Loss—Project cost]	605100 Payroll allocation [Profit&Loss—Project payroll allocation]	$8,000
Estimate		
165401 Earned Value Estimate [BalanceSheet—Project WIP sales value]	165402 Earned Value Estimate Offset [BalanceSheet—Project accrued revenue sales value]	$65,665

Figure 3-53 Vouchers created for sample project with modified setup

The only difference between the vouchers that are illustrated in Figure 3-53 and those that have been presented further above in Figure 3-35 can be found in the estimate postings. Those postings or vouchers are recorded on statistical accounts that are not included in the company's balance sheet and income statement. For that reason, the company's profitability is not affected by those transactions. However, as they are posted on ledger accounts, one can use them for analytical purposes even through the trial-balance form or the management reporter. In other words, one does not need BI instruments for executing an EV analysis.

3.2.4.4. Summary

The previous illustrations and modifications of the estimate calculation demonstrated the sensitivity of the POC measure and its influence on the calculated EV and variance measures. Before one applies the EVA technique, much consideration needs, thus, to be put into the setup of the cost template, especially in regard to the main progress driver and how it can be measured. In addition, much thought needs to be put on the completion method and the basis for the POC calculation. If no single progress driver can be identified, the use of a combined one—as illustrated above—or a manual estimation might be required.

Even if one does not want to make use of the EVA—possibly because one shuns the time and effort required for the set up and processing of those projects—one should at least make use of the cost and progress percentage figures that are automatically recorded in the project-tracking forms to analyze the progress of long-term projects. This comparison—which has been made in Figure 3-30—does not necessarily result in theoretically "correct" progress measures. It might, however, be sufficient for getting a first indication that something is wrong with the project that requires some attention and possibly counteractive measures.

3.3. Parallel Accounting

Previously, the major differences between the Completed Contract (CC) and Percentage of Completion (POC) accounting methods have been explained. For details, please see chapter 2.7.2.

Companies that operate in an international environment are regularly confronted with the situation that local accounting standard setters require them to evaluate their projects according to the CC method, while group accounting policies specify that their projects need to be evaluated according to the POC method.

Let's assume that local accounting regulations require a company to apply the CC method with a BS accounting setup and a SV estimate, while group accounting policies require the use of the POC method with a P&L accounting setup and a SV estimate for the evaluation of long-term projects.

Note The differences in the setup and postings generated for those project types have been illustrated in chapters 2.7.2.4.8 and 2.7.2.6.8. For details, please see there.

3.3.1. Setup

Because the project module does not have parallel valuation models or functionalities implemented, a mixed valuation approach has to be used. This mixed valuation approach makes use of a project group that follows the POC accounting method and uses separate ledger accounts that are assigned to the company's BS or IS depending on the accounting policy to be applied.

For the following illustrations, a newly set up project group that makes use of the completed percentage (POC) revenue recognition method is used. This project group is illustrated in Figure 3-54 and is set up in the very same way as in chapter 2.7.2.6.

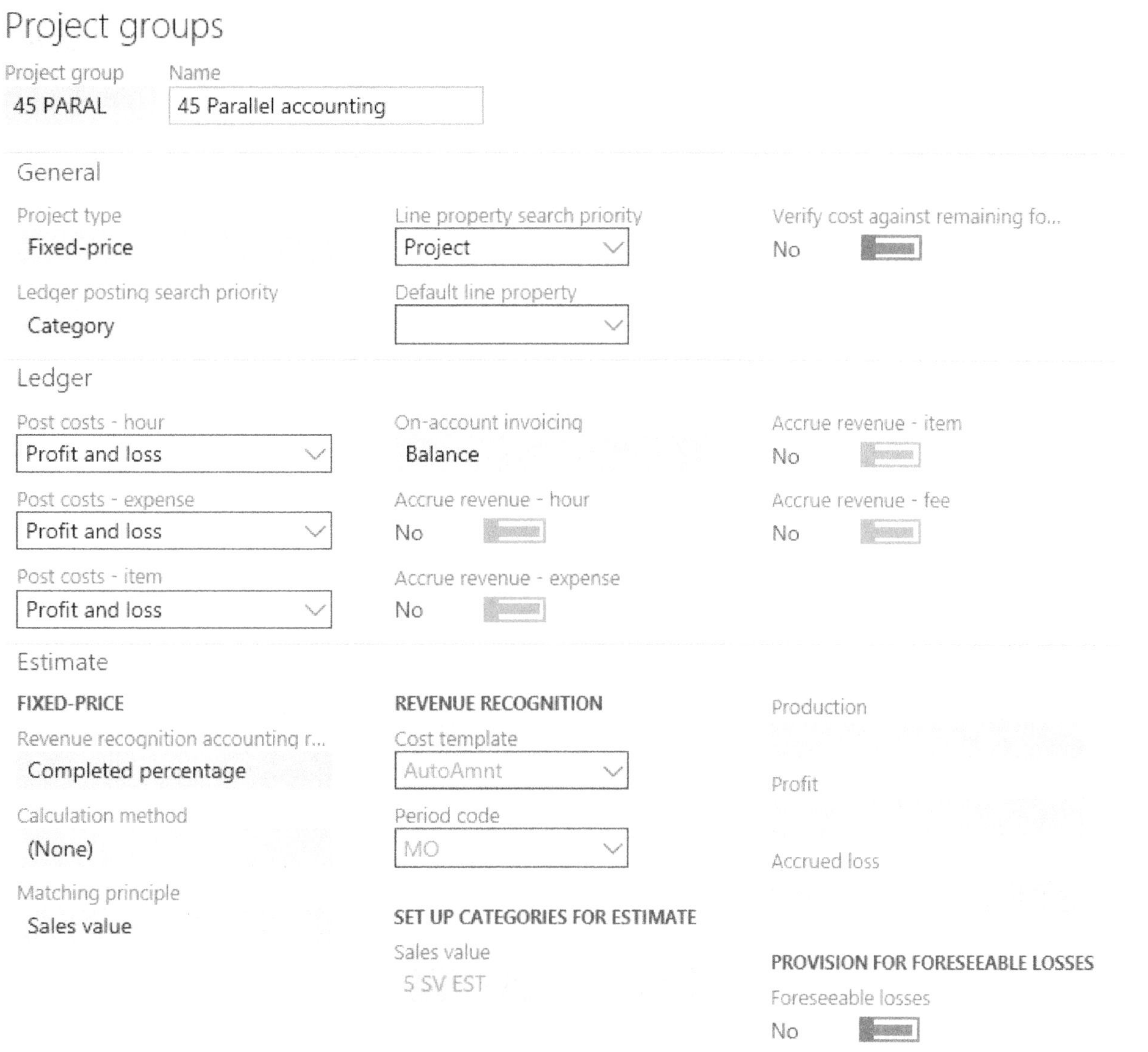

Project groups

Project group | Name
45 PARAL | 45 Parallel accounting

General

Project type
Fixed-price

Ledger posting search priority
Category

Line property search priority
Project ∨

Default line property
∨

Verify cost against remaining fo...
No ▭

Ledger

Post costs - hour
Profit and loss ∨

Post costs - expense
Profit and loss ∨

Post costs - item
Profit and loss ∨

On-account invoicing
Balance

Accrue revenue - hour
No ▭

Accrue revenue - expense
No ▭

Accrue revenue - item
No ▭

Accrue revenue - fee
No ▭

Estimate

FIXED-PRICE

Revenue recognition accounting r...
Completed percentage

Calculation method
(None)

Matching principle
Sales value

REVENUE RECOGNITION

Cost template
AutoAmnt ∨

Period code
MO ∨

SET UP CATEGORIES FOR ESTIMATE

Sales value
S SV EST

Production

Profit

Accrued loss

PROVISION FOR FORESEEABLE LOSSES

Foreseeable losses
No ▭

Figure 3-54 Project-group setup used for parallel project evaluation

For this project group, special ("mixed") ledger accounts are set up, which will be assigned either to the BS or IS depending on the valuation approach (POC or CC) that is applied.

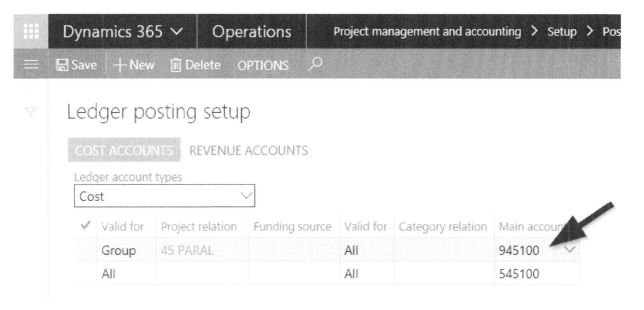

Figure 3-55 Project cost account setup for parallel project evaluation

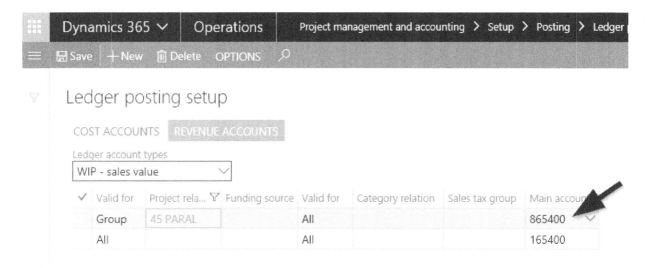

Figure 3-56 WIP sales-value account setup for parallel project evaluation

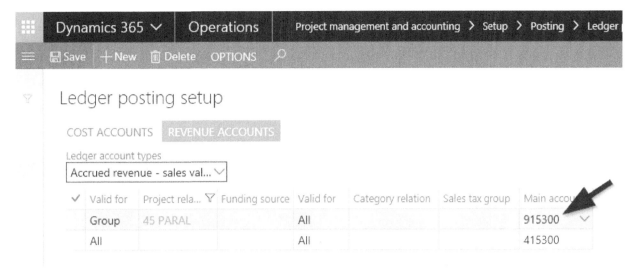

Figure 3-57 Accrued revenue-sales value account setup for parallel project evaluation

3.3.2.   Example

For the following illustrations and explanations, the same sample data that have been used in chapter 2.7.2. will be used. Figure 3-58 shows those data once again to make it easier for the reader to follow the subsequent demonstrations.

	Period 1	Period 2	Period 3	Total
Planned cost				
Hour	5 hours ($500)		2 hours ($200)	$700
Expense		$100		$100
Item			2 items ($200)	$200
Total	**$500**	**$100**	**$400**	**$1,000**
Actual cost				
Hour	5 hours ($500)	4 hours ($400)	1 hour ($100)	$1,000
Expense		$150		$150
Item			1 item ($100)	$100
Total	**$500**	**$550**	**$200**	**$1,250**

Figure 3-58 Sample data parallel project evaluation

3.3.2.1.   Period 1

Please note that a fixed milestone payment for a total amount of $3,000 is posted in the first period. The resulting project invoice voucher is shown in Figure 3-59.

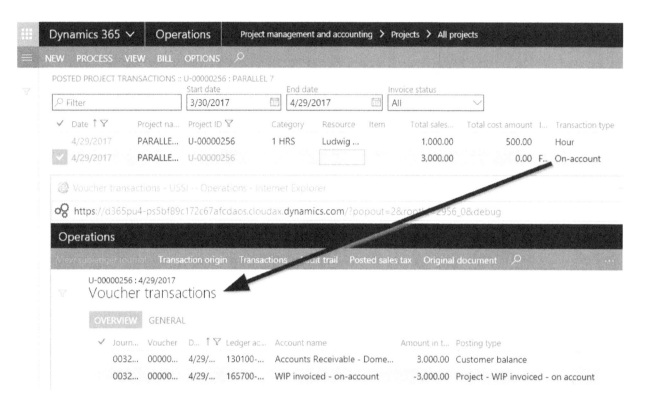

Figure 3-59 Project invoice voucher—parallel project evaluation

While the created invoice voucher is identical to what has been shown in chapter 2.7.2.6., the voucher that is created for the recorded project hours makes use of a different ledger account for recording the debit transaction.

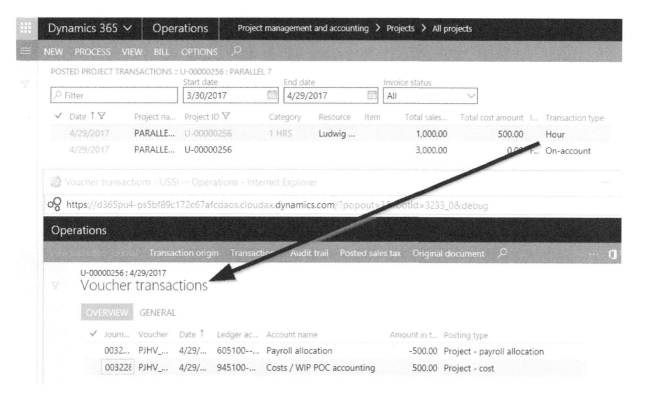

Figure 3-60 Hour transaction and voucher—parallel project evaluation

The voucher that is created for the posting of the project estimate also uses different ledger accounts compared to the ones that have been used in chapter 2.7.2.6. For details, please compare Figure 3-61 with Figure 2-207.

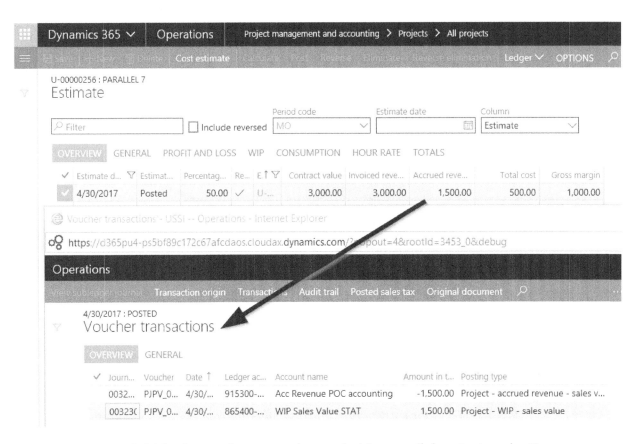

Figure 3-61 Project-estimate voucher period 1—parallel project evaluation

Similar to what has been shown in the previous chapters, all accounting vouchers that have been created in the first period are summarized in Figure 3-62.

DEBIT	CREDIT	AMOUNT
PERIOD 1		
Customer invoice		
130100 Accounts Receivable [BalanceSheet—Customer Balance]	165700 WIP Invoiced on-account [BalanceSheet—Project WIP invoiced on-account]	$3,000
Hours		
945100 WIP / Project costs [P&L/BS—Project cost]	605100 Payroll allocation [Profit&Loss—Project payroll allocation]	$500
Estimate		
865400 WIP sales value [P&L/BS—Project WIP sales value]	915300 Accrued revenue sales value [Profit&Loss—Project accrued revenue sales value]	$1,500

Figure 3-62 Summary accounting vouchers period 1

Figure 3-63 shows the resulting BS and IS reports that have been prepared based on the vouchered transactions in period 1.

Reporting Tree ∨   Show ∨   Zoom ∨   Publish   Currency ∨   Export   Report Options   Print

Search in report   Previous   Next

	YTD		YTD
Completed Contract Method		**Percentage of Completion Method**	
Balance Sheet		**Balance Sheet**	
130100 - Accounts Receivables	3,000.00	130100 - Accounts Receivables	3,000.00
165700 - WIP Invoiced	(3,000.00)	165700 - WIP Invoiced	(3,000.00)
945100 - WIP Cost	500.00	865400 - WIP Sales Value	1,500.00
200100 - Accounts Payable		200100 - Accounts Payable	
140200 - Inventory		140200 - Inventory	
Total	*500.00*	*Total*	*1,500.00*
Income Statement		**Income Statement**	
605100 - Payroll Allocation	(500.00)	605100 - Payroll Allocation	(500.00)
865400 - WIP Sales Value	1,500.00	945100 - Cost	500.00
915300 - Accrued Revenue	(1,500.00)	915300 - Accrued Revenue	(1,500.00)
945200 - Realized Project Costs		945200 - Realized Project Costs	
Total	*(500.00)*	*Total*	*(1,500.00)*

Figure 3-63 BS and IS according to CC and POC accounting method

On the left-hand side of Figure 3-63, one can identify the BS and IS information that have been prepared in line with the completed contract accounting method. Please note that account no. 945100 that was debited when posting the hours transactions is included in the BS for the CC method. This has been done in order to neutralize the cost effect of the hour transaction. Expressed differently, account no. 945100 represents a WIP account for the CC accounting method.

The WIP sales-value account no. 865400 and the accrued revenue account no. 915300 are included in the IS for the CC accounting method. As the total balance of these accounts adds up to $0, no profit effect from the accrued revenue posting that has been recorded with the project estimate arises.

In summary, by treating the debit account that has been used for posting the hour transaction as a WIP account and by assigning the WIP sales-value and the accrued revenue account to the IS, financial statements that are in line with the CC accounting method can be created.

For the illustration of the POC accounting method, the WIP and cost and accrued revenue accounts are assigned to the BS and IS, as one would expect. For details, please see the BS and IS section on the right-hand side of Figure 3-63.

3.3.2.2.   Period 2

Figure 3-64 summarizes the accounting vouchers that have been created for the hour and expense transactions in the second period.

DEBIT	CREDIT	AMOUNT
PERIOD 2		
Hours		
945100 WIP / Project costs [P&L/BS—Project cost]	605100 Payroll allocation [Profit&Loss—Project payroll allocation]	$400
Expenses		
945100 WIP / Project costs [P&L/BS—Project cost]	200100 Accounts Payable [BalanceSheet—Vendor balance]	$150
Estimate		
865400 WIP sales value [P&L/BS—Project WIP sales value]	915300 Accrued revenue sales value [Profit&Loss—Project accrued revenue sales value]	$1,020

Figure 3-64 Summary accounting vouchers—period 2

By applying the same principles as before, the following financial statements for the CC and POC accounting method result.

	YTD		YTD
Completed Contract Method		**Percentage of Completion Method**	
Balance Sheet		**Balance Sheet**	
130100 - Accounts Receivables	3,000.00	130100 - Accounts Receivables	3,000.00
165700 - WIP Invoiced	(3,000.00)	165700 - WIP Invoiced	(3,000.00)
945100 - WIP Cost	1,050.00	865400 - WIP Sales Value	2,520.00
200100 - Accounts Payable	(150.00)	200100 - Accounts Payable	(150.00)
140200 - Inventory		140200 - Inventory	
Total	*900.00*	*Total*	*2,370.00*
Income Statement		**Income Statement**	
605100 - Payroll Allocation	(900.00)	605100 - Payroll Allocation	(900.00)
865400 - WIP Sales Value	2,520.00	945100 - Cost	1,050.00
915300 - Accrued Revenue	(2,520.00)	915300 - Accrued Revenue	(2,520.00)
945200 - Realized Project Costs		945200 - Realized Project Costs	
Total	*(900.00)*	*Total*	*(2,370.00)*

Figure 3-65 BS and IS according to CC and POC accounting method—period 2

3.3.2.3.   Period 3

Except for the transaction types, no differences between the previously recorded project transactions can be identified in the third project period. The resulting accounting vouchers and financial statements are illustrated in Figures 3-66 and 3-67, respectively.

DEBIT	CREDIT	AMOUNT
PERIOD 3		
Hours		
945100 WIP / Project costs [P&L/BS—Project cost]	605100 Payroll allocation [Profit&Loss—Project payroll allocation]	$100
Items		
945100 WIP / Project costs [P&L/BS—Project cost]	140200 Finished Goods [BalanceSheet—Inventory issue]	$100
Estimate		
865400 WIP sales value [P&L/BS—Project WIP sales value]	915300 Accrued revenue sales value [Profit&Loss—Project accrued revenue sales value]	$257.78

Figure 3-66 Summary accounting vouchers—period 3

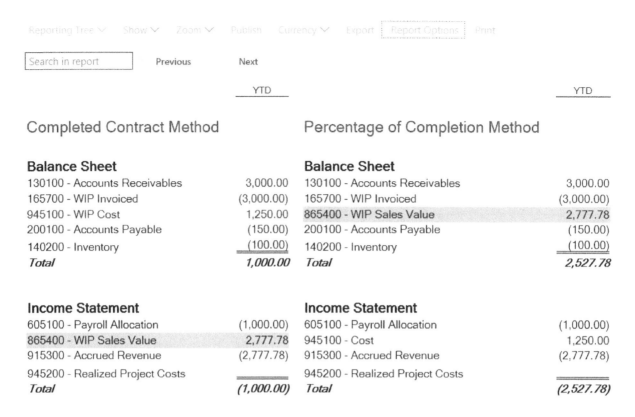

	YTD		YTD
Completed Contract Method		**Percentage of Completion Method**	
Balance Sheet		**Balance Sheet**	
130100 - Accounts Receivables	3,000.00	130100 - Accounts Receivables	3,000.00
165700 - WIP Invoiced	(3,000.00)	165700 - WIP Invoiced	(3,000.00)
945100 - WIP Cost	1,250.00	865400 - WIP Sales Value	2,777.78
200100 - Accounts Payable	(150.00)	200100 - Accounts Payable	(150.00)
140200 - Inventory	(100.00)	140200 - Inventory	(100.00)
Total	*1,000.00*	*Total*	*2,527.78*
Income Statement		**Income Statement**	
605100 - Payroll Allocation	(1,000.00)	605100 - Payroll Allocation	(1,000.00)
865400 - WIP Sales Value	2,777.78	945100 - Cost	1,250.00
915300 - Accrued Revenue	(2,777.78)	915300 - Accrued Revenue	(2,777.78)
945200 - Realized Project Costs		945200 - Realized Project Costs	
Total	*(1,000.00)*	*Total*	*(2,527.78)*

Figure 3-67 BS and IS according to CC and POC accounting method—period 3

3.3.2.4.   Period 4 and Elimination

At the end of the project, the final estimate and the elimination are posted. Figure 3-68 summarizes the respective vouchers.

DEBIT	CREDIT	AMOUNT
END OF PROJECT		
Final Estimate		
865400 WIP sales value [P&L/BS—Project WIP sales value]	915300 Accrued revenue sales value [Profit&Loss—Project accrued revenue sales value]	$222.22
Elimination		
165700 WIP invoiced on account [BalanceSheet—Project WIP invoiced on account]	865400 WIP sales value [P&L/BS—Project WIP sales value]	$3,000

Figure 3-68 Summary accounting vouchers—end of project (1)

From Figure 3-68, one can identify that the elimination voucher clears the balance on the WIP sales-value account no. 865400. As no similar clearance occurs for the accrued revenue account no. 915300, a total of $3,000 remains in the IS that has been prepared in line with the CC accounting method. Details thereof can be identified from the IS that is illustrated on the left-hand side of Figure 3-69.

	YTD		YTD

Completed Contract Method

Balance Sheet

130100 - Accounts Receivables	3,000.00
165700 - WIP Invoiced	
945100 - WIP Cost	1,250.00
200100 - Accounts Payable	(150.00)
140200 - Inventory	(100.00)
Total	*4,000.00*

Income Statement

605100 - Payroll Allocation	(1,000.00)
865400 - WIP Sales Value	
915300 - Accrued Revenue	(3,000.00)
945200 - Realized Project Costs	
Total	*(4,000.00)*

Percentage of Completion Method

Balance Sheet

130100 - Accounts Receivables	3,000.00
165700 - WIP Invoiced	
865400 - WIP Sales Value	
200100 - Accounts Payable	(150.00)
140200 - Inventory	(100.00)
Total	*2,750.00*

Income Statement

605100 - Payroll Allocation	(1,000.00)
945100 - Cost	1,250.00
915300 - Accrued Revenue	(3,000.00)
945200 - Realized Project Costs	
Total	*(2,750.00)*

Figure 3-69 BS and IS according to CC and POC accounting method—end of project (1)

286

3.3.2.5. Final Adjustment

Please note that a difference between the CC and POC financial statements remains even after posting the elimination. This can easily be identified from the difference in the financial statement totals in Figure 3-69.

The underlying reason for this difference is that the project costs that have been recorded on ledger account no. 945100 are assigned to the BS for the CC accounting method.

To get this corrected, an adjustment posting is required, which shifts those costs from the BS to the IS. Figure 3-70 illustrates the adjustment voucher that has been created for the example by posting a manual adjustment in a general ledger journal.

DEBIT	CREDIT	AMOUNT
END OF PROJECT		
Adjustment posting		
945200 Realized project costs [Profit&Loss—Ledger journal]	945100 Project costs [P&L/BS—Ledger journal]	$1,250

Figure 3-70 Summary accounting vouchers—end of project (2)

Note
For the use in a live environment, a system modification is required that automatically creates this voucher once a project is finished.

After the adjustment is posted, the financial statements that follow the CC and POC accounting methods match, as Figure 3-71 proves.

	YTD		YTD
Completed Contract Method		**Percentage of Completion Method**	
Balance Sheet		**Balance Sheet**	
130100 - Accounts Receivables	3,000.00	130100 - Accounts Receivables	3,000.00
165700 - WIP Invoiced		165700 - WIP Invoiced	
945100 - WIP Cost		865400 - WIP Sales Value	
200100 - Accounts Payable	(150.00)	200100 - Accounts Payable	(150.00)
140200 - Inventory	(100.00)	140200 - Inventory	(100.00)
Total	*2,750.00*	*Total*	*2,750.00*
Income Statement		**Income Statement**	
605100 - Payroll Allocation	(1,000.00)	605100 - Payroll Allocation	(1,000.00)
865400 - WIP Sales Value		945100 - Cost	
915300 - Accrued Revenue	(3,000.00)	915300 - Accrued Revenue	(3,000.00)
945200 - Realized Project Costs	1,250.00	945200 - Realized Project Costs	1,250.00
Total	*(2,750.00)*	*Total*	*(2,750.00)*

Figure 3-71 BS and IS according to CC and POC accounting method—end of project (2)

3.3.3. Summary

Figures 3-72 and 3-73 summarize and compare the WIP cost and revenue data for the sample project that follows the CC and POC accounting method and prove that both accounting methods can be applied in parallel with a "special" ledger accounting setup and treatment.

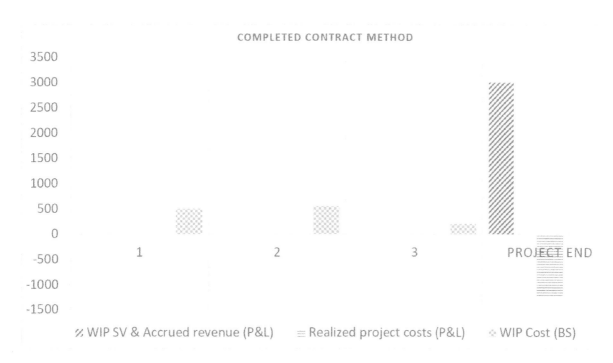

Figure 3-72 Graphical accounting summary—parallel project evaluation (1)

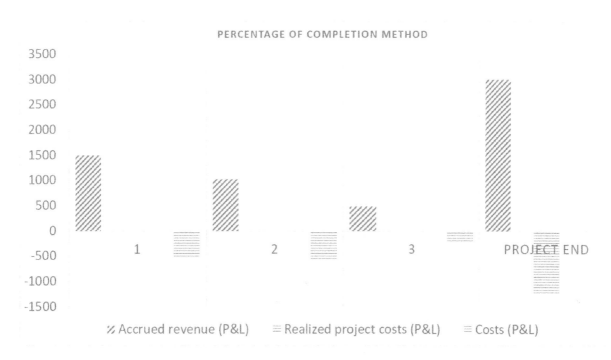

Figure 3-73 Graphical accounting summary—parallel project evaluation (2)

3.4. Activity-Based Costing (ABC)

3.4.1. Background

Increasing technological and productivity improvements have reduced the relative portion of direct costs, such as labor and materials, but increased the relative portion of indirect costs. As the relative portion of indirect costs rose, traditional cost-accounting systems that allocated indirect costs based on direct labor costs, floor space, or machine time became increasingly unreliable. This unreliability was caused by the fact that product costs became very sensitive to changes in the allocation percentages, as the allocation basis shrank and the allocation percentages increased. It thus became increasingly difficult to identify the "true costs" of an item and those products that were profitable and those that were not. Let's have a look at a simplified example—adopted from business-case-analysis.com (https://www.business-case-analysis.com/activity-based-costing.html)—that illustrates the issue.

	Product A	Product B	Sum
Units produced and sold	900,000	2,100,000	
Sales price / unit	$3.00	$2.00	
Total revenue	**2,700,000.00**	**4,200,000.00**	**$6,900,000**
Direct labor costs / unit	$0.50	$0.50	
Total direct labor costs	$450,000	$1,050,000	$1,500,000
Direct material costs / unit	$0.75	$0.50	
Total direct material costs	$675,000	$1,050,000	$1,725,000
Total direct costs / unit	$1.25	$1.00	
Total direct costs	**$1,125,000**	**$2,100,000**	**$3,225,000**
Indirect costs / unit	$0.47	$0.47	
Total indirect costs	**$426,750**	**$995,750**	**$1,422,500**
Total costs / unit	$1.72	$1.47	
Total costs	**$1,551,750**	**$3,095,750**	**$4,647,500**
Margin / unit	$1.28	$0.53	
Total margin	**$1,148,250**	**$1,104,250**	**$2,252,500**
Margin in % of revenue	43%	26%	

Figure 3-74 Example traditional cost-accounting approach

In this example, two products A and B are produced. Both products have direct labor costs of $0.50 per unit but different material costs of $0.75 per unit. Based on the units produced and sold, different total labor and material costs result.

In addition to the direct costs, $1,422,500 indirect costs arose. Those costs are allocated to product A and B based on the total labor costs of $1,500,000.

Indirect costs product = Total indirect costs / $\sum$ Labor costs * labor costs product   (33)

Indirect costs product A = $1,422,500 / 1,500,000 * $450,000 = $426,750   (34)

Indirect costs product B = $1,422,500 / 1,500,000 * $1,050,000 = $995,750   (35)

As the allocation of the indirect costs is made on the basis of the total direct labor costs, the same indirect costs per unit can be identified for both products irrespective of the complexity of the product, the time required for designing and developing the product, the time and effort required for purchasing the different components of the products, and so forth.

After the indirect costs are allocated to product A and product B, total costs of $1.72 and $1.47 are calculated, which result in a margin of $1.28 and $0.53 per unit of product A and B. Stated differently, based on the traditional cost-accounting approach, product A is more profitable than product B.

After exploring the traditional cost-accounting approach and how it deals with indirect costs, let's have a quick look at how the ABC approach deals with indirect costs.

The major difference in the treatment of indirect costs when applying the ABC costing method is that the ABC approach does not spread the indirect costs evenly across all products but rather tries to identify activity pools and cost drivers for those activity pools in a first step.

Note An activity pool is a set of activities that are required to complete a task. Examples comprise processing purchase orders, testing machines, creating product designs, and so forth.

The adopted example continues in a way that the following activity pools and cost drivers are identified for product A and B.

Activity pool	Cost driver activity units	Cost driver unit costs	Total activity product A	Total indirect costs A	Total activity product B	Total indirect costs
Purchase orders	No. of purchase orders	$1,800	75	$135,000	25	$45,000
Machine setups	No. of setups	$1,500	150	$225,000	100	$150,000
Product packaging	No. of product packages packed	$0.20	900,000	$180,000	500,000	$100,000
Machine testing and calibration	No. of tests	$100	1,000	$100,000	2,000	$200,000
Maint. and cleaning	No. of runs	$1,150	200	$230,000	50	$57,500
Total				$870,000		$552,500

Figure 3-75 Example ABC approach (1)

Based on the specified cost drivers and cost driver unit costs, indirect costs of $870,000 for product A and $552,000 for product B are calculated. If one adds those costs to the direct costs—which are identical for the traditional and the ABC approach—the following costs and margins result.

	Product A	Product B	Sum
Units produced and sold	900,000	2,100,000	
Sales price / unit	$3.00	$2.00	
Total revenue	**2,700,000.00**	**4,200,000.00**	**$6,900,000**
Direct labor costs / unit	$0.50	$0.50	
Total direct labor costs	$450,000	$1,050,000	$1,500,000
Direct material costs / unit	$0.75	$0.50	
Total direct material costs	$675,000	$1,050,000	$1,725,000
Total direct costs / unit	$1.25	$1.00	
Total direct costs	**$1,125,000**	**$2,100,000**	**$3,225,000**
Indirect costs / unit	$0.97	$0.26	
Total indirect costs	**$870,000**	**$552,500**	**$1,422,500**
Total costs / unit	$2.22	$1.26	
Total costs	**$1,995,000**	**$2,652,000**	**$4,647,500**
Margin / unit	$0.78	$0.74	
Total margin	**$705,000**	**$1,547,000**	**$2,252,500**
Margin in % of revenue	26%	37%	

Figure 3-76 Example ABC approach (2)

A comparison of the total costs and margins illustrates that the ABC approach results in a completely different (more accurate) outcome where product B is now more profitable than product A.

3.4.2. Application D365

After illustrating the differences in the treatment of the indirect costs in a traditional and ABC costing approach, you might have asked the question, how those cost-accounting approaches are related to the project-management and accounting module?

This question can be answered by referring to the previously used definition of an activity pool as a set of activities that is required to complete a task and for which a cost driver can be identified.

As projects are tracking activities that are required to complete a task, the project-management module can be used as a building block of a comprehensive cost-accounting system that provides additional insights into the indirect costs of a company. Especially in administrative and supportive process areas where the working time is the main cost driver, the incorporation of the project-management module can help improving the accuracy of indirect cost allocations.

As an example, rather than spreading the costs of the product management evenly across all products or cost centers, recorded project hours of the product managers can be used for allocating the costs of the product management. The same holds for employees working in other indirect cost areas, as long as those employees are recording their working time based on cost objects, such as cost centers, products, and the like.

Within the following, a comprehensive but still simplified example will be presented that illustrates the incorporation of the project module into a cost-accounting system for a bike producing company. Please note that the following example focuses primarily on another cost object (cost centers rather than products) for reasons of simplicity, which does, however, not limit the use of the ABC approach in D365 to cost centers only.

3.4.2.1.   Sample Data

Let's start with the sample data illustrated in Figure 3-77 that will be used for the following illustrations.

Ledger accounts	Cost centers								Total
	110 Supplies	120 Car pool	130 Product management	210 Purchasing	220 Production Mountain Bikes	230 Production City Bikes	240 Admin	250 Sales	
851000 Material costs				$150.000					$150.000
852000 Production wages					$ 100.000	$104.000			$204.000
853000 Salaries & other wages	$ 2.000	$ 3.000	$ 25.000	$ 14.000			$18.000	$15.000	$ 77.000
854000 Electricity, water & supplies	$30.000								$ 30.000
855000 Repairs		$ 5.500		$ 500					$ 6.000
856000 Advertisement								$ 8.000	$ 8.000
857000 Insurance							$25.000		$ 25.000
Total direct costs	$32.000	$8.500	$ 25.000	$164.500	$ 100.000	$104.000	$43.000	$23.000	$500.000

Figure 3-77 Sample data ABC in D365

The first column of Figure 3-77 lists different ledger accounts—so-called cost elements in cost-accounting terminology. The costs of those cost elements can be found in the column of the respective cost center. The first three cost centers (110, 120, and 130) are indirect or supportive cost centers, which are required to support the other operative processes of the company.

For that reason, the indirect costs that are recorded on those cost centers are allocated to the other operative or main cost centers no. 210 to 250. The allocation of those indirect costs is exemplified in Figure 3-78.

Ledger accounts	Cost centers								Total
	110 Supplies	120 Car pool	130 Product management	210 Purchasing	220 Production Mountain Bikes	230 Production City Bikes	240 Admin	250 Sales	
Total direct costs	$ 32,000	$ 8,500	$ 25,000	$ 164,500	$ 100,000	$ 104,000	$ 43,000	$ 23,000	$500,000
Headcount			*1*	*2*	*3*	*40*	*42*	*4*	*2*	
Allocation 110 Supplies	$ -32,000	$ 340	$ 681	$ 1,021	$ 13,617	$ 14,298	$ 1,362	$ 681	$ -
No of company cars			*1*	*2*	*0*	*1*	*1*	*3*	
Allocation 120 Car pool		$ -8,840	$ 1,105	$ 2,210	$ -	$ 1,105	$ 1,105	$ 3,315	$ -
No of bikes produced					*60000*	*70000*			
Allocation 130 Product management			$ -26,786		$ 12,363	$ 14,423			$ -
Total costs	$ -	$ -	$ -	$ 167,731	$ 125,980	$ 133,826	$ 45,467	$ 26,996	$500,000
Indirect cost as % of total costs				1.96%	25.98%	28.68%	5.74%	17.37%	

Figure 3-78 Cost allocation indirect costs

The cost allocations that are shown in Figure 3-78 follow the traditional cost-accounting approach, where an allocation key (headcount, number of company cars, and number of bikes produced) is used to shift the costs from the indirect to the main cost centers.

Note Please note that the allocation is done iterative. That is, the indirect cost centers do not directly and fully allocate their costs to the main cost centers (210-250) but also allocate a part of their direct costs to the other indirect cost centers. Take cost center 110 as an example, which shifts $340 and $681 to the other indirect cost centers 120 and 130. From there, those costs are further allocated to the other cost centers until all costs of the indirect cost centers are shifted to the main cost centers.

Once all costs have been allocated from the indirect to the main cost centers, indirect cost percentages can be calculated, which are, for example, required for the product cost calculation.

3.4.2.2. Implementation Cost-Accounting Module

3.4.2.2.1. Setup Cost Accounting—Part 1

Even though the cost-accounting module is not in the major focus of this book, the set up of this module is nevertheless illustrated here because understanding how the traditional cost-accounting approach is incorporated in D365 is important for the subsequent differentiation of the ABC approach.

So, let's get started with the set up of the first part of the cost-accounting module, which requires the set up of various dimensions that are shown in Figure 3-79.

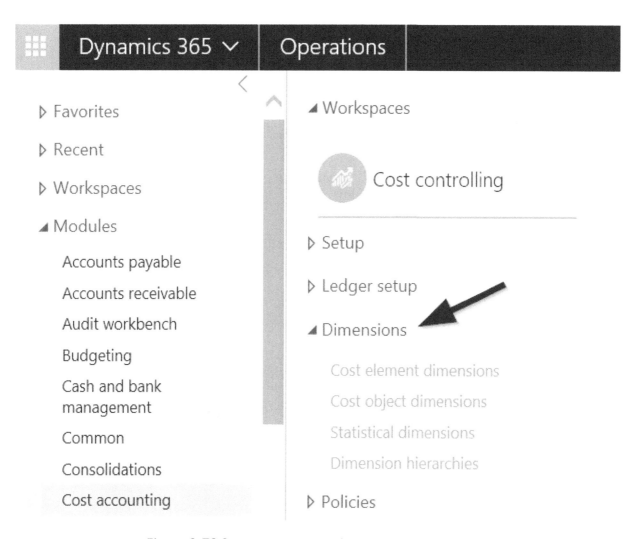

Figure 3-79 Setup cost accounting—part 1: Dimensions

3.4.2.2.1.1. Cost Element Dimension

The first dimension that needs to be set up is the cost element dimension that holds the ledger accounts that are illustrated in the first column of Figure 3-77. To get those ledger accounts incorporated into the cost-accounting module, one has to specify and configure a data connector for the dimension member provider first.

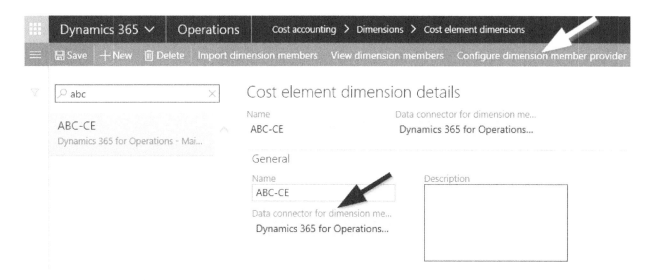

Figure 3-80 Specification and configuration of cost element dimension provider

Configuring this data connector requires that one specifies the chart of accounts (COA) and the ledger accounts that shall be transferred from the ledger to the cost-accounting module. This is shown in Figure 3-81.

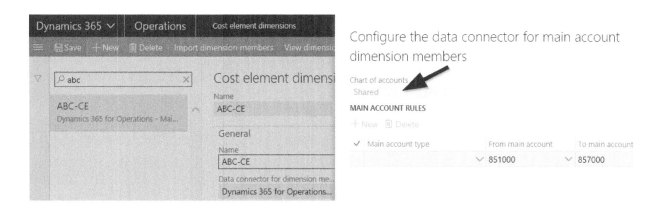

Figure 3-81 Configuration data connector cost element dimension

After the data connector is configured, the ledger accounts or cost elements can be imported and viewed in the respective form.

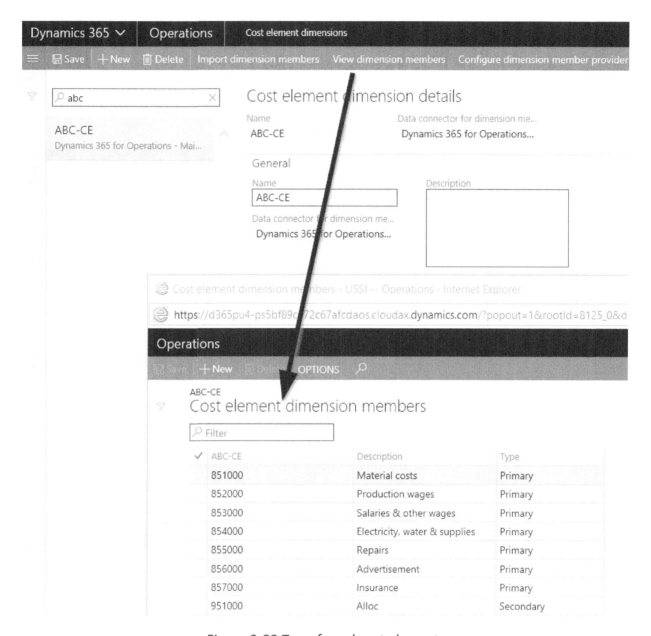

Figure 3-82 Transferred cost elements

Note Please note that the cost elements that are transferred from the general ledger are classified as primary cost elements. Users can additionally create secondary cost elements that are needed, for example, for tracking cost allocations. The use of secondary cost elements is explained in more detail further below.

3.4.2.2.1.2.   Cost Object Dimension

The next dimension that needs to be set up is the cost object dimension, which defines the cost centers that are illustrated column-wise in Figure 3-77. Transferring those cost center information from the ledger to the cost-accounting module follows the same principles that have been shown before. That is, a data connector needs to be configured first before cost objects (financial dimensions) can be transferred to the cost-accounting module. Figures 3-83 to 3-86 exemplify this transfer process.

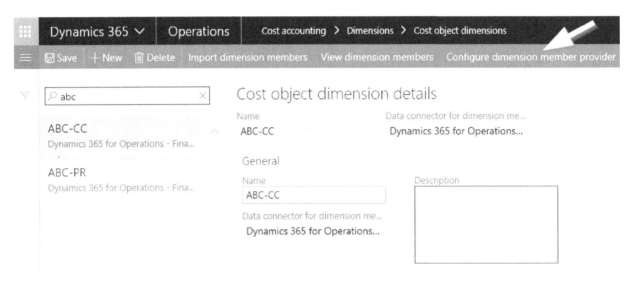

Figure 3-83 Specification and configuration of cost object dimension provider

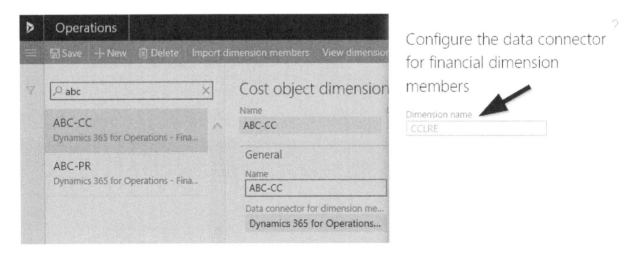

Figure 3-84 Configuration data connector cost object dimension

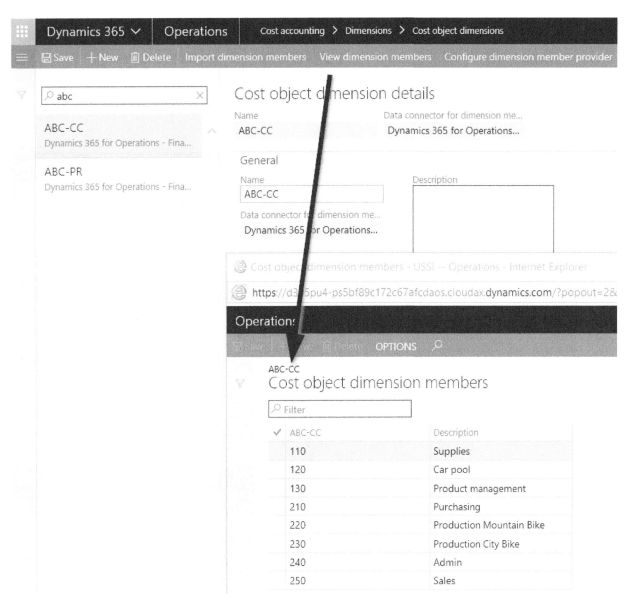

Figure 3-85 Transferred cost objects

Note Any financial dimension can be transferred to the cost-accounting module through the configuration of a data connector. Figure 3-86 shows the product cost object that has been created through the transfer of a product-related financial dimension.

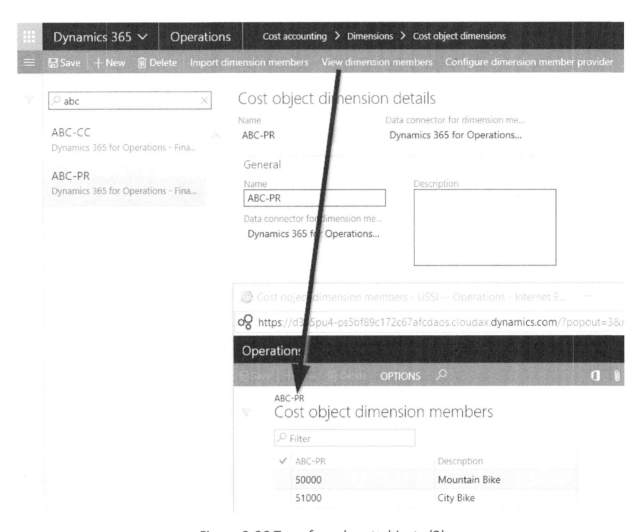

Figure 3-86 Transferred cost objects (2)

3.4.2.2.1.3. Statistical Dimension

The third dimension required to be set up is the statistical dimension, which holds the statistical elements that are required for allocating the costs from the indirect cost centers to the main operative cost centers.

Those statistical elements represent the allocation keys that are shown in Figure 3-78, and because there are only three elements used in the example, the set up of the statistical dimension and its elements has been done manually as shown in Figure 3-87.

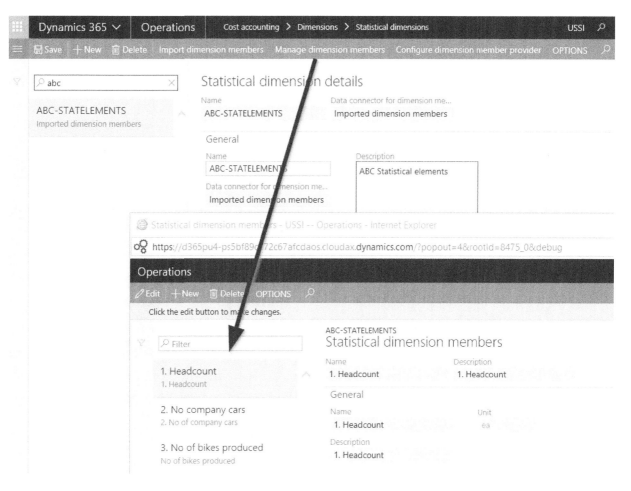

Figure 3-87 Statistical dimension and elements

3.4.2.2.1.4.   Dimension Hierarchies

The last dimension-related setup concerns the set up of dimension hierarchies that are required for structuring the cost elements and cost objects. In line with the previous set up dimensions and their elements, three different hierarchies are set up. The first one for structuring cost centers (ABC-CCH), the second one for structuring cost elements (ABC-CEH), and the last one for structuring products (ABC-PRH).

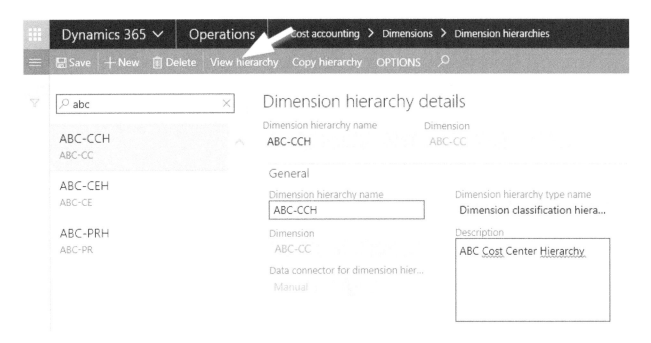

Figure 3-88 Dimension hierarchies

Once the required dimension hierarchies are defined, the structure of those hierarchies and the assignment of the structural elements with the cost elements and cost objects can be made. This assignment is shown in Figures 3-89 and 3-90 for the three-dimension hierarchies used.

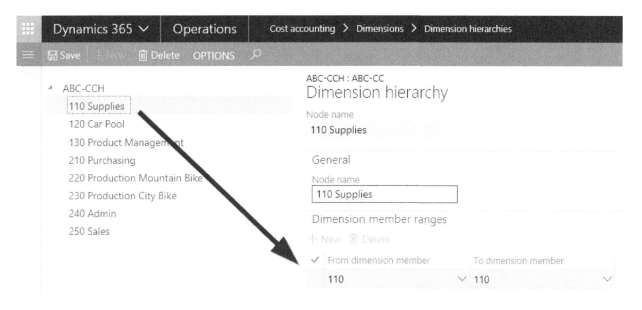

Figure 3-89 Cost center dimension hierarchy

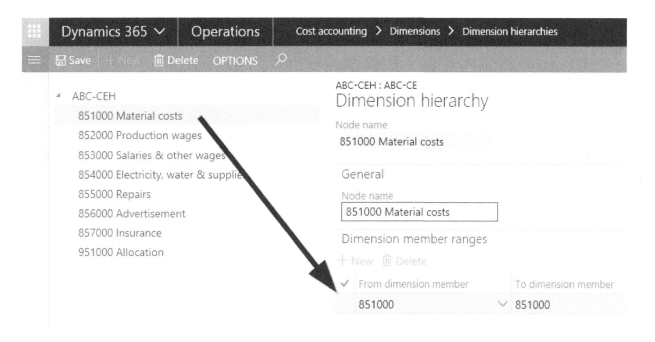

Figure 3-90 Cost element dimension hierarchy

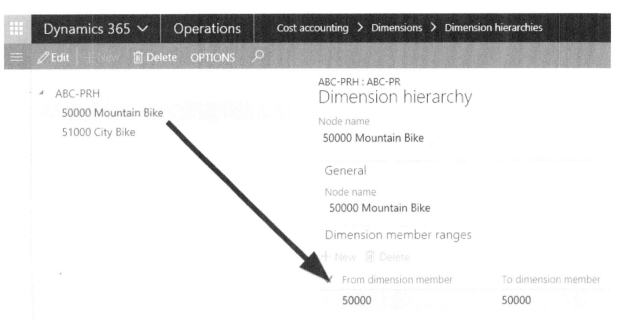

Figure 3-91 Product dimension hierarchy

3.4.2.2.2.   Setup Cost Accounting—Part 2

3.4.2.2.2.1.   Import Statistical Dimension Data

After the cost-accounting dimensions are set up, the processing of the data in the cost-accounting module can begin. The first data that need to be processed or imported are the statistical elements, which are used as allocation keys for the allocation of the indirect costs.

The respective statistical data are prepared in an Excel document and imported by making use of the *imported statistical measures* data entity that is illustrated together with its target fields in Figure 3-92.

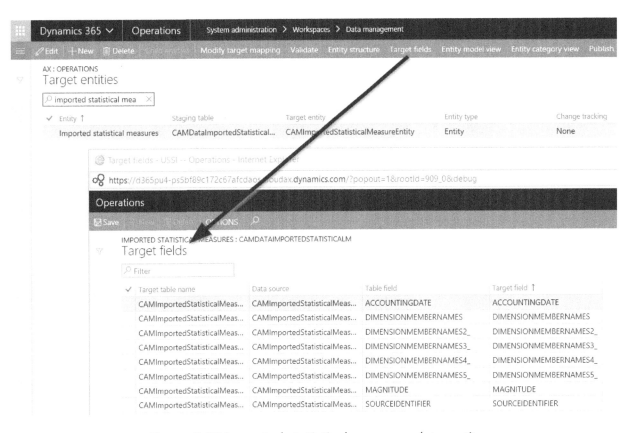

Figure 3-92 Imported statistical measures data entity

Figure 3-93 shows the prepared Excel data. Please note, especially, the data in column C that establish a link between the statistical measures and the cost centers.

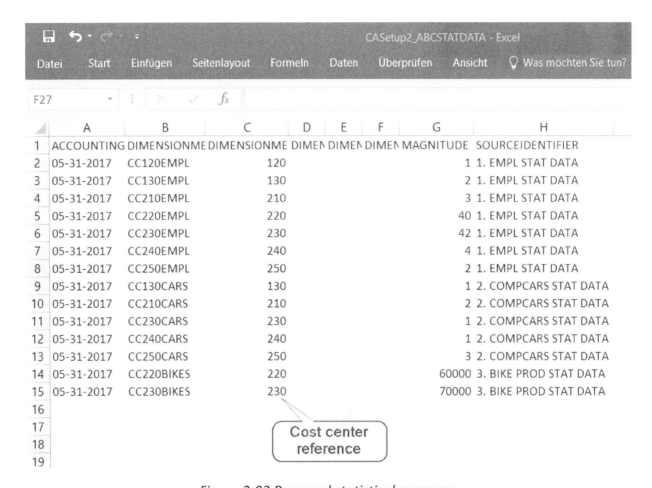

Figure 3-93 Prepared statistical measures

After the data are prepared, the statistical measures can be imported and identified in the staging tables. Figures 3-94 and 3-95 document this import process.

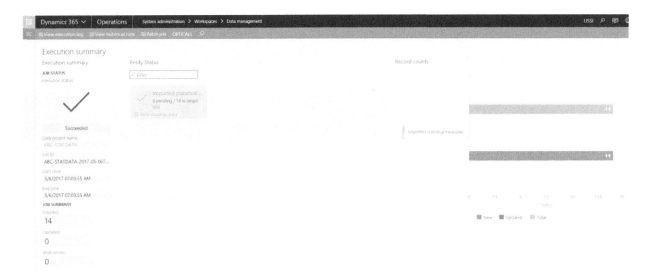

Figure 3-94 Data import execution summary for statistical measures

ABC-STATDATA-2017-05-06T07:03:54-33603775FAF54D35B8C5549682

Imported statistical measures :

Select	S...	Transfer status	Record-ID	Accounting da...	Dimension member name 1	Dimension member name 2	D...	D...	D...	Import source identifier	Magnitude
☐	⊘	Completed	5637144715	5/31/2017	CC120EMPL	120				1. EMPL STAT DATA	1.00
☐	⊘	Completed	5637144716	5/31/2017	CC130EMPL	130				1. EMPL STAT DATA	2.00
☐	⊘	Completed	5637144717	5/31/2017	CC210EMPL	210				1. EMPL STAT DATA	3.00
☐	⊘	Completed	5637144718	5/31/2017	CC220EMPL	220				1. EMPL STAT DATA	40.00
☐	⊘	Completed	5637144719	5/31/2017	CC230EMPL	230				1. EMPL STAT DATA	42.00
☐	⊘	Completed	5637144720	5/31/2017	CC240EMPL	240				1. EMPL STAT DATA	4.00
☐	⊘	Completed	5637144721	5/31/2017	CC250EMPL	250				1. EMPL STAT DATA	2.00
☐	⊘	Completed	5637144722	5/31/2017	CC130CARS	130				2. COMPCARS STAT DATA	1.00
☐	⊘	Completed	5637144723	5/31/2017	CC210CARS	210				2. COMPCARS STAT DATA	2.00
☐	⊘	Completed	5637144724	5/31/2017	CC230CARS	230				2. COMPCARS STAT DATA	1.00
☐	⊘	Completed	5637144725	5/31/2017	CC240CARS	240				2. COMPCARS STAT DATA	1.00
☐	⊘	Completed	5637144726	5/31/2017	CC250CARS	250				2. COMPCARS STAT DATA	3.00
☐	⊘	Completed	5637144727	5/31/2017	CC220BIKES	220				3. BIKE PROD STAT DATA	60.000.00
☐	⊘	Completed	5637144728	5/31/2017	CC230BIKES	230				3. BIKE PROD STAT DATA	70.000.00

Figure 3-95 Imported statistical measures

3.4.2.2.2.2.   Setup Cost Accounting Ledger and Cost Allocation Policy

After all statistical measures are imported, a couple of additional setups are required before costs can be allocated between cost objects (cost centers). Figure 3-96 summarizes those additional setup steps that will be explained in detail below.

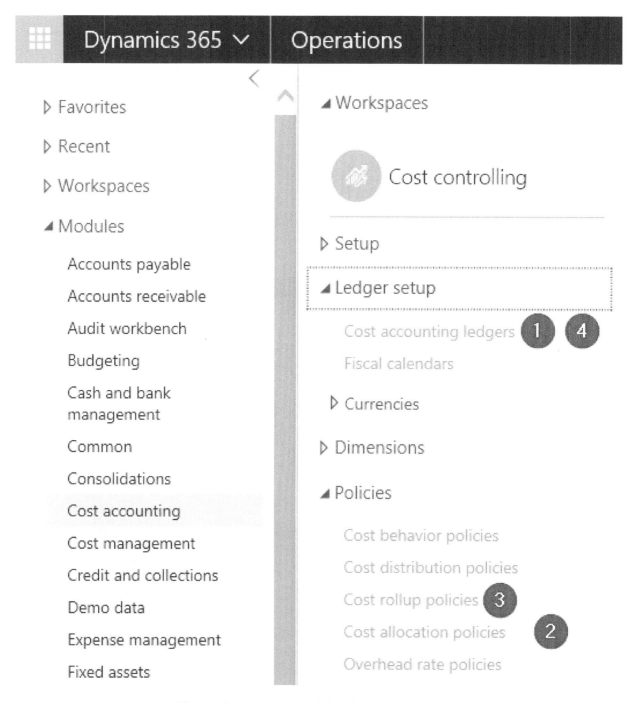

Figure 3-96 Additional setup required for the execution of cost allocations

Setup Step 1: Basic Cost Accounting Ledger Setup

Configuring a basic cost-accounting ledger setup is the first required additional setup.

Note A cost-accounting ledger defines processes and rules for measuring costs on cost objects. It handles cost transactions and manages documents that log the changes in values and quantities that cost transactions produce.

The basic cost-accounting ledger setup requires the assignment of a cost element dimension, which represents the lines in the costing overview shown in Figure 3-77. In addition, the statistical dimension needs to be specified together with the other, more general parameters, such as the exchange rate type and the fiscal calendar. For details, please see Figure 3-97.

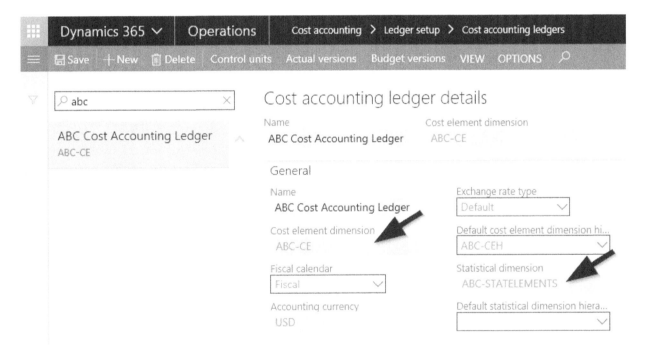

Figure 3-97 Basic cost-accounting ledger setup

Finally, the cost objects—in the example, cost centers—need to be set up in the cost control unit form, as exemplified in Figure 3-98.

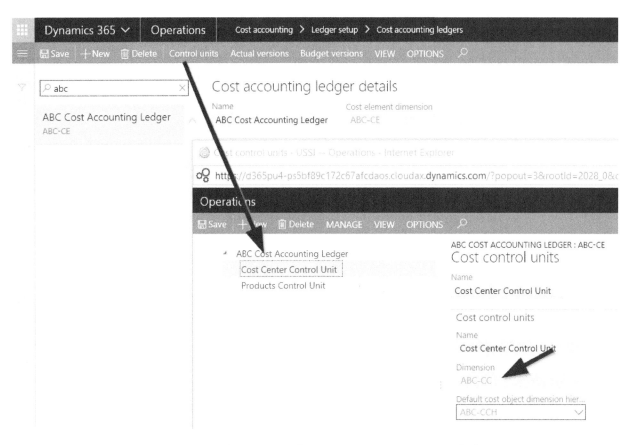

Figure 3-98 Linkage cost objects to cost-accounting ledger

Setup Step 2: Setup Cost Allocation Policy

After the cost-accounting ledger is set up, cost allocation policies need to be created, which determine how a specific cost object dimension value is allocated. As an example, the costs of cost center 110 are allocated to the other cost centers based on the statistical measure *Headcount* and the costs of cost center 120 are allocated to the other cost centers based on the statistical measure *No. of company cars*. Figure 3-99 illustrates the allocation policies used in the example.

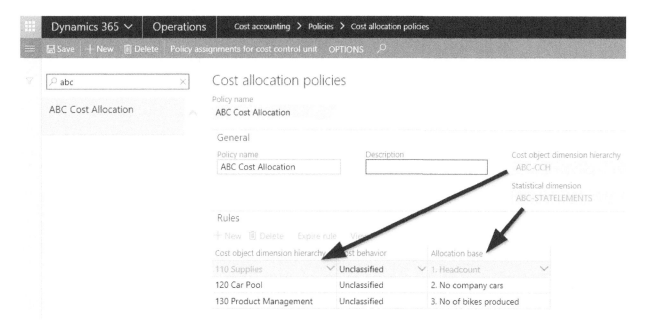

Figure 3-99 Allocation policy rules

Before an allocation policy can be used and processed, it needs to be assigned to a cost-accounting ledger cost control unit. Without this assignment, the policy will never be applied and the allocation never be executed. Figure 3-100 shows the assignment of the cost allocation policy to the previously set up cost center control unit of the cost-accounting ledger.

313

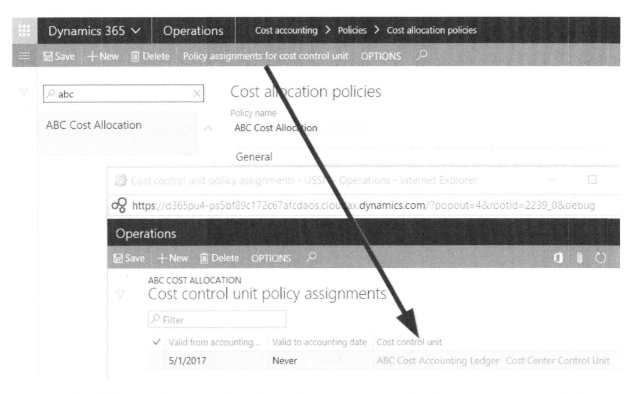

Figure 3-100 Association cost allocation policy to cost control unit in cost-accounting ledger

Setup Step 3: Setup Cost Rollup Policy

A cost rollup policy allows differentiating between primary and secondary cost elements when allocating costs. If no cost rollup policy is set up, costs are simply shifted from one cost object to another without having the chance to differentiate between primary and secondary costs, that is, between costs that originate from the accounting ledgers and those that originate from the cost-accounting module.

In the example shown below, all cost allocations that are made for the cost centers included in the hierarchy ABC-CCH are recorded on the secondary cost element 951000 that allows differentiating them from the other primary costs.

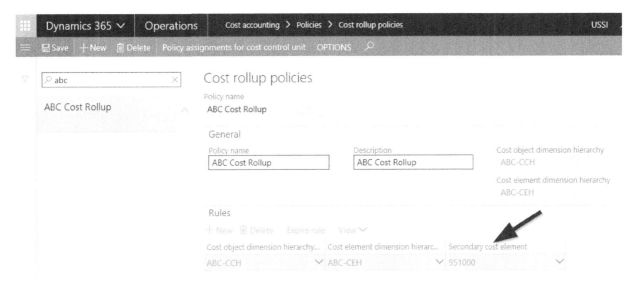

Figure 3-101 Cost rollup policy

Similar to cost-accounting policies, cost rollup policies must be associated to the cost control unit that has been specified in the cost-accounting ledger. This is shown in Figure 3-102.

Figure 3-102 Association cost rollup policy to cost control unit in cost-accounting ledger

Setup Step 4: Finalize Cost-Accounting Ledger Setup

The last additional setup step relates once again to the cost-accounting ledger set up that needs to be finalized. This finalization consists of two parts: the configuration of the general ledger data provider (A) and the configuration of the statistical measures data provider (B).

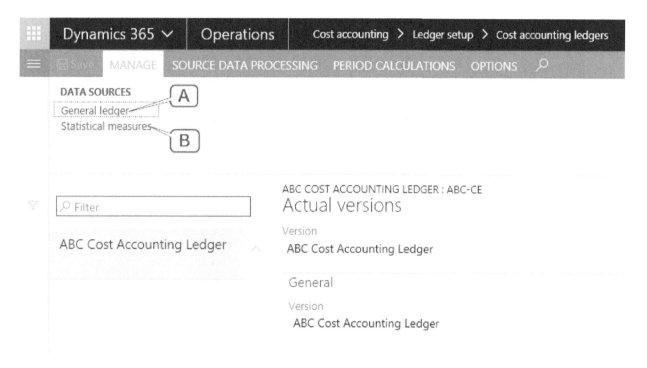

Figure 3-103 Finalization cost-accounting ledger setup

The first part—the configuration of the general ledger data provider—requires the specification of the legal entity and the posting layer only, which are needed for the identification of the data that shall be transferred from the ledger to the cost-accounting module. Please see Figure 3-104 for details.

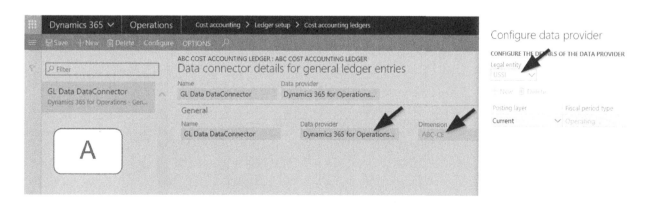

Figure 3-104 Configuration general ledger data provider

Thereafter, the data connector for the statistical measures needs to be set up. When making this setup, a reference to the source identifier and the financial dimension that have been specified in the Excel import template—please see Figure 3-93—needs to be made. For details, please see Figure 3-105.

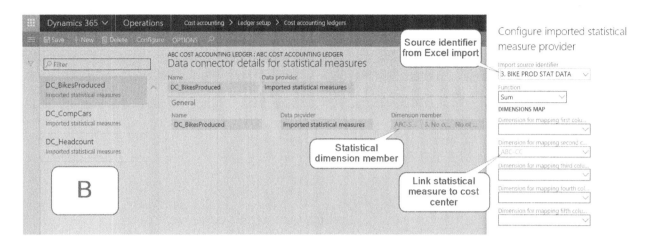

Figure 3-105 Configuration statistical measure data provider

3.4.2.2.3.   Process Cost-Accounting Data Sources

With all those setups in place, the general ledger and statistical measure data can be processed, that is, imported into the cost-accounting ledger. The next figures illustrate this import and the resulting cost-accounting journals that have been created.

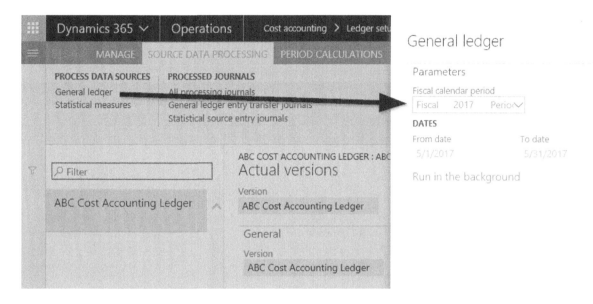

Figure 3-106 Transfer general ledger data to cost-accounting ledger

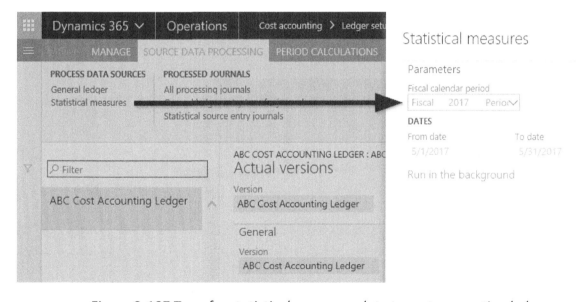

Figure 3-107 Transfer statistical measures data to cost-accounting ledger

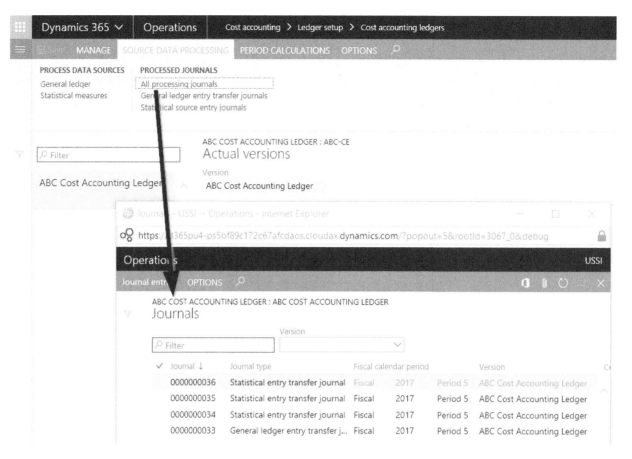

Figure 3-108 Created cost-accounting process journals

After the general ledger and statistical measures data have been imported into the cost-accounting ledger, the overhead calculation can be started. Starting the overhead calculation creates all the cost allocations that are illustrated in Figure 3-78.

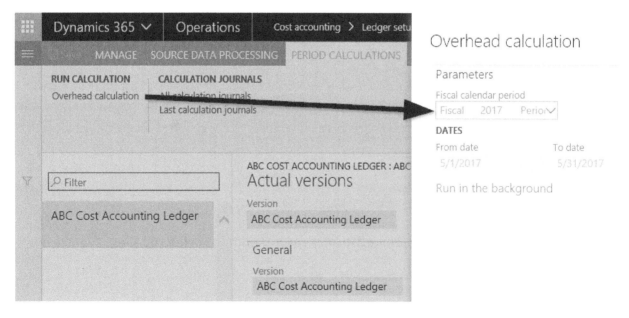

Figure 3-109 Overhead calculation cost-accounting module

3.4.2.2.4. Cost-Controlling Workspace

The outcome of the overhead calculation can be analyzed by using the cost-controlling workspace, which needs to be set up first.

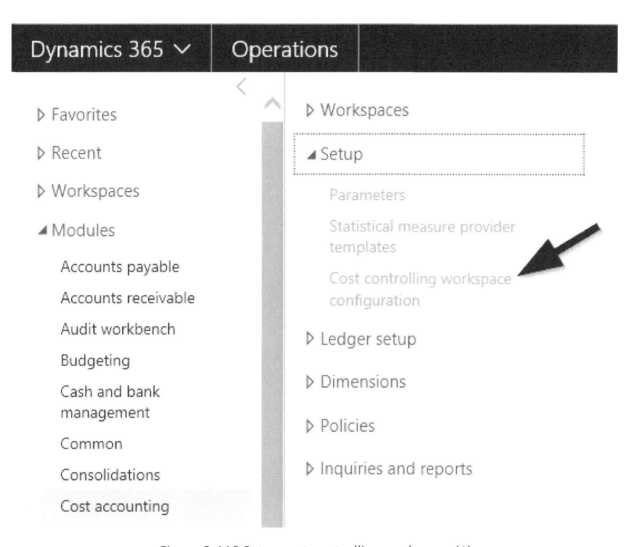

Figure 3-110 Setup cost-controlling workspace (1)

The set up of the cost-controlling workspace requires the selection of the cost control unit from the cost-accounting ledger. In addition, the cost elements and cost element hierarchies need to be selected, which represent the columns and lines of the costing overview shown in Figure 3-78. Finally, the actual version of the executed overhead calculation must be selected in order to illustrate the allocated costs in the cost-controlling workspace. Figure 3-111 highlights the aforementioned elements that need to be set up with the cost-controlling workspace configuration.

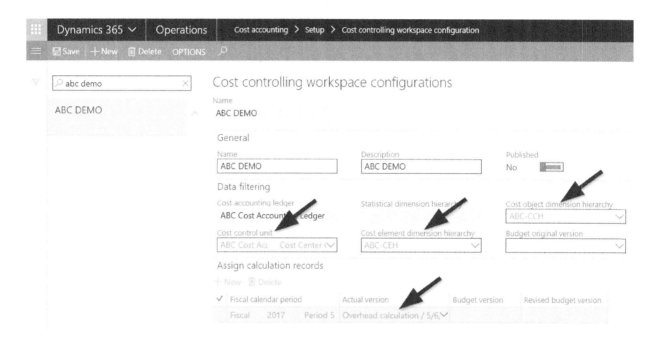

Figure 3-111 Setup cost-controlling workspace (2)

After the set up of the cost-controlling workspace is finished, the total costs for all the cost centers can be identified. Figures 3-112 to 3-116 show those costs for the sample data used.

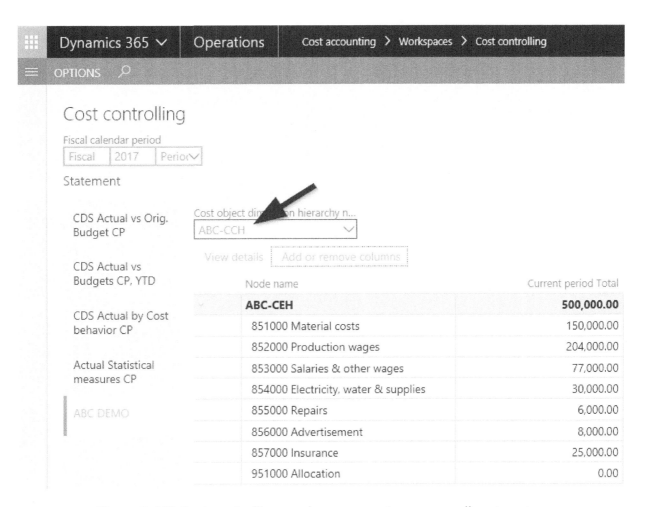

Figure 3-112 Cost-controlling workspace—cost summary all cost centers

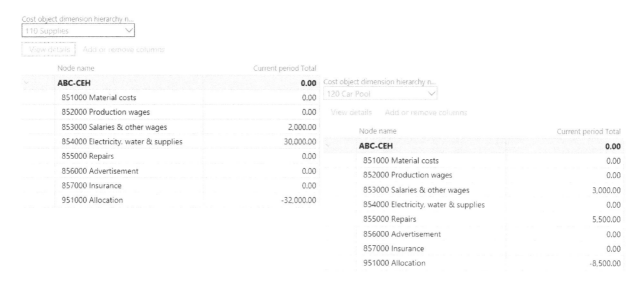

Figure 3-113 Cost-controlling workspace—cost summary cost centers 110 and 120

Figure 3-114 Cost-controlling workspace—cost summary cost centers 130 and 210

Cost object dimension hierarchy n...
| 240 Admin | ∨ |

View details   Add or remove columns

Node name	Current period Total
ABC-CEH	**45,466.76**
851000 Material costs	0.00
852000 Production wages	0.00
853000 Salaries & other wages	18,000.00
854000 Electricity, water & supplies	0.00
855000 Repairs	0.00
856000 Advertisement	0.00
857000 Insurance	25,000.00
951000 Allocation	2,466.76

Cost object dimension hierarchy n...
| 250 Sales | ∨ |

View details   Add or remove columns

Node name	Current period Total
ABC-CEH	**26,996.01**
851000 Material costs	0.00
852000 Production wages	0.00
853000 Salaries & other wages	15,000.00
854000 Electricity, water & supplies	0.00
855000 Repairs	0.00
856000 Advertisement	8,000.00
857000 Insurance	0.00
951000 Allocation	3,996.01

Figure 3-116 Cost-controlling workspace—cost summary cost centers 240 and 250

Note
Different from what has been shown in Figures 3-77 and 3-78, only single cost centers can be selected and analyzed in the cost-controlling workspace. A column-wise comparison of the various cost centers requires the use of Power BI tools. The same applies for the calculation and illustration of the indirect cost percentage measures that are shown in Figure 3-78.

3.4.2.3.   ABC Approach For Dealing with Indirect Costs

Previously it has been explained that posting-hour transactions on projects can be considered as a cost allocation from the department or cost center of the respective employee to the department or cost center that has been set up with the project.

This cost-allocation effect can be used for incorporating an ABC approach in those areas where the working time is the main cost driver. In the following, it is assumed that this is the case for the product development team that is responsible for the management of the current and the design of new products.

To illustrate how the ABC approach can be incorporated in D365, the previously used example is slightly modified in a way that the product management cost are not allocated to the other operative cost centers by referring to the items produced but rather by referring to the hour postings of the product managers in the project module. Within the following subchapters, the necessary setups in the project and cost-accounting modules are explained.

3.4.2.3.1. Project-Module Setup and Processing

Let's start with the required setups in the project module, where a new project (*U-00000262*) with two subprojects is created. The first subproject is thereby assigned to the cost center of the mountain bike production and the second one to the city bike production cost center. Figure 3-117 exemplifies this setup for the first subproject.

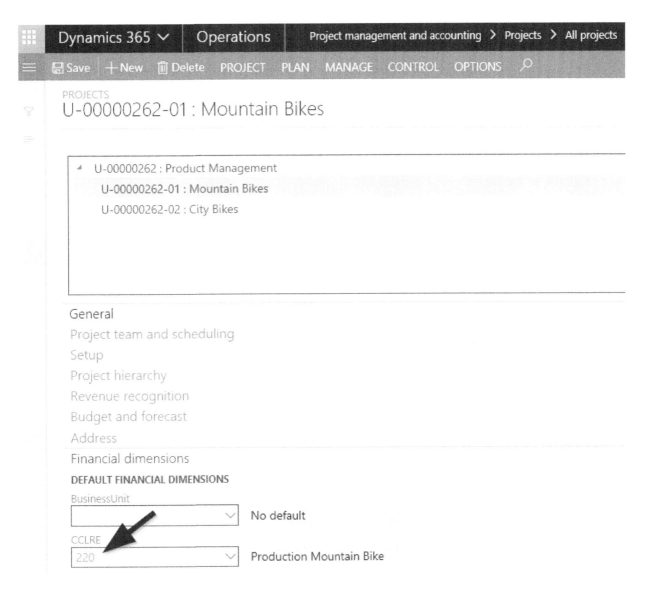

Figure 3-117 Project setup ABC approach

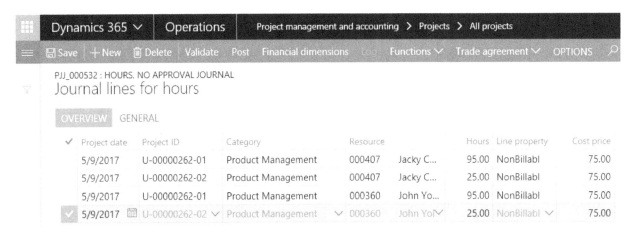

Note The main project is set up only for grouping the other projects, and no transactions are recorded on the main project.

The next setups—not shown for reasons of brevity—are the set up of a project category *Product Management* and the set up of a cost price of $75 for this newly created project category.

According to what has been explained before (see chapter 3.4.1.), the hourly cost price represents the cost driver unit cost that are determined—in the example—by the hourly cost price of an external product manager.

With those setups in place, the two product managers record their working time on the two subprojects, as exemplified in Figure 3-118.

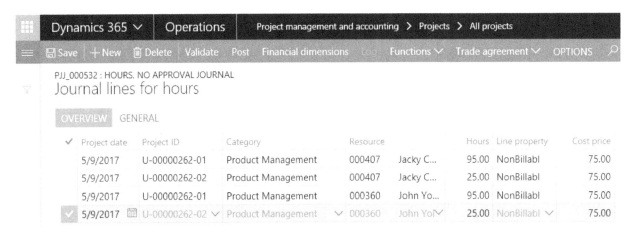

Figure 3-118 Product management time recording

The resulting voucher transactions and accounting voucher of those postings are summarized in Figures 3-119 and 3-120.

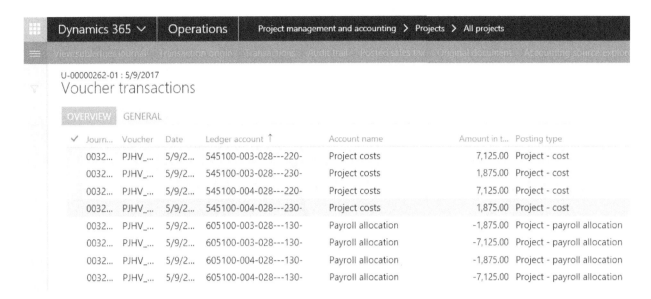

Figure 3-119 Resulting hour transactions

DEBIT		CREDIT		AMOUNT
Account	Cost Center	Account	Cost Center	
545100 Project costs	220 Production Mountain Bikes	605100 Payroll allocation	130 Product management	$14,250
545100 Project costs	230 Production City Bikes	605100 Payroll allocation	130 Product management	$3,750

Figure 3-120 Resulting accounting voucher

Figure 3-120 has been prepared in a way that the ledger accounts and the cost centers can be identified. An analysis of the cost centers shows that the project hour transactions are shifted from cost center 130 to the production cost centers 220 and 230.

3.4.2.3.2.   Cost-Accounting Module Setup and Processing

The next setups required for the analysis of the cost center costs relate once again to the cost-accounting module. There the ledger accounts (cost elements) that have been used for posting the project hour transactions are included in a newly set up cost element dimension (ABC-CE2), which is shown in Figure 3-121.

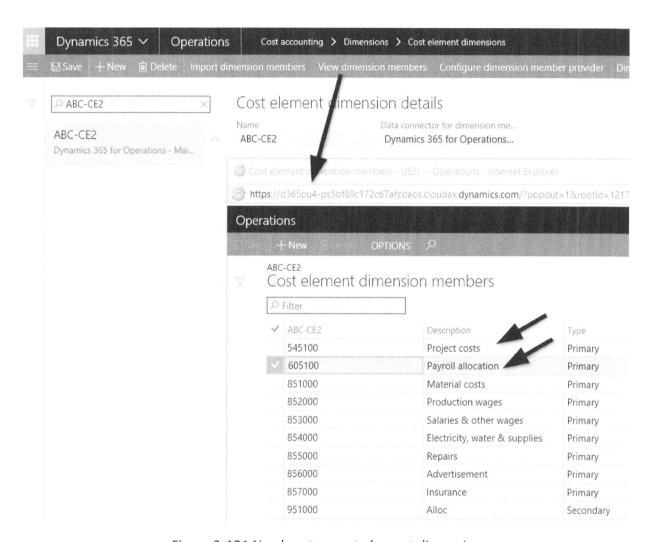

Figure 3-121 Newly setup cost element dimension

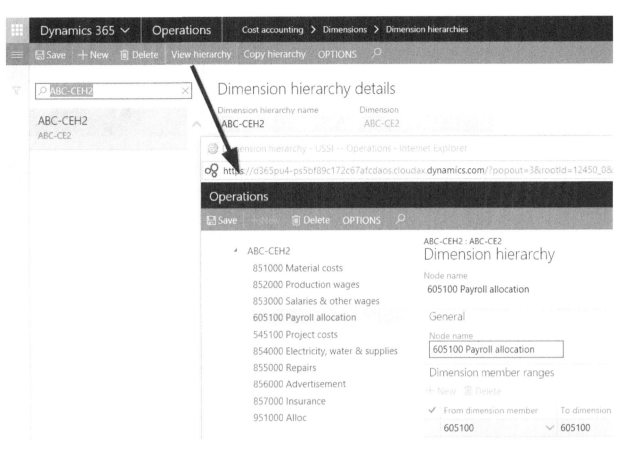

Figure 3-122 Newly setup cost element dimension hierarchy

Next, a new cost-accounting ledger (*ABC Cost Accounting Ledger2*) has been set up in a similar way to what has been shown further above in chapter 3.4.2.2.

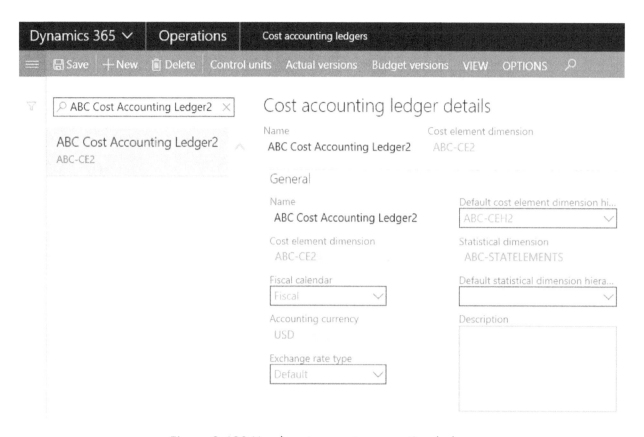

Figure 3-123 Newly setup cost-accounting ledger

Note
To conserve space, not all of the required cost-accounting setups are illustrated here because they have already been shown in detail before. A focus is consequently made on those things that differ from the previously used setup shown in chapter 3.4.2.2.

The main difference to the previously used setup can be found in the cost allocation policy form that only includes allocation policy rules for the cost centers 110 and 120.

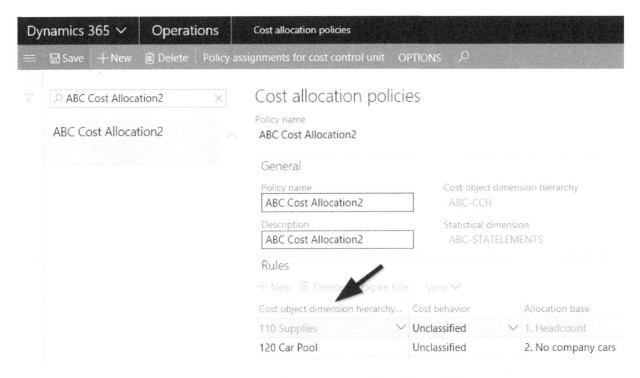

Figure 3-124 Newly setup cost allocation policies

If those policies are processed, the following costs for the company as a whole and the various cost centers can be identified in the cost-controlling workspace.

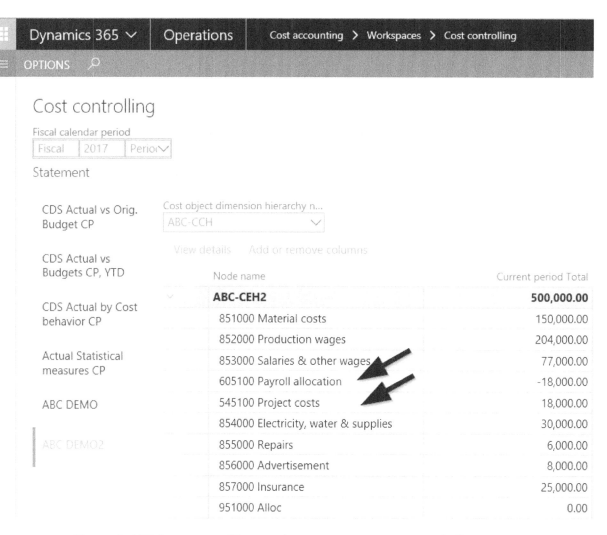

Figure 3-125 Cost-controlling workspace—cost summary of all cost centers

Figure 3-126 Cost-controlling workspace—cost summary cost centers 110 and 120

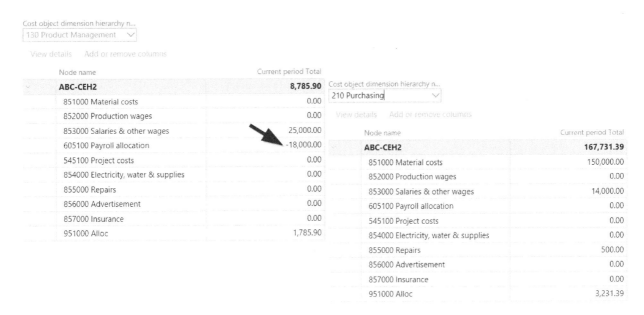

Figure 3-127 Cost-controlling workspace—cost summary cost centers 130 and 210

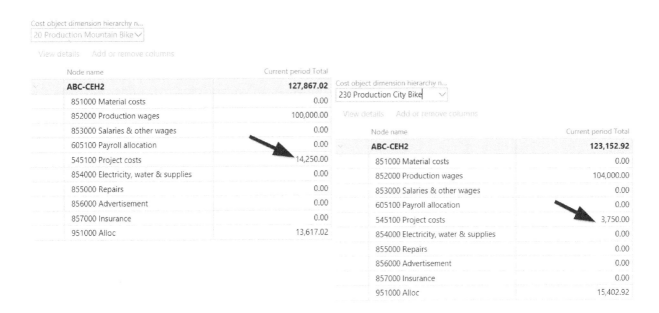

Figure 3-128 Cost-controlling workspace—cost summary cost centers 220 and 230

Figure 3-129 Cost-controlling workspace—cost summary cost centers 240 and 250

To compare the newly created cost data easier with the prior results, the cost and allocation data have been summarized in Figures 3-130 and 3-131.

Ledger accounts	110 Supplies	120 Car pool	130 Product management	210 Purchasing	220 Production Mountain Bikes	230 Production City Bikes	240 Admin	250 Sales	Total
851000 Material costs				$ 150,000					$150,000
852000 Production wages					$ 100,000	$ 104,000			$204,000
853000 Salaries & other wages	$ 2,000	$ 3,000	$ 25,000	$ 14,000			$ 18,000	$ 15,000	$ 77,000
Hours total			*240*		*190*	*50*			
Cost price / hour			*$ 75*		*$ 75*	*$ 75*			
605100 Payroll allocation			$ -18,000						
545100 Project costs					$ 14,250	$ 3,750			
854000 Electricity, water & supplies	$ 30,000								$ 30,000
855000 Repairs		$ 5,500		$ 500					$ 6,000
856000 Advertisement								$ 8,000	$ 8,000
857000 Insurance							$ 25,000		$ 25,000
Total direct costs	$ 32,000	$ 8,500	$ 7,000	$ 164,500	$ 114,250	$ 107,750	$ 43,000	$ 23,000	$500,000

Figure 3-130 Summary costs ABC costing approach (1)

Ledger accounts	Cost centers 110 Supplies	120 Car pool	130 Product management	210 Purchasing	220 Production Mountain Bikes	230 Production City Bikes	240 Admin	250 Sales	Total
Total direct costs	$ 32,000	$ 8,500	$ 7,000	$ 164,500	$ 114,250	$ 107,750	$ 43,000	$ 23,000	$500,000
Headcount		*1*	*2*	*3*	*40*	*42*	*4*	*2*	
Allocation 110 Supplies	$ -32,000	$ 340	$ 681	$ 1,021	$ 13,617	$ 14,298	$ 1,362	$ 681	$ -
No of company cars			*1*	*2*	*0*	*1*	*1*	*3*	
Allocation 120 Car pool		$ -8,840	$ 1,105	$ 2,210	$ -	$ 1,105	$ 1,105	$ 3,315	$ -
No of bikes produced									
Allocation 130 Product management			$ -		$ -	$ -			$ -
Total costs	$ -	$ -	$ 8,786	$ 167,731	$ 127,867	$ 123,153	$ 45,467	$ 26,996	$500,000
Indirect cost as % of total costs			1.96%	24.39%	17.78%	5.74%	17.37%		

Figure 3-131 Summary costs ABC costing approach (2)

The first thing that one can identify from the previous summary figures is that the payroll allocation and the project cost account are included in the direct costing section. Even though this is not fully correct from a cost-accounting perspective, both accounts have been included there to get a better differentiation between those costs that originate from the ledger modules and those that originate from the cost-accounting module.

The second thing that can be identified from the summary figures shown above is that $8,786 remain on the product management cost center. That is because the $75 cost driver unit cost price that has been set up is seemingly too low to cover all direct and indirect costs of the product management. Assuming that the $75 are an external benchmark or market cost price, it can be concluded that the internal product management is comparatively too expensive.

Note
If one does not want to have unallocated direct costs remaining on the product management cost center, the effective labor rate functionality that has been explained in the first part of this book can be applied. In addition, the indirect costs that are allocated from other cost centers can also be eliminated either by modifying the allocation key or by making use of a cost allocation policy that distributes those secondary costs to the other cost centers.

The third major difference between the ABC and the traditional cost-accounting approach is that the overall costs of the mountain bike production are higher than the costs of the city bike production. That is because the complexity of the products and the time required to manage them has not been incorporated into the production volume-related allocation key that has been used with the traditional cost-accounting approach.

3.4.3. Summary

The previous illustrations and comparisons of the traditional and ABC approach showed that the ABC approach could be incorporated into a comprehensive cost-accounting framework through the use of the project module.

Even though the ABC approach might not be used for each and every section of a company, its application might shed some light into the often-intransparent indirect costing block and can help companies identifying those products and process that add value and those that don't.

Irrespective of the fact whether one plans to use the project module for ABC costing purposes or not, two major things need to be clarified when it comes to the combined use of the cost-accounting and project module:

1) Whether project hour transactions shall be posted on ledger accounts or not?
   (Please also see chapter 2.7.2.10.1.1. for details.)
2) Where and how project-related costs should be allocated—"directly" in the project module or "indirectly" in the cost-accounting module.

Answering those questions beforehand is crucial for a successful implementation of the project and the cost-accounting module.

3.5. Indirect Cost Allocations

3.5.1. Background

Often companies do not only want to analyze the direct costs of their projects but also want to get a picture of the full or true costs of their projects. Obtaining this picture requires that indirect costs are recorded at the project level.

Note Indirect costs are those that are not directly accountable to a cost object, such as a particular project, function or product. Examples of indirect costs comprise costs for management, insurance, taxes, and alike.

3.5.2. Application D365

Before one allocates indirect costs to projects, two questions need to be answered:

1.) Whether allocating indirect costs to projects is allowed, and
2.) What instrument or functionality is used for making those allocations?

The first question relates to the accounting standards a company follows and whether those standards allow allocating indirect costs to projects. This question cannot fully be answered here, as the author is not familiar with all accounting standards around the world. By referring to the major accounting standard setters (IASB and FASB), it can, however, be stated that in general only those indirect costs that are attributable to specific projects can be allocated to them. Examples comprise insurance-related costs, costs of design, and technical assistance and construction overhead costs.

The second question relates to the instrument or module that is used for allocating indirect costs to projects. Here, the following instruments are available:

a.) The indirect project cost functionality,
b.) The use of the project adjustment functionality, or
c.) The use of general ledger or cost-accounting allocations.

3.5.2.1. Indirect Project Cost Functionality

The indirect project cost functionality allows—among others—specifying a percentage- or unit-based cost rate that is posted together with recorded project hours. Let's have a look at an example, where each project hour transaction gets an additional 1.15% sick-leave costs assigned.

To make use of the indirect project cost functionality, an indirect project category needs to be set up first. Setting up this category requires the activation of the indirect cost component parameter that is shown in Figure 3-132.

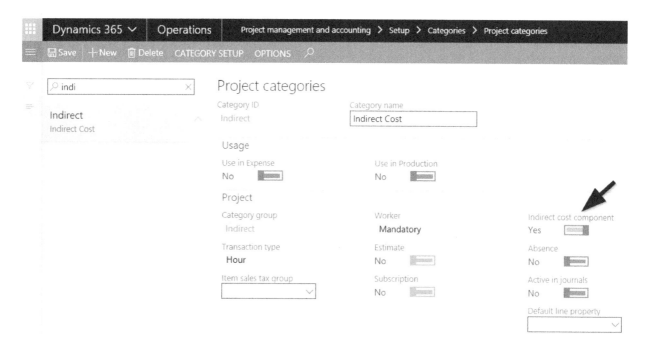

Figure 3-132 Setup indirect project category

Once the indirect project category is set up, an indirect cost component needs to be created. This indirect cost component is then linked to the previously set up indirect project category. Figure 3-133 shows several examples of indirect cost components and their linkage to the indirect cost category.

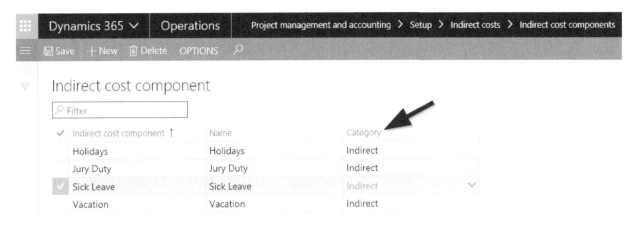

Figure 3-133 Indirect cost components

Note To keep things as simple as possible, only the *sick leave* component will be used in the following.

The third setup required for the use of the indirect project cost functionality relates to the indirect cost component groups that allow the specification of a percentage- or unit-based cost rate.

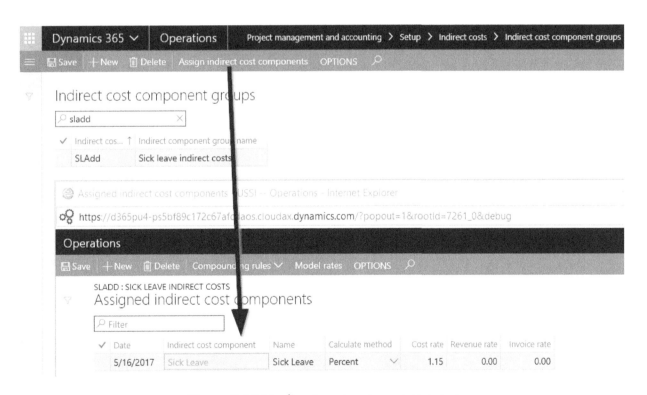

Figure 3-134 Indirect cost component group

As only one single indirect cost component (*sick leave*) is used in the example, the compounding rules functionality that can be identified in Figure 3-134 does not need to be set up. The same applies for the use of the model rates functionality.

Through the specification of revenue and invoice rates, additional indirect revenue and invoice rates—that are charged to the project customer—can be specified. Those functionalities won't be used in the following. If required, some additional information on their usage can be found on the author's blog.

The last setup required for making use of the indirect project cost functionality is assigning the indirect cost component group to one or more of the elements shown in Figure 3-135.

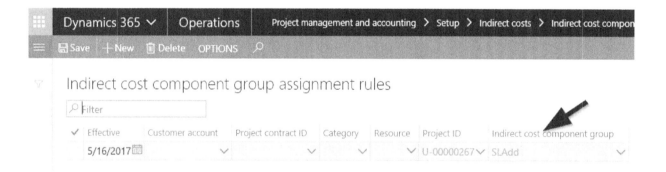

Figure 3-135 Assignment indirect cost component group

Recording project hours with all those setups in place will finally result in a voucher that has the additional indirect costs included. Figure 3-136 illustrates this for an hour transaction with an original cost price of $100.

Figure 3-136 Sample hour transaction with indirect costs

Even though the indirect project cost functionality allows recording indirect costs on projects, it falls short of allocating indirect costs that are not directly related to project hour transactions. Indirect costs, such as insurance costs that are related to multiple projects cannot be allocated to projects through the indirect project cost functionality because no causal relationship between those costs and project hour transactions exists.

Let's thus take a look at the other available instruments that can be used for allocating indirect costs to projects.

3.5.2.2. Project Adjustment Functionality

The second standard functionality that can be used for allocating indirect costs to projects is the project adjustment functionality. Making use of the project adjustment functionality for allocating indirect costs to projects follows a two-step process. Within the first process step, indirect costs are posted on a summary project from where the indirect costs are then allocated to the various other projects. Figure 3-137 illustrates this two-step process.

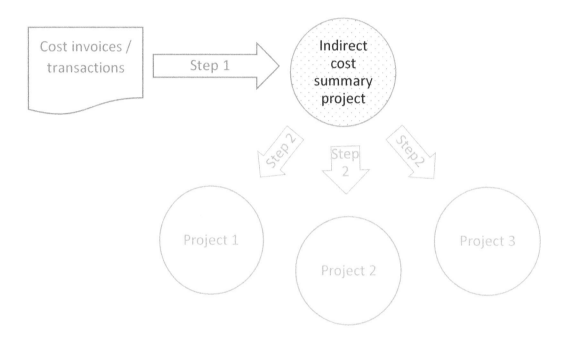

Figure 3-137 Two-step project adjustment functionality

Within the following, the two-step allocation process is exemplified based on the following simplified project structure. Please see Figure 3-138.

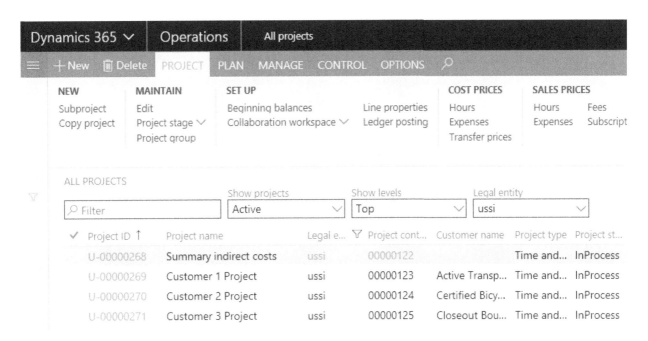

Figure 3-138 Project structure two-step allocation process

Figure 3-138 shows the indirect cost summary project (*U-00000268*) together with the three external customer projects (*U-00000269* to *U-00000271*) that are used in this example.

For the illustration of the two-step allocation process, an insurance-related vendor invoice that covers the insurance costs for all projects is recorded in the pending vendor invoice form first. In line with what has been mentioned before, this invoice is posted on the summary project *U-00000268*.

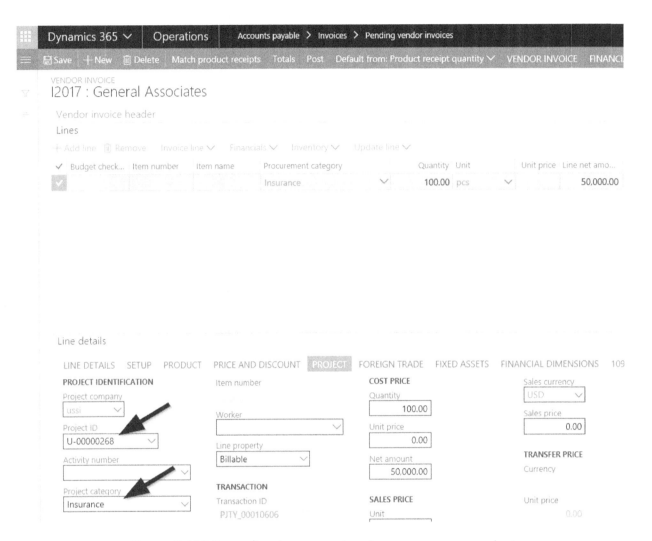

Figure 3-139 Recording insurance invoice on summary project

Once the vendor invoice has been recorded, all costs that have been accumulated on the summary project are allocated to the other projects by making use of the project adjustment functionality. This is exemplified in Figures 3-140 and 3-141.

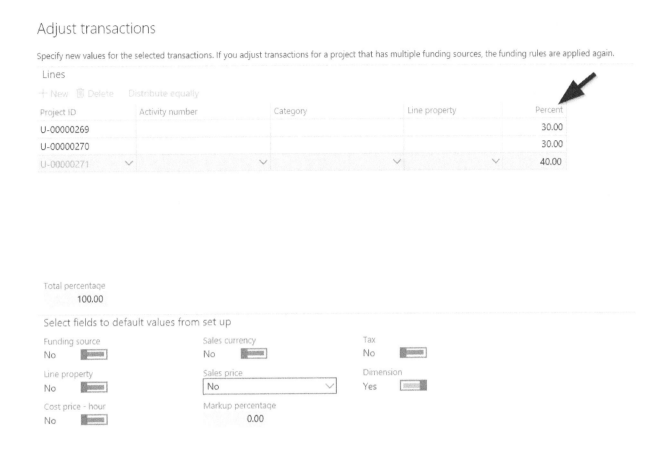

Figure 3-140 Allocate costs from summary project to other external customer projects (1)

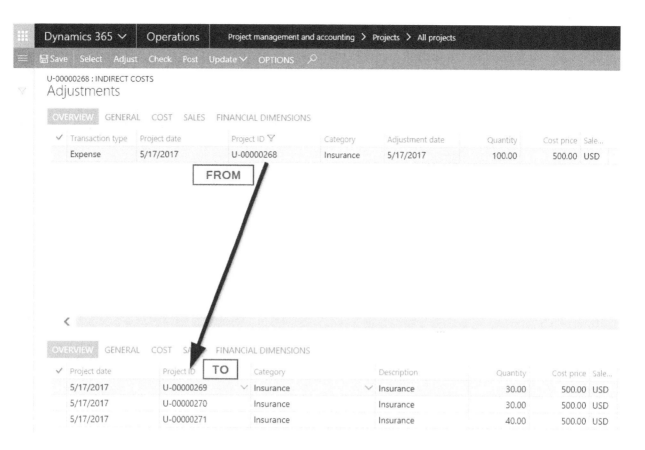

Figure 3-141 Allocate costs from summary project to other external customer projects (2)

Note In the standard application, the selection of the projects to which the costs shall be allocated to needs to be made manually. In other words, no predefined allocation key can be set up that can be used for making those allocations. If one wants to make the allocations automatically based on a predefined allocation key, a modification of the standard project adjustment functionality is required.

After posting the adjustment, the summary project is cleared of all costs, which have been shifted to the external customer projects. This is illustrated in Figure 3-142.

348

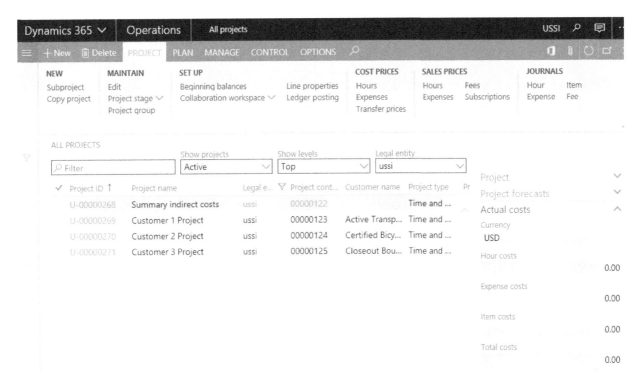

Figure 3-142 Resulting costs on summary project

Overall it can be summarized that the two-step allocation process that makes use of the project adjustment functionality is not perfect in the sense that the allocations are not fully automated. However, in comparison to the previously shown indirect cost functionality, the two-step allocation process does not only allow allocating hour-related project transactions but also can be used for allocating all kind of indirect costs. In addition, the already existing standard functionalities provide a good basis for implementing a more advanced and automated project allocation functionality that is required in companies where indirect costs need to be allocated to a large number of projects.

Note The allocation approach that makes use of the project adjustment functionality can also be applied for indirect cost allocations across companies. An example how this can be realized can be found on the following website: https://dynamicsax-fico.com/2016/10/23/project-related-intercompany-cost-allocations-1. As long as contractual agreements exist that detail what indirect costs need to be covered by which company, the approach illustrated on the aforementioned website is fine. It can even be used in cases where no contractual agreements exist or where allocations need to be made on statistical ledger accounts because the applicable accounting regulations do not allow recording those indirect costs on projects.

3.5.2.3. General Ledger or Cost-Accounting Allocations

Often, a company's management does not want to record indirect management costs directly on projects but only wants to analyze them internally. In those cases, the allocations can still be made either on statistical accounts that are not part of the external financial statements or in the cost-accounting module. This will be presented below based on the following scenario.

Scenario: The management of the company is—among others—responsible for overseeing the projects that are operated in all companies of the group. For that reason, it has been decided that a fraction of the total management costs ($100,000) shall be allocated to the projects they oversee. The basis for making those allocations are the total costs that have been recorded on those projects. From an organizational perspective, the management is employed in company USSI and the projects are operated in company FRSI and GBSI. Figure 3-143 illustrates the corporate structure and the way in which the management costs shall be allocated.

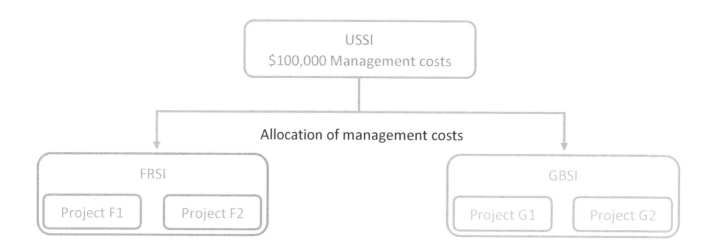

Figure 3-143 Sample corporate structure

Let's start with the indirect cost allocation through general ledger allocation rules. Figure 3-144 shows the different tabs—overview, general, and offset—of the intercompany allocation rule that is set up in company USSI and used for allocating the $100,000 management costs to the other companies, respectively, projects.

Ledger allocation rule

OVERVIEW GENERAL OFFSET

✓	Rule ↑ ▽	Description	Effective date	Expiration date	Active
	PROJ-IC	Project IC			☑

Ledger allocation rule

OVERVIEW GENERAL OFFSET

IDENTIFICATION

Rule
PROJ-IC

Description
Project IC

ADMINISTRATION

Effective date

Expiration date

Active
Yes

Date last run
5/18/2017

Intercompany rule
Yes

Allocation method
Basis

JOURNAL SETTINGS

Journal name
Allocation

Description
Ledger Allocations

SOURCE

Data source
Fixed value

Fixed value
100,000.00

Mathematical operation
None

Amount
0.00

Date interval code

DESTINATION

Keep account from
User specified

Keep dimension from
User specified

Ledger allocation rule

OVERVIEW GENERAL OFFSET

ACCOUNT

Offset account
602102

Figure 3-144 Intercompany general ledger allocation rule

Please note that the basis allocation method is used in this example, which allocates the management costs based on the costs recorded on the different projects. The allocation basis itself needs thus to refer to the different projects, respectively, their financial dimensions and the cost accounts that are used for recording project costs. In other words, the general ledger allocation functionality requires the setup and usage of a project financial dimension.

Figure 3-145 exemplifies the set up of the allocation basis for a project in company FRSI.

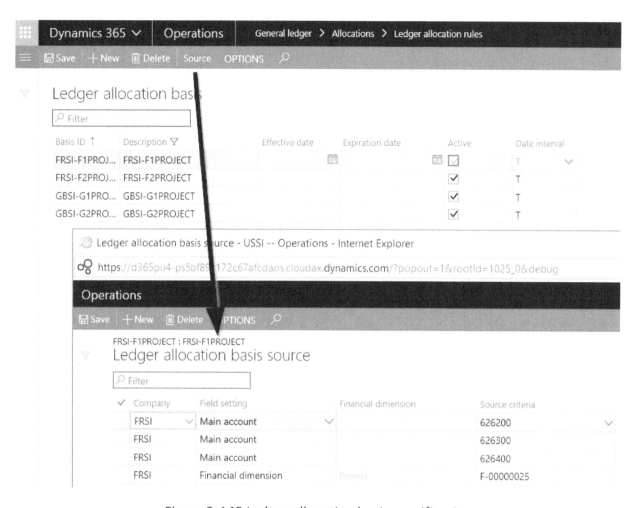

Figure 3-145 Ledger allocation basis specification

After the basis for the cost allocations has been set up, the ledger allocation destinations can be established. Those destinations define to which account and financial dimension combination the management costs are allocated to. Figure 3-146 shows an example of this setup.

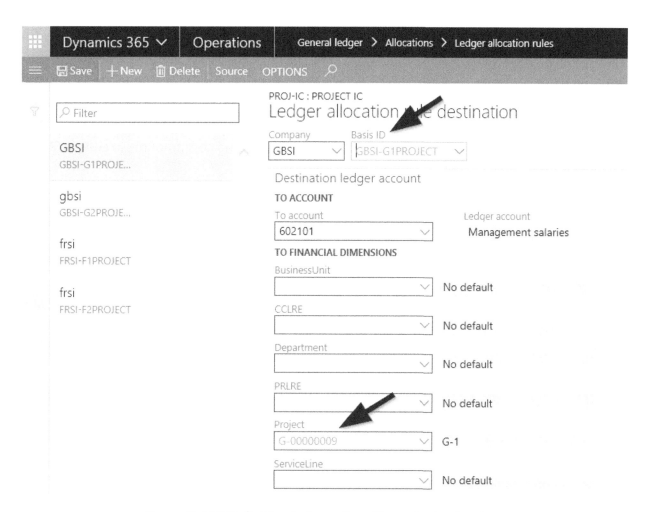

Figure 3-146 Definition ledger allocation rule destinations

Before the general ledger allocation rules can be processed, project costs need to be recorded on the various projects in company FRSI and GBSI because those costs will later on be used as the basis for the management cost allocations.

In the example illustrated, 25,000 and 50,000 GBP are recorded on the projects in company GBSI and 125,000 and 200,000 EUR on the projects in company FRSI. As the general ledger allocation process is initiated from company USSI, those cost values are converted into USD—the accounting currency of company USSI. At the time the intercompany allocation journal is posted, the USD amounts are once again converted back into the currencies of the affiliated companies where the cost amounts are posted. Figure 3-146 summarizes the project costs and allocated cost amounts in GBP, EUR, and USD.

Company-Project	Project Costs in GBP / EUR	Exchange Rate	Project Costs in USD	Allocated Management Costs in USD	Allocated Management Costs in GBP/EUR
GBSI-G1	25,000.00 GBP	0.6347	39,388.69 USD	6,991.60 USD	4,437.57 GBP
GBSI-G2	50,000.00 GBP	0.6347	78,777.38 USD	13,983.20 USD	8,875.14 GBP
FRSI-F1	125,000.00 EUR	0.7300	171,232.88 USD	30,394.31 USD	22,187.84 EUR
FRSI-F2	200,000.00 EUR	0.7300	273,972.60 USD	48,630.89 USD	35,500.55 EUR
			563,371.55 USD	100,000.00 USD	

Figure 3-147 Project costs and allocations

Processing the general ledger allocation rule in company USSI consequently results in the following allocation journal voucher.

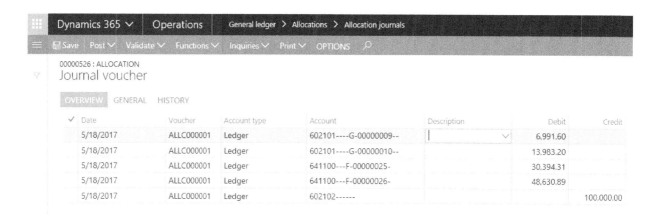

Figure 3-148 Allocation journal voucher company USSI

Posting the allocation journal does not increase the project costs. Figure 3-149 illustrates this for the first project in company FRSI.

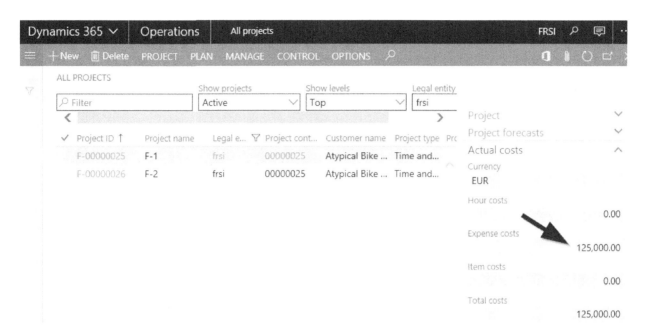

Figure 3-149 Project costs company FRSI

The underlying reason for this outcome is the fact that ledger allocation rules are executed at the ledger account-financial dimension combination level only. As a result, the total costs of the project can be identified in the general ledger trial balance that is illustrated below for company FRSI.

MainAccount	Project	Name	Opening bala...	Debit	Credit	Closing balan...
410000	F-00000025	Clients et Comptes Rattaches-F-1	0.00	0.00	22,187.85	-22,187.85
410000	F-00000026	Clients et Comptes Rattaches-F-2	0.00	0.00	35,500.55	-35,500.55
625100	F-00000025	Frais de Vols-F-1	0.00	0.00	125,000.00	-125,000.00
625100	F-00000026	Frais de Vols-F-2	0.00	0.00	200,000.00	-200,000.00
626400	F-00000025	Coût du projet - dépenses-F-1	0.00	125,000.00	0.00	125,000.00
626400	F-00000026	Coût du projet - dépenses-F-2	0.00	200,000.00	0.00	200,000.00
641100	F-00000025	Charges de management-F-1	0.00	22,187.85	0.00	22,187.85
641100	F-00000026	Charges de management-F-2	0.00	35,500.55	0.00	35,500.55

Figure 3-150 General ledger trial balance company FRSI

The last two lines in Figure 3-150 show the allocated indirect project costs in EUR currency for company FRSI. By filtering on the respective financial project dimension value, the total direct and indirect costs of a project can be analyzed.

Note Please note that also other standard reporting tools, such as the Management Reporter can be used as an alternative to the previously illustrated trial balance form for analyzing the different projects from a financial perspective.

Even though the general ledger allocation rules can be used for allocating indirect project costs within or across companies, the required manual set up of those rules is quite cumbersome if cost allocations to many projects are required. What is more, the general ledger allocation rules are quite limited in the way how indirect costs are allocated, as the standard application ships only with a limited and predefined number of general ledger allocation methods (basis, fixed percentage, fixed weight, and equally).

Note The illustrated general ledger cost allocations can also be executed from the cost-accounting module. This can, however, not be presented here, as the required cost-accounting functionalities will publicly become available with the so-called spring release that has not been released at the time when writing this book.

3.5.3.   Summary

Within this chapter different instruments that can be used for allocating indirect project costs have presented. The first one—the indirect project cost functionality—can be used for allocating those indirect costs that are directly related to project hour transactions. If no relationship between indirect costs and project hour transactions can be established, the project adjustment functionality can be used. Finally, if one does not want to show indirect costs in the project-management and accounting module, general ledger or cost-accounting module allocations can be used.

4. Conclusion

The second part of this two-part series on the D365 project-management and accounting module detailed the project accounting setups that are available for the different project types in D365. This description together with the accounting- and controlling-related scenarios that have been presented in the third chapter of this book provide the reader with easy to grasp scenarios that can be extended and implemented in D365 live environments.

Index

A

Activity Based Costing 290, 292, 293, 294, 297, 326, 338

C

Completed Contract 110, 192, 272, 280
Cost Allocation 20, 188, 294, 296, 299, 310, 313, 315, 320, 326, 333, 337, 339, 349, 350, 353, 354, 356
Cost Projects 18, 19, 20, 21, 22, 23, 24, 25, 27, 28, 31, 38, 46, 69, 118
Cost Variance 230, 244, 247, 253, 254, 257, 258, 267

E

Earned Value Analysis 229, 230, 234, 238, 240, 244, 245, 247, 250, 252, 253, 255, 256, 257, 259, 266, 267, 270, 271

F

Fix-Price Projects 101, 110, 111, 112, 115, 116, 118, 122, 131, 132, 133, 143, 144, 145, 146, 152, 153, 156, 157, 161, 163, 168, 170, 171, 175, 179, 184, 214, 237, 239

I

Indirect Costs 290, 291, 292, 293, 294, 295, 307, 326, 337, 339, 340, 341, 342, 343, 344, 349, 356
Internal Projects 25, 26, 27, 28, 30, 31, 32, 33, 34, 35, 36, 37, 38, 40, 41, 46, 47, 54, 57, 92, 188, 191

Investment Projects 41, 42, 44, 45, 46, 47, 48, 53, 54, 56, 57, 58, 59, 60, 61, 62, 188, 192, 214

P

Parallel Accounting 272, 289
Percentage of Completion 110, 111, 113, 123, 126, 127, 152, 154, 156, 157, 159, 160, 161, 162, 164, 168, 170, 175, 177, 178, 184, 195, 201, 204, 205, 207, 214, 240, 243, 244, 246, 247, 252, 253, 254, 255, 256, 257, 258, 259, 260, 261, 262, 263, 266, 267, 271, 272, 273, 281, 282, 287, 288, 289
Project Category 42, 61, 112, 202, 210, 217, 233, 260, 328, 340
Project Group 13, 18, 26, 32, 44, 53, 66, 81, 91, 101, 115, 133, 138, 147, 152, 162, 170, 178, 188, 195, 212, 234, 252, 256, 272

S

Schedule Variance 230, 244, 247, 259
Standard Reporting Tools 215, 216, 217, 218, 219, 220, 223, 227

T

Time & Material Projects 66, 67, 72, 75, 81, 82, 89, 90, 91, 95, 97, 98, 99, 100, 161, 188, 191, 192, 193, 239
Time Projects 13, 14, 15, 16

W

Work Breakdown Structure 116, 219, 235, 237, 261, 262

Made in the USA
Las Vegas, NV
02 October 2024

96116798R10203